The Good-to-Go Cookbook

W9-CDL-199

THE Good-to-Go COOKBOOK

Take-Along Food, Quick Suppers, and
Satisfying Snacks for *On-the-Go Families*

Kathleen Cannata Hanna

Storey Publishing

To Chris, Joe, and Lisa

And to all of the families who laugh together and
appreciate what each person brings to the table.

The mission of Storey Publishing is to serve our customers by
publishing practical information that encourages
personal independence in harmony with the environment.

Edited by Margaret Sutherland and Molly Jackel
Art direction and cover design by Alethea Morrison
Page design by Simona Bortis and Patrick Barber/McGuire Barber Design

Illustrations by © Moira Millman
Indexed by Christine Lindemer, Boston Road Communications

© 2008 by Kathleen Cannata Hanna

All rights reserved. No part of this book may be reproduced without written permission from the publisher,
except by a reviewer who may quote brief passages or reproduce illustrations in a review with appropriate
credits; nor may any part of this book be reproduced, stored in a retrieval system, or transmitted in any form
or by any means — electronic, mechanical, photocopying, recording, or other — without written permission
from the publisher.

The information in this book is true and complete to the best of our knowledge. All recommendations are
made without guarantee on the part of the author or Storey Publishing. The author and publisher disclaim
any liability in connection with the use of this information. For additional information, please contact Storey
Publishing, 210 MASS MoCA Way, North Adams, MA 01247.

Storey books are available for special premium and promotional uses and for customized editions. For
further information, please call 1-800-793-9396.

Printed in the United States by R.R. Donnelley
10 9 8 7 6 5 4 3 2 1

Library of Congress Cataloging-in-Publication Data

Cannata Hanna, Kathleen.
  The good-to-go cookbook / Kathleen Cannata Hanna.
    p. cm.
  Includes index.
  ISBN 978-1-60342-076-1 (pbk. : alk. paper)
  1. Quick and easy cookery. I. Title.
TX833.5.C36375 2008
641.5'55—dc22
                              2008026547

Contents

Acknowledgments

It takes many hands to complete a work . . .

It is almost impossible to explain how many people it took to put this book together. I also don't know how to thank them all, but I will try.

To my husband, Chris, thank you for believing in me and my abilities. To our teens, Joe and Lisa, you have tasted and tested more food than you would ever have wished to taste and test. From now on I will try very hard **not** to say, "Oh, a little of this and a little of that . . . " in response to your question, "Mom, what's for dinner?"

To Jane and Tim, who helped me to stabilize my thought processes — I will be forever indebted to both of you.

Thanks to Mom and Dad Cannata for supporting me in so many ways and teaching me how to be independent and confident. I have passed these skills along to our children — I love you. And Mom, thanks for being such an outstanding cook and teaching me more in the kitchen than I can ever list. I am very lucky to have worked beside you all those years in your Italian kitchen. And yes, Mom, you will come to New York City with me! To Mom and Dad Hanna — your patience, support, prayer, and unconditional love through the years have been more than anyone could ask — I love you.

To my sisters, Cindy and Gina, thank you for loving me just the way I am! To my lawyer friends Tom Hall and Pat Corbett, thank you for working through the contracts with me. To Bill and Nancy, you are comfort to my soul. To John, Lauren, Patti, and Judy, thank you for being there when I needed you most. To Earl — you probably didn't think that I would mention you — but your gentle nudging, genuine concern, and confidence in my ideas and my abilities have helped more than you know. I would like to thank all of my friends, neighbors, and family from the bottom of my heart; you were essential in testing recipes and giving hints, comments, directions, corrections, options, opinions, and observations. Linda and Tom, Shawn and Gretchen — no one in the world could ask for better neighbors than you. Thank you for the long driveway talks and the endless hours of food testing. Barb and Tim Mansfield and Chris Coady — all three of you have outstanding knowledge of food; your honest, sophisticated, helpful, and tender suggestions helped to make this book "taste great." Thanks for being my friends. I have traveled far to find friends as genuine as Hott Rhonda and Kathleen. I love you both and thank you for all your laughter, tears, support, and knowledge, and for the crash course in edi tor language.

Sam, cheap coffee is not the same without you — you are the guardian angel given to me by God. Thank you to Sam Speigel of Partners and Rhoda at Schuler books; you always had the time to help answer questions and guide me through the book-selling process. Thanks to Dr. Monish Jain for your knowledge and wisdom when discussing the eating habits and styles of adolescents and teens. Richard Baldwin, you have been a wealth of knowledge and inspiration, and an unending source of information. Without you and your class, I know I would not have written this book. Thank you!

And Storey Publishing — wow, you guys are great. Thanks for believing in me and having the vision for this book. Pam Art, Dan Reynolds, Jessica Richard, Stephanie DiSantis, Maribeth Casey, Maryellen Mahoney, Deborah Balmuth, Margaret Lennon, Kim Corey, Wes Seeley, Alethea Morrison, and everyone else who has made me feel so at home at Storey — thank you. In particular, thanks to my editor, Margaret Sutherland, for her patience and calming nature.

And most of all, thanks to God — without your help, guidance, and eternal love and forgiveness I would not be here!

"Come on, we gotta GO!!!"

Sound familiar? Every day, millions of parents yell these words to their kids while running out the door armed with baseball bats, shin guards, book bags, trumpet cases, and water bottles. Juggling careers and family activities has become a way of life for many of us and, unfortunately, nutrition often falls by the wayside. Eating out is okay once in a while or when you're in a pinch, but nutritionally speaking, it's lousy — not to mention how fast it can blow a family's budget or waistlines! An important step toward keeping your family healthy and fit is to think about how to have good, fun, nutritious, economical, home-prepared food replace fast food and concession-stand snacks.

I decided to write *The Good-to-Go Cookbook* after my children started school and I helped to serve lunch in the school cafeteria. At the time, I could not believe what I was seeing in children's lunch boxes. The school lunch program was no better, and teachers were using candy in the classroom as a way to motivate students. Wake up and smell the dental bills!

This book is filled with delicious, healthy, easy-to-follow recipes for busy families. The recipes are for kids of all ages, but they're especially geared toward teenagers. There are so many books out there on feeding children, but far fewer seem to address the older kids in the house.

We *must* be as passionate about the food we prepare and serve to our families as we are about our jobs, hobbies, fitness regimens, or sports teams. To say "I can't cook" is no excuse. You don't have to be Martha Stewart to prepare healthy meals at home. All it takes are some good recipes and a new attitude.

Where to start? Right at your local grocery store. As you walk through the aisles, be more aware of the choices you make. Don't favor "quick" and "fast" over nutrition. How healthy can a food item be when the ingredients listed include salt, corn syrup, or a multitude of things you can't pronounce? Eating well doesn't have to be hard, and it's the best thing that you can do for your family. Act smart, start simple, and think nutrition — and get ready for some fun, delicious, and (pssst!) *healthy* food.

Make a Plan and Get Organized

To provide nutritious meals for your family on a daily basis, you have to have a plan. I suggest making up a weekly dinner menu. List each main dish, vegetable, salad, and carbohydrate. Then organize your weekly grocery shopping around this list. This helps you to see easily the balance of proteins, vegetables, fats, and carbs of each day's menu. Pin this menu up in the kitchen for all to see, allowing the whole family a glimpse of the week and how they can plan around it and help out.

Remember too to plan each dinner menu around your planned activities, so that you are not scheduled to make an involved meal on the night that you have a soccer tournament overlapping with parent-teacher conferences.

Your menu plan will enable you to shop more efficiently, take advantage of coupons, and stick to your budget. You will make fewer last-minute trips to the grocery store, and impulsive purchases will be much easier to avoid.

Treat Yourself

I have a very busy life, but I always take a bit of time every day for myself. This time might consist of reading the newspaper with a cup of tea, reading one of my cooking magazines, or sitting on our deck for a few minutes listening to the barn owls and watching the birds dine at the bird feeder. Once a week I also treat myself to something special, like giving myself a pedicure, shopping for a new tube of lipstick, or visiting the local bookstore to see the latest cookbooks. I encourage you to do the same, even during your craziest weeks; it will rejuvenate your spirit and give you a renewed sense of self that you need to be able to give to your family.

Break It Down

Finally, when life gets too big to get my hands around it, I tend to break things down into small bites (I can't help using a food analogy!), and I'm not talking about eating. I'm referring instead to managing the day-to-day operations of my life's big categories. In no particular order, they are: 1. Family; 2. Personal life; 3. Marriage; 4. Faith. I pray first, then I consider what the most important things are in each of the other categories. I break down the necessary stuff into small bites, and the rest always seems to fall into place.

Menu Plans for Every Need

I try to write down a dinner menu plan for the week each Sunday that coincides with the family schedule: sport practice, music lessons, late business meetings, studies, presentations, and whatever else comes along. This helps me with my grocery list and helps my teens and husband to begin a meal or two if I arrive at home late during the week. Here are some menu ideas that have worked well for me over the years and that might be handy for you some week.

Great Menu Ideas in under 30 Minutes

- Texas Ranch Steak (page 162) with Stove Top Zucchini (page 261)
- Barbecued Salmon Fillets (page 140) with Spring Salad (page 117)
- Salsa Corn Pasta (page 232) with a green salad
- Cobb Salad Pitas (page 131) with celery and carrot sticks
- High-Protein Tomato Soup (page 98) with Best-Ever Grilled Cheese Sandwich (page 123) and carrot sticks
- Sweet and Spicy Glazed Chicken (page 141) with Better Buttered Noodles (page 240) and a green salad
- Curry Peanut Sauce or Garlic Peanut Sauce on pasta (page 251) with Seasoned Green Beans (page 278)
- Fresh Herb Turkey Burgers (page 133) with Microwave Potatoes (page 272) and steamed broccoli
- Cheesy Linguine (page 242) with Italian-Style Green Bean Sauté (page 256)
- Red Beans and Rice (page 176) with a fruit salad
- Master-Mix Pancakes (page 36) with Bananas and Cream (page 19) and Warm Drink for a Cold Soccer Game (page 65)
- Bow Ties with Caesar (page 241) with Stove Top Zucchini (page 261)

Great Menu Ideas in under 45 Minutes

- Quick and Tender Chicken (page 188) with Tarragon Carrots (page 258)
- Rockin' Sockin' Soccer Sauce (page 252) and a green salad

- Fast Brunch Eggs (page 21) with Red Eye Muffins (page 30) and fresh fruit
- Savory San Antonio Pork Cutlets (page 167) with a Monster Potato Pancake (page 266) and a green salad
- Ultimate Salami Sandwich (page 122) with sliced veggies and ranch dip
- BLT Pie (page 223) with Tooty-Fruity Smoothies (page 20)
- Hearty Chowder (page 215) with Mandarin Salad (page 104)
- Can-You-Keep-a-Secret Chicken (page 187) with Italian-Style Green Bean Sauté (page 256)

Great Menu Ideas for Family Meals

- Neighborhood Chicken (page 184) with Seasoned Biscuits (page 279) and Greens and Cheese (page 256)
- Sunshine Chicken Kabobs (page 156) with Quick Potato Bake (page 267) and Kickin' Southwest Bean Bake (page 265)
- Tomato Tart (page 179) with a green salad and crusty bread
- Baked French Toast Soufflé (page 28) and Fruit Kabobs with Yogurt Dip (page 45)
- Chicken Curry Casserole (page 219) with a green salad
- Family Party Chicken (page 189) with Seasoned Green Beans (page 278)
- Family Meeting Pot Roast (page 198) with Zesty Baked Carrots (page 257)
- Crockpot Hungarian Beef (page 202) with Cheddar Onion Pudding Pie (page 259)

One-Dish Main Dishes

Family Meals and One-Pot Deals

Zucchini Lasagna (page 205)

Veggie Chili (page 218)

Tuna Swiss Pie (page 207)

Baked Pasta (page 220)

Tortilla Casserole (page 222)

Pasta, Please!

Salsa Corn Pasta (page 232)

Summer Chopped Veggie Pasta (page 234)

Easy-Cheesy Pasta Salad (page 239)

Bow Ties with Caesar (page 241)

Cheesy Linguine (page 242)

Shells and Cheese (page 244)

Spinach Feta Mostaccioli (page 245)

Fast Skillet Pasta (page 246)

Quick, Hot Pasta Salad (page 247)

Peas, Cheese, and Pasta Bake (page 248)

Duo of Peanut Sauces (page 251)

White Clam Sauce (page 253)

My Favorite No-Fail Family Keeper Recipes

Try to develop at least five no-fail family keeper meals. These are meals that you know the family loves and that can be prepared easily in less than 45 minutes, start to finish. Readily accessible ingredients are the key to this trick. Here are my favorites. I know I can always depend on these foods to taste great and satisfy my family:

Italian Country Sandwich (page 121)

Quickest Meatloaf in the West (page 163)

Salsa Corn Pasta (page 232)

Chicken Salad Barbecue (page 144)

Barbecued Salmon Fillets (page 140)

Sweet and Spicy Glazed Chicken (page 141)

Meatless Recipes

Fast Breakfast

Fresh Fruit Cups (page 17)

Best Breakfast Sandwich (page 24)

Grab and Go

Kid's Burrito (page 82)

Pizza Pockets (page 84)

The Lunch Crunch

Texas Corn Chowder (page 94)

Pita Antipasto (page 118)

15-Minute Dishes

Veggie Mix Salad (page 132)

Modern Mamma's Pierogi (page 139)

30-Minute Dishes

Speedy Gonzales Chili (page 168)

Red Bean Burgers (page 175)

Tomato-Cheese Pie (page 177)

Tomato Tart (page 179)

Ma's Frittata (page 180)

Cooking for and with Your Teens

Textures play an important role for children and other picky eaters. Explore the different textures of foods (especially vegetables). One kid may eat only raw carrots, while another may want them cooked; others may prefer refried beans instead of whole beans in a chili. I remember not liking roasted potatoes as a child, but I loved mashed potatoes. So my mother would take the carrots, onions, and potatoes from the roasting pan and mash them with a chunk of butter, and I was happy.

Involve your kids in preparing meals and snacks with you in the kitchen. They will learn from your example and will be much more willing to try foods that they had a hand in making. This may take a bit more time and make more of a mess, but the payoff is a hundredfold for you and your children for the rest of their lives.

Grocery List Help

About two weeks before the start of a new school year I ask my teens to list five different types of lunches that they would like to take to school. The lunches must be nutritionally balanced (I help them to make this assessment) and reasonable to carry in a sack, thermos, or thermal lunch bag. This gives me a sense of their changing tastes and appetites and allows me some time to start stocking up on lunch items. If you have smaller children, sit down and make a list with them; it's a guarantee that their lunches will be eaten instead of thrown into the school trashcan.

I also have my teens add their own items to the weekly grocery list. This may include a specific flavor of yogurt, a type of hair shampoo they need, or a kind of deli meat they prefer for their lunches. This really helps me to take the guesswork out of shopping for my teens.

Teen Cooks

Get your teens involved in planning weekly dinner menus. Allow them (or encourage them) to make dinner once a week. They can go through this book and choose recipes, create a balanced menu, give you a list of ingredients to purchase, make the meal, and clean up afterwards (which includes taking out the garbage and sweeping the kitchen floor). You'll be surprised by how much fun they will have picking out recipes and creating the menu. Just make sure that you work with them so that they don't bite off more than they can chew. Remember to convey the following important principles to them: "Less is more" and "Keep it simple."

Fancy-Shmancy

If you have an extra five minutes, serve your family a simple meal on your good dishes, complete with cloth napkins, tablecloth, candles, and glassware. Every time I do this, for some mysterious reason, the table manners of my teens improve immensely.

Teen-Friendly Recipes

Organizing Your Kitchen

Less is more. Do you have clutter in your cupboards and kitchen drawers? Keep things simple and try not to get lured into buying gadgets and kitchen tools when you already have a cupboard full of them. Here are the basics:

Everyday Stuff

- 2 sets of nesting mixing bowls: 1 stainless and 1 glass, plastic, or ceramic (microwave-safe). These also function as serving bowls.
- 2 sets of measuring spoons
- 1 vegetable peeler
- 1 pair of kitchen shears
- 1 box-style cheese grater
- 1 multi-purpose hand-operated can opener
- 1 set of measuring cups, plus 2 extra stainless 1-cup measuring cups with graduated marks on the sides

- 1 large Pyrex measuring container — at least 4-cup capacity
- 2 rubber or silicone spatulas (I like to have 2 different sizes: one to get into skinny jars and a fatter one for scraping mixing bowls and pans. The silicone varieties are heat-resistant.)
- 1 stainless steel mixing spoon
- 1 slotted spoon
- 1 ladle
- 1 large two-prong fork
- 2 pancake turners
- 1 potato masher
- 1 pastry blender
- 1 rolling pin
- 1 flour sifter or metal strainer
- 3 wooden spoons
- 1 pair tongs
- 2 whisks: one big and one small
- 1 set of plastic cutting boards, in different colors so that you can keep the raw-meat cutting surface separate from the rest — and the fruit separate from the garlic

Special Stuff

- 2 large (10- by 15-inch or 11- by 17-inch) baking sheets with 1-inch sides
- 1 large colander for draining pasta and rinsing vegetables. This can also function as a fruit bowl for the kitchen table.
- 1 set of 2 nesting ceramic baking dishes. These can also function as serving bowls.
- 1 roasting pan with rack and lid
- 1 9-inch pie plate: ceramic, metal, or Pyrex
- 2 round cake pans
- 1 9- by 5-inch loaf pan
- 1 9- by 13-inch baking pan
- 1 12-cup muffin tin
- 1 large lasagna pan with high sides
- 1 decent set of pots and pans (I prefer stainless steel with an aluminum core. Yes, they should be heavy. All-Clad makes a fabulous line and you can get a basic set pretty cheaply during a holiday sale.)

☑ 1 large nonstick skillet (Invest in a good one. The cheaper you go, the faster the finish will wear off.)

☑ 1 steamer basket

Sharp Stuff

Last but not least, the knives. Don't invest in an entire set of knives if you don't plan to use all of them. Here are the three basic styles that will get you through almost any cutting process in the kitchen:

☑ 4- to 5-inch paring knife

☑ 6- to 9-inch serrated knife for cutting through tomatoes and crusty bread

☑ 8- to 12-inch chef's knife for chopping and multipurpose use — the one indispensable item in your kitchen

Notes on Ingredients

Here are some helpful things to keep in mind when using this book:

If you don't have a specific spice listed in a given recipe, try something similar. (I wouldn't, however, recommend this when baking.)

Garlic in a jar: I'm Italian and I love using fresh garlic in my recipes. In the interest of being quick, however, the recipes in this book rely on prepared chopped garlic, which you can find in a jar in the produce section of the grocery store. It's great and it works, but when you have a free minute or two, use the fresh stuff — it can't be beat.

Olive oil is used frequently in my recipes. I always use the extra-virgin variety because of the warm, fruity flavor it imparts to any dish. Cold-pressed extra-virgin olive oil is the oil from the first pressing of the olives. This is the purest, cleanest olive oil, with only 1% acid. You can use vegetable oil instead for cooking. There will be a difference in taste, but it will do in a pinch.

I love the taste of sharp cheddar cheese. A little goes a long way because of the strong flavor and tanginess. But feel free to choose a milder cheese if you prefer.

Old-fashioned rolled oats are used in these recipes instead of quick oats. They are very similar, but if you are cooking with quick oats, reduce each full cup of oats by two tablespoons.

Most of the recipes in these pages have been tested with 2 percent milk. There are a few, however, that specifically call for nonfat milk or whole milk. Sometimes a recipe needs a precise fat level to produce the proper consistency or texture.

"Optional" *means* optional. You truly do not have to add ingredients marked as such to make any recipe taste right. They are only suggestions for good complements to the recipes.

Fresh lemon juice cannot be recreated. I would use bottled lemon juice only if I lived at the North Pole and had no access to lemons.

Use my book — and I mean *use* it. Scribble notes in the columns, mark your additions, cross off what you don't like. Modify the salt, pepper, and spices. Use the inside cover to record your favorites and what occasions you made them for so that you'll have a record of that Christmas morning French toast dish that was a hit six years ago.

Quick Chicken

Many of the recipes in this book include boneless, skinless chicken breast halves. Following are some tips for buying, storing, thawing, and cooking chicken.

Buying

For recipes that call for chopped cooked chicken, here are some guidelines for how much to purchase:

4 boneless, skinless chicken breast halves (1 to 1½ pounds total) yield 3 to 4 cups of chopped cooked chicken.

4 chicken tenders (about 8 ounces total) yield 1 to 1½ cups of chopped cooked chicken.

4 boneless, skinless chicken thighs yield 1½ to 2 cups of chopped cooked chicken.

1 broiling/frying chicken (about 3 pounds) yields 3 to 4 cups of chopped cooked chicken.

Cooking Tips

- If the recipe calls for the chicken to be cut up, cut it into equal-size pieces to ensure even cooking.
- If your boneless chicken breast is too thick, pound it with a mallet between two pieces of plastic wrap until the desired thickness is achieved.
- Boneless chicken that is too thick can also be cut horizontally with a sharp knife.
- Try chicken tenders, which are usually of uniform size. When substituting tenders for breast halves in a recipe, remember to cut the cooking time in half.

BASIC CHICKEN PREP
RECIPES

Here are three simple methods to use for dishes that call for cooked chicken. When you have some extra time, you may want to cook and freeze a big batch to have on hand for when you need a super-quick, low-fat, high-protein meal. Following each recipe are easy, tasty suggestions from other chapters for dishes that use cooked chicken.

1. MICROWAVE CHICKEN

Prep time About 3 minutes
Cook time About 6 minutes

> 2 boneless, skinless chicken breast halves, of similar weight and thickness
> Italian seasoning (if salt-free, add salt to taste)

1 Place the chicken on a microwave-safe plate (a bit of moisture on the chicken is okay), sprinkle lightly with herbs, and wrap in microwave-safe plastic wrap.

2 Cook in the microwave on high for 3 minutes; check for doneness.

3 Cook 2 to 3 minutes longer, checking every minute for doneness, or until the chicken reaches an internal temperature of 160°F.

4 Let stand, covered, for 5 minutes.

RECIPE SUGGESTIONS:
- Chicken and Cherry Salad (page 110)
- Peas, Cheese, and Pasta Bake (page 248)
- Bowties with Caesar (page 241)

2. POACHED CHICKEN

Prep time About 5 minutes
Cook time About 30 minutes

> 4–5 cups low-sodium chicken broth
> 4 boneless, skinless chicken breast halves
> Freshly ground black pepper

1 Add ½ inch of chicken broth to a large skillet and bring to a simmer over medium heat. Generously pepper one side of the chicken. Place the chicken pepper-side down in the simmering broth; immediately sprinkle the top of the chicken with pepper.

2 Bring the broth back to a simmer and cook for 14 minutes. Turn the chicken over and add ½ inch of broth to the skillet.

3 Cook 14 minutes longer — occasionally adding broth to keep the pan from becoming dry — or until juices run clear when the thickest part of the chicken is pierced with a knife.

RECIPE SUGGESTIONS:
- Stuffed Chicken Crescents (page 85)
- Cheese-Baked Chicken Enchiladas (page 192)
- Quick Asian Chicken Salad (page 112)

3. CROCKPOT CHICKEN

Prep time 2 minutes
Cook time 8 hours

Use this recipe if you want to cook a number of chicken breasts at one time. The chicken comes out moist and tender, and it shreds very easily for recipes calling for shredded chicken. It does take several hours to cook, but prep time is only a few minutes. Follow the recipe carefully to ensure that the chicken does not overcook.

> **6–8 frozen boneless, skinless chicken breast halves**
>   **Italian seasoning (or seasoning of choice)**
>   **½ cup chicken broth**

1 Generously season each piece of chicken and stack them on top of each other in the crockpot.

2 Add broth to the crockpot, cover, and cook on low heat for 8 hours, turning and rearranging the meat halfway through the cooking time.

RECIPE SUGGESTIONS:
- **Seven-Layer Chicken Salad (page 111)**
- **Hot Chicken Salad (page 194)**
- **Kids-Love-This-Pasta Pasta (page 240)**

SIZE MATTERS

Boneless, skinless chicken breast halves are available fresh or frozen. The breast halves can vary quite a bit in size and weight. Some can be as thick as two and a half inches and weigh as much as twelve ounces. Others might be one inch thick with a good individual portion weight of four ounces. The recipes in this book are based on an average half breast weight of four to six ounces. This average half breast will yield approximately three quarters of a cup of sliced or diced raw meat.

Temperature

An instant-read meat thermometer is a practical item to have in your kitchen toolbox. As of this writing, the USDA recommends that chicken be cooked to an internal temperature of 165°F. Note, though, that the chicken will rise in temperature at least 5 degrees after it's off the heat.

Storing

If you are cooking chicken for the purpose of storing it in the freezer for future use, here are some general guidelines:

- Cool the cooked chicken quickly by removing it from the heat source and from the hot pan. You can then choose to chop, dice, shred, or leave whole.
- Store desired amounts in ziplock freezer bags. Mark the bags with type, style, and/or flavor of the chicken, the number it serves, and the date.
- Cooked chicken will keep in the refrigerator no longer than 3 days. Store it in the freezer for up to 2 months.

Thawing

Thawing boneless, skinless chicken is easy. Here are two methods:

1. Place covered, frozen chicken in the refrigerator the night before you plan to cook. Put the meat on a plate or in a bowl to avoid drips.

2. In just minutes, you can defrost chicken using the defrost option on your microwave. If you use the microwave, make sure that you cover the chicken with waxed paper and rotate the meat frequently to avoid actually cooking it. I usually remove chicken from the microwave when it's still a bit frozen in the middle.

Survival Cooking Tips

Here are some simple, useful food preparation facts that will help you to save time and money, as well as add flavor and nutrition to your family's diet.

Microwave Cooking

Microwave wattage varies from as low as 550 watts to as high as 1500 watts. Frozen bread rolls become unpalatable rubber balls in a matter of 30 seconds in some higher-wattage ovens. The higher the wattage, the faster the food thaws, cooks, bubbles, melts, and explodes. So take it slow until you get to know your microwave.

Money-Saver

When they go on sale, buy several pounds of deli meat, bacon, chicken, or pork loin, portion them out into ziplock freezer bags, and freeze. Separate deli meats into 4 or 5 separate ziplock freezer bags, mark the bags with their contents, and pop them into the freezer. The sliced meat keeps in the freezer for up to 2 months. When my kids make their lunches in the morning before leaving for school, they can pull out a bag of their favorite deli meat and thaw it in the microwave for 30 to 40 seconds. The rest of the bag lasts for 2 or 3 days in the refrigerator. You can take out what you need when you need it, and you've saved yourself time and money.

Flavorful Seasonings

Smell your dried herbs and spices periodically — if you can't smell anything, they surely won't add any taste to your dish. Discard them and buy new ones. Kitchen shelf-life for spices is about 6 months. Freezing a fresh jar will prolong the flavor for up to 2 years.

Fresh Baking

Plan to use most of your baking ingredients within 2 months of purchase to guarantee fresh baked goods. Whole-wheat flour should be kept in the refrigerator or freezer if you don't use it often because it becomes rancid quickly at room temperature.

Time-Savers

If your budget allows for them, there are many prepared ingredients such as sliced mushrooms, matchstick carrots, bagged salads, and pre-chopped vegetable mixes available in the produce section of the grocery store. You will pay a premium for these items, but if purchasing them means getting nutritious vegetables onto your family's table in significantly less time, take advantage of them.

The Best Way to Start the Day — Easy, Nutritious Morning Fare

Why *not* eat breakfast? Too busy, too tired, or not hungry?

We all know the benefits of eating a good breakfast. But do we really follow the rules? Are you practicing what you preach? I figured that if I was going to tell my kids to eat a good breakfast, it had to begin with me. I explained to my kids that just like cars, their bodies perform and respond based on how they treat them. This means that if you need your car to start every morning, you have to treat it right, and if you want your body and mind to respond at the beginning of the day, then start each day with a smart breakfast.

Some teens think that skipping breakfast is a way to stay slim. Actually, skipping breakfast is a good way to gain weight. If you don't give your body the right fuel in the morning to burn an entire day's calories, your metabolism slows down and you will burn fewer calories — hence, weight gain. Eating a simple but smart breakfast containing grain, protein, and fruit is a good place to begin. If your teens want to be lean, mean cruising machines, it all starts at the breakfast table.

Donuts and pastries are *not* included among my breakfast recipes; I try not to rely on them as breakfast foods. They are high in calories, sugar, and fat, and leave you feeling hungry in a matter of hours — not exactly the right kind of fuel for your body. Instead, buy whole grain breads and bagels; they toast deliciously. Look, too, for cold cereals that have less sugar, such as Cheerios, Great Grains, or Rice Krispies. Sweeten these cereals by adding chopped pears, peaches, berries, or dried fruit. Revisit hot cereals such as oatmeal or Cream of Wheat by adding peanut butter, pure maple syrup, or fresh fruit.

A FEW VERY SIMPLE
BREAKFAST IDEAS

THE SIMPLE BREAKFAST

- Cold cereal, low-fat milk, and a handful of berries or raisins on top.

- Hot cereal, a handful of dried raisins or cherries, chopped pecans, or chopped dates, and a small sprinkle of brown sugar.

- Whole grain toast, bagel, or English muffin with a spread of low-fat cream cheese and teaspoon of all-fruit jam.

THE "RUN OUT
THE DOOR" BREAKFAST

- Yogurt in one hand and a whole grain bagel in the other.

- Bag of trail mix (nuts, dried fruit, pretzels, crackers, and dry cereal) with an apple on the side.

- Fruit smoothie and a handful of whole grain crackers.

- Cottage cheese mixed with your favorite jam — full of protein!

THE TRADITIONAL
HEARTY BREAKFAST

- Eggs, whole grain toast, and orange slices. Stay away from greasy egg preparations. Instead poach, hard-boil, or fry in 1 teaspoon of olive oil in a nonstick skillet (this makes for an easy cleanup, too).

- French toast, waffles, or pancakes (try whole-wheat or other whole grain varieties). Use some all-fruit jam as a spread instead of gobs of syrup.

FRESH FRUIT CUPS

Here's a clever way to serve fresh fruit. The ice cream cone adds a touch of sweetness and makes it easy to hold. These cones are also a refreshing summertime dessert.

Vegetarian

Prep time 10 minutes **Yield** 4 cones

4 cups sliced fresh fruit (strawberries, bananas, apples, cherries, grapes, kiwi, peaches, nectarines, plums, or whatever you like)

4 large waffle cones or waffle cups

1½ cups sliced strawberries, optional

Shredded coconut or chopped nuts, optional

1 Divide the fruit evenly among the four waffle cones.

2 Purée strawberries in a blender and drizzle over the fruit, if desired.

3 Sprinkle with coconut and nuts, if desired, and serve immediately.

QUICK TIPS:

- **Try mixing fruit with a low-fat vanilla yogurt before filling cups or add shredded coconut, chopped peanuts, walnuts, almonds, mini-marshmallows, dried cherries, or nonfat whipped topping when serving for dessert.**

- **Filling the cones is much easier if you place them in tall glasses before adding the fruit.**

vegetarian

ENERGY-BOOST PARFAIT

This is a great way for kids to eat yogurt and have fun doing it.

Prep time 5 minutes **Yield** 1 serving

1 **(6-ounce) container low-fat yogurt, any flavor**
¾ **cup cut-up fruit, such as fresh peaches, fresh or frozen berries, dried cranberries, cherries, or apricots**
6 **tablespoons packaged granola**

1 In a clear 12-ounce glass, layer ¼ cup yogurt, ¼ cup fruit, and 2 tablespoons cereal.

2 Continue layering until you reach the top of the glass; top with a layer of granola. Serve immediately.

QUICK TIPS:

• Make a big batch of mini-parfaits in 6-ounce freezer-safe bowls with lids. Kids can grab them whenever they need a healthy, high-protein snack.

• This is a great place to try my Great Granola Crumble (page 69).

FOR KEEPS: Store in the refrigerator for 1 day.

BANANAS AND CREAM

This recipe is very easy to put together. My kids make this and have a great snack without a lot of effort. It's fresh, healthy, and quick.

 teen-friendly

Prep time 2 minutes **Yield** 4–6 servings

- **1 (12-ounce) can frozen orange-pineapple juice concentrate, thawed**
- **1 (32-ounce) container plain low-fat yogurt**
- **4 bananas, sliced**

Whisk juice concentrate and yogurt in a medium bowl. Serve over the bananas.

QUICK TIPS:

- If you're out of bananas, you can use canned, drained fruit.
- Sliced pineapple, orange segments, sliced peaches, or strawberries work well too.

FOR KEEPS: The yogurt topping keeps for 1 week in the refrigerator. Add the bananas when ready to serve.

TWO QUICK
BREAKFAST DRINKS

TOOTY-FRUITY SMOOTHIE

Prep time **5 minutes**
Yield **4 servings**

A light, refreshing drink for the summer-time — thirst-quenching and rich in vitamins. It takes only minutes to put together. I have spent many hot summer days sitting with the kids on the deck sipping this refreshing beverage.

> **2 cups chilled cran-raspberry juice**
> **2 whole fresh bananas, sliced**
> **12 medium strawberries, hulled and halved**
> **10–12 ice cubes**

Place all ingredients in a blender; blend until smooth, rich, and frothy. Pour into tall glasses and serve.

QUICK TIP: **Try cran-grape or cran-apple juice for a slightly different flavor.**

CHOCOLATE BANANA FROSTY

Prep time **5 minutes**
Yield **2 servings**

A high-energy and high-vitamin shake that needs no ice cream. Perfect for those very ripe bananas when you don't have time to use them in banana bread! Great for the chocolate lover in the house.

> **3 very ripe frozen bananas, sliced**
> **4 tablespoons unsweetened cocoa**
> **1 teaspoon vanilla extract**
> **2 tablespoons confectioners' sugar**
> **1 cup skim milk**

Place all ingredients in the blender and blend until smooth, about 30 seconds; serve.

QUICK TIP: **When bananas are so ripe that they are about to walk off of the counter, remove the skins, wrap the bananas in plastic, and store them in the freezer. They are ready to use (frozen or thawed) as directed in recipes such as banana bread, muffins, frozen drinks, milk shakes, or the recipe above.**

FAST BRUNCH EGGS

A fast and easy dish. Serve with fresh orange or apple slices and toast.

Prep time 5 minutes **Cook time** 25 minutes **Yield** 4 servings

- 5 eggs, beaten
- 2 cups shredded sharp cheddar cheese (about 8 ounces)
- 1 cup cottage cheese
- 4 tablespoons butter, melted and cooled
- ¼ cup all-purpose flour
- ½ teaspoon baking powder
- ⅛ teaspoon salt

1 Preheat the oven to 350°F. Coat an 8-inch square glass baking dish with cooking spray.

2 Combine all of the ingredients in a large bowl; mix well.

3 Transfer the mixture to the prepared baking dish and bake for 25 to 30 minutes, or until it's golden brown and a butter knife inserted in the center comes out clean.

4 Cool for 5 minutes before serving.

QUICK TIPS:

- For variety, add to the egg mixture: olives, artichokes, green chiles, or thin slices of pepperoni. When making additions, increase the cooking time by 5 minutes.

- For a great lunch on the run, roll up the leftovers in a flour tortilla (with some sliced pickles, salami slices, and roasted red pepper, if you like).

KITCHEN 411: If you are using a metal pan or ceramic baking dish instead of a glass baking dish, change the oven temperature to 375°F.

BREAKFAST PIZZA

I call this Breakfast Pizza, but it's great for lunch or dinner as well. It's perfect to take "on the go" because it slices easily and the filling stays in place well.

Prep time **20 minutes**   **Cook time** **20 minutes**   **Yield** **8 servings**

1 **pound frozen pizza dough, thawed**

4 **eggs**

¼ **teaspoon salt**

⅛ **teaspoon black pepper**

1 **tablespoon sesame seeds**

¼ **cup milk**

¼ **cup diced deli ham**

1 **bunch scallions (white and tender green parts), thinly sliced**

1 **cup grated sharp cheddar cheese (about 4 ounces)**

1   Preheat the oven to 375°F.

2   Line a 12- to 14-inch round pizza pan or 9- by 13-inch baking pan with foil, generously overlapping the sides of the pan. Coat with cooking spray.

3   On a lightly floured surface, roll out the dough in a suitable shape to fit in the pan that you're using. Use your hands to stretch out the dough if necessary. Pinch the edges to form a lip.

4   Beat the eggs, salt, and pepper in a medium bowl until blended.

5   Brush a little of the egg mixture around the edge of the dough and sprinkle with sesame seeds.

6   Transfer the crust to the oven and bake for 5 minutes.

7   Meanwhile, add the milk, ham, and scallions to the remaining egg mixture and mix well.

8   Remove the crust from the oven. With the overlapping foil, make a collar 1 inch higher than the edge of the crust by gently folding and rolling foil around the pizza's edge. This collar will help to keep the egg mixture from escaping.

9   Pour the egg mixture into the crust and return it to the oven immediately. Bake 20 minutes longer or until the egg is set.

10 Remove the pizza from the oven and top with the cheese. Let it stand for 2 minutes or until the cheese is melted. Cut into 8 wedges and serve hot, warm, or chilled.

QUICK TIP: **You can add any number of items to the egg mixture. Try pepperoni, onion, mushrooms, or even cooked breakfast sausage. Your baking time should increase by 5 minutes when you add multiple ingredients.**

brown-bag special

BEST BREAKFAST SANDWICH

Better tasting by far than any fast-food breakfast sandwich — but an even bigger plus is that the ingredients are nutritionally *miles ahead*.

Prep time 5 minutes   **Cook time** 3 minutes   **Yield** 1 sandwich

1 teaspoon olive oil
1 egg
   Salt and pepper
1 slice smoked deli ham
1 slice sharp cheddar cheese
2 slices sourdough bread, toasted and, if you
   like, lightly buttered

1   Heat the olive oil in a small skillet over medium-high heat. Fry the egg, breaking the yolk to cook faster and to ensure that it is fully cooked. Season with salt and pepper to taste.

2   When the egg is almost done, add the ham to the pan beside the egg and cook each side for 30 seconds.

3   Place the ham on the egg and top with the cheese. Sandwich the stack between the 2 slices of toast, and serve or wrap it to go.

HAM CRESCENTS

teen-friendly

I made this recipe for the fifth-grade girls' soccer team. They ate them so quickly that I will double the batch next time.

Prep time	10 minutes	Cook time	13 minutes	Yield	6 servings

- 1 (8-ounce) container refrigerated reduced-fat crescent dinner rolls
- 8 thin slices deli ham
- 5 teaspoons Dijon mustard
- 1¼ cups grated sharp cheddar cheese (about 5 ounces)

1. Preheat the oven to 375°F.
2. Unroll the dough on a work surface. You will have a slab of dough made up of 8 perforated triangles. Divide the dough into 4 separate rectangles, each formed by 2 triangles. Press the perforated seams between the 2 triangles in each rectangle firmly together with your fingers.
3. Divide the ham evenly among the 4 rectangular pieces of dough and spread with mustard. Sprinkle each with cheese.
4. Starting at a short end, roll each one like a jelly roll; press the edges to seal. Cut each roll into 3 slices and transfer, filling-side down, to a baking sheet.
5. Bake for 13 to 15 minutes or until golden brown. Transfer immediately to a wire rack to cool. Serve warm or at room temperature.

QUICK TIP: For a vegetarian option, omit the ham and add a thin layer (2 tablespoons) of refried beans and 1 tablespoon spicy salsa per rectangle. Sprinkle with cheese and continue with recipe directions.

FOR KEEPS: The rolls can be assembled and sliced, and frozen on a baking sheet. When frozen solid, remove them from the baking sheet and store in a ziplock freezer bag. To serve, transfer the frozen rolls to a baking sheet and bake for 18 to 20 minutes.

vegetarian

WAFFLE SANDWICH TO GO

A great grab-and-go meal that I invented one morning when I woke up and realized that the power had gone out during the night. My alarm clock had failed to sound, and we had exactly 10 minutes before the school bus was due to arrive.

Prep time	2 minutes	Cook time	3 minutes	Yield	1 serving

- **2 whole-grain waffles**
- **1 tablespoon peanut butter**
- **1 tablespoon all-fruit jam**

1 Toast the waffles. (If the power is out, slide waffles under the broiler in a gas oven.) Spread one side of one waffle with peanut butter and spread one side of the other waffle with jam.

2 Make a sandwich and eat on the run.

POTATO PIE

This is a very flexible dish. I have served it for breakfast with fresh fruit, as a side dish for dinner, and as an after-school snack for the kids.

vegetarian

Prep time 8 minutes **Cook time** 40 minutes **Yield** 6 servings

- 6 **eggs**
- ½ **cup milk**
- 1 **(16-ounce) bag frozen hash brown potatoes, any style**
- 1 **bunch scallions (white and tender green parts), thinly sliced**
- ½ **teaspoon salt**
- 2–3 **dashes hot sauce, such as Tabasco**
- 1½ **cups grated sharp cheddar cheese (about 6 ounces)**

1. Preheat the oven to 350°F. Coat a 9-inch pie pan with cooking spray.

2. Beat the eggs and milk in a large bowl; stir in the remaining ingredients. Pour the mixture into the prepared pan.

3. Bake for 40 to 45 minutes, or until the center is set.

4. Remove the pie from the oven and let it stand for 5 minutes before serving.

QUICK TIP: You can add any of these items to the beaten eggs: ⅓ cup bacon bits; ½ cup precooked breakfast sausage, diced; ¼ cup each sautéed chopped onion and green bell pepper; ½ cup sautéed sliced mushrooms; ½ cup precooked baby shrimp; ½ cup canned, smoked salmon, drained and flaked.

vegetarian

BAKED FRENCH TOAST SOUFFLÉ

If you are like me and can never remember to make these overnight casseroles the night before, this recipe is very forgiving. You can make it in the morning, let it rest 45 minutes (or more if you have the time) before baking, and it will still turn out crisp on the edges and yummy inside. And with this recipe, you don't need syrup!

Prep time	20 minutes	Chill time	45 minutes–8 hours
Cook time	35 minutes	Yield	10 servings

1 (1 pound) loaf of Italian bread, cut into
   ½-inch-thick slices
8 eggs, lightly beaten
3 cups milk
2 tablespoons granulated sugar
1 teaspoon vanilla
¼ teaspoon salt
½ teaspoon ground cinnamon
¼ teaspoon ground nutmeg

TOPPING

1 cup firmly packed brown sugar
1 cup chopped pecans
½ cup (1 stick) butter, at room temperature
2 tablespoons light corn syrup
½ teaspoon cinnamon
¼ teaspoon ground nutmeg

1. Preheat the oven to 350°F. Coat a 10- by 15-inch baking dish with cooking spray.

2. Arrange the bread in the prepared baking dish, overlapping slices to fit.

3. Combine the eggs, milk, sugar, vanilla, salt, cinnamon, and nutmeg in a medium bowl. Pour the mixture over the bread; cover and chill for 45 minutes to 8 hours.

4. To make the topping combine the brown sugar, pecans, butter, corn syrup, cinnamon, and nutmeg in a small bowl; mix with a fork until a paste forms. Spread the sugar mixture over the bread.

5. Transfer to the oven and bake for 35 to 40 minutes, or until browned. Serve immediately.

QUICK TIP: It is important that your butter is at room temperature — not melted. Melting will cause the butter to separate and the mixture will not spread properly. The softened butter mixture will spread across the slices of soaked bread and create the proper texture and syrup once baked. If you're pressed for time, place a chilled stick of butter between two sheets of waxed paper and pound with a rolling pin or heavy skillet two or three times on each side to soften it.

RED-EYE MUFFINS

Simple to make and the perfect combination of tart and sweet.

Prep time 10 minutes   **Cook time** 25 minutes   **Yield** 18 muffins

2 cups all-purpose flour
1 cup sugar
1½ teaspoons baking powder
½ teaspoon baking soda
1 teaspoon ground cinnamon
½ teaspoon ground nutmeg
½ teaspoon ground ginger
½ cup (1 stick) butter, melted

¾ cup orange juice
2 teaspoons vanilla extract
2 eggs
1½ cups cranberries, fresh or frozen
1 cup chopped walnuts or pecans, optional

1 Preheat the oven to 350°F. Coat 2 muffin pans with cooking spray.

2 Stir the flour, sugar, baking powder, baking soda, cinnamon, nutmeg, and ginger together in a large bowl; add the butter and mix with a fork until coarse crumbs form.

3 Whisk the orange juice, vanilla, and eggs in a small bowl; add to the dry ingredients and stir just until moist, about 30 seconds. The batter will look slightly lumpy. Gently fold in the cranberries and the nuts, if desired.

4 Divide the batter among the prepared muffin cups. Put a little water in each of the empty muffin cups so the pan does not bake dry. Bake for 25 minutes, or until golden brown on top.

QUICK TIP: Frozen raspberries or blueberries can be used in place of cranberries. Just toss the berries with 1 additional tablespoon of flour before folding into the batter.

FOR KEEPS: These muffins freeze well for up to 2 months. For freezing, cool the muffins completely. Transfer them to a ziplock freezer bag or container. If you layer the muffins, use waxed paper between the layers. If you are using a ziplock bag, press out as much air from the bag as possible without crushing the muffins.

MUFFINS MADE EASY

A milk-free muffin that's perfect for anyone who is lactose intolerant. The key to terrific muffins is to just *moisten* the batter when you combine the wet ingredients with the dry — do not beat or you will make one tough muffin!

Prep time 10 minutes   **Cook time** 20 minutes   **Yield** 12 muffins

2 eggs	1¼ cups plus 1 tablespoon all-purpose flour
½ cup sugar	1 teaspoon baking soda
¾ cup vegetable oil	¼ teaspoon salt
1 teaspoon grated lemon peel	1 cup frozen blueberries
3 tablespoons fresh lemon juice	

1. Preheat the oven to 350°F. Coat a muffin pan with cooking spray.

2. Combine the eggs, sugar, and vegetable oil in a large bowl; whisk for 2 minutes. Add the lemon peel and juice, stirring to blend.

3. Stir together 1¼ cups of the flour, the baking soda, and the salt in a small bowl. Add the dry ingredients to the wet ingredients; mix with a wooden spoon just until combined.

4. Toss the frozen blueberries with the remaining 1 tablespoon flour and add them to the batter, stirring once or twice just until incorporated.

5. Divide the batter among the prepared muffin cups. Bake for 20 to 22 minutes, until golden brown on top.

QUICK TIPS:

- **Add ½ teaspoon each of nutmeg and ginger to the dry ingredients for a spicier flavor.**
- **If you're using fresh blueberries in place of frozen, there's no need to toss them with flour.**

FOR KEEPS: **These muffins freeze well for up to 2 months; follow the For Keeps instructions on page 30.**

BLUEBERRY WHEAT MUFFINS

Not too sweet and very satisfying, these muffins are a great way to start the day. They're also a welcome addition to lunch boxes, a satisfying after-school snack, a quick pre- or post-game snack . . . get the picture?

Prep time 10 minutes **Cook time** 20 minutes **Yield** 12 muffins

¾ **cup all-purpose flour**
¾ **cup whole-wheat flour**
½ **cup firmly packed brown sugar**
1½ **teaspoons baking powder**
½ **teaspoon salt**
1¼ **cups blueberries, frozen**
1 **egg**
½ **cup milk**
½ **cup (1 stick) butter, melted**

1. Preheat the oven to 400°F. Coat a muffin pan with cooking spray.

2. Stir together the flours, brown sugar, baking powder, and salt in a large bowl; add the blueberries, tossing to coat.

3. Beat the egg, milk, and butter in a small bowl; add to the dry ingredients, stirring just until combined.

4. Divide the batter among the prepared muffin cups. Bake for 20 minutes, or until golden brown on top.

QUICK TIP: Any kind of fresh or frozen berries — blueberries, raspberries, blackberries — can be used in this recipe.

FOR KEEPS: These muffins freeze well for up to 2 months; follow the For Keeps instructions on page 30.

WHOLE GRAIN MASTER MIX

This is my original mix and the basis for the recipes on pages 34 through 38. This mix can be prepared in advance and stored at room temperature. It keeps well for up to two months. Measure it as you would flour. This mix is very handy when you need to make biscuits, pancakes, waffles, or muffins in a snap.

Prep time 10 minutes **Yield** About 7 cups

- 2 cups all-purpose flour
- 2 cups whole-wheat flour
- ¾ cup nonfat dry milk powder
- ½ cup old-fashioned rolled oats
- ½ cup cornmeal (white or yellow)
- 2 tablespoons baking powder
- 2 tablespoons sugar
- 1 teaspoon salt
- ½ cup vegetable oil

Combine the flours, dry milk, oats, cornmeal, baking powder, sugar, and salt in a large bowl. Using a pastry blender or 2 forks, cut in the oil until a coarse meal forms.

FOR KEEPS: Store the mix in a covered container at room temperature or in the refrigerator for up to 2 months.

KITCHEN 411: I cannot begin to tell you how excited my kids become when I have this mix on hand. They are able to make pancakes, waffles, and muffins very easily. I simply tape the recipes to the lid of the container that holds the mix — they're so easy, even my husband can prepare them. This mix is infinitely better than any purchased version, and should be substituted in any recipe that calls for the latter.

MASTER-MIX BISCUITS

These biscuits are rich and hearty and perfect for a sausage or ham breakfast sandwich.

Prep time **5 minutes** **Cook time** **10 minutes** **Yield** **15–20 biscuits**

3 **cups Whole Grain Master Mix (page 33)**
⅔ **cup water**

1 Preheat the oven to 400°F.

2 Combine the master mix and water; knead ten times.

3 Roll out the dough to a ½-inch thickness on a lightly floured surface. Using a lightly floured 2-inch-diameter biscuit cutter or drinking glass, cut out biscuits. Transfer them to an ungreased baking sheet.

4 Bake for 10 minutes or until light golden brown.

QUICK TIP: **Dip the biscuit cutter into flour to keep dough from sticking.**

MASTER-MIX MUFFINS

A great start before a long cross-country ski outing, these muffins are hearty and dense with dried fruit, nuts, or berries.

Prep time **5 minutes**   **Cook time** **18 minutes**   **Yield** **12 muffins**

3 **cups Whole Grain Master Mix (page 33)**

2 **tablespoons sugar**

1 **cup water**

1 **egg, beaten**

¾ **cup dried fruit, chopped nuts, or frozen blueberries or raspberries**

1   Preheat the oven to 400°F. Coat a muffin pan with cooking spray.

2   Combine all of the ingredients in a large mixing bowl; stir just until barely moistened.

3   Fill the muffin cups two-thirds full and bake for 18 minutes.

QUICK TIPS:

- **If you're using frozen berries toss them with 1 tablespoon of flour before folding them into the batter.**

- **For a sweet crunchy topping, sprinkle some cinnamon sugar over the muffins before baking.**

MASTER-MIX PANCAKES AND WAFFLES

These hearty pancakes and waffles will hold up to any kind of syrup or jam.

Prep time 2 minutes   **Cook time** 3 minutes
Yield About 16 four-inch pancakes or 6 waffles

> 3 **cups Whole Grain Master Mix (page 33)**
> 1½ **cups water**
> 1 **egg**

1. Combine all of the ingredients in a large bowl, whisking just until blended and lumps barely disappear, 10 to 15 seconds (do not mistake the oats for lumps in the batter; you do not want to overmix).

2. Set a nonstick griddle or skillet over medium-high heat or preheat an electric griddle or waffle iron. Before cooking, test your griddle with a drop of water — it should sizzle and evaporate in a few seconds.

3. Pour pancake batter onto the griddle and cook until bubbles appear on the surface and begin to pop, about 2 minutes. Flip the pancakes and cook until golden brown on the bottom, about 1 minute longer. Repeat with the remaining batter.

4. Serve hot with butter and warm syrup.

QUICK TIP: For a lunch idea, spread leftover pancakes with cottage cheese, egg salad, or chicken salad.

FOR KEEPS: Make a batch and stack the cooled pancakes between waxed paper; store in ziplock freezer bags, pressing out any excess air from the bags. Freeze up to 2 months. Pop into the toaster oven to heat for a quick meal or snack.

MASTER-MIX
PANCAKE VARIATIONS

Here are some additional pancake batter recipes.

PUMPKIN SPICE PANCAKES

A great recipe for any time of year, but the pumpkin pie spice especially evokes the smells of Thanksgiving and Christmastime.

> **3 cups Whole Grain Master Mix (page 33)**
>
> **1½ cups water, or slightly more for a thinner batter**
>
> **1 egg**
>
> **½ cup plain canned pumpkin**
>
> **1 tablespoon sugar**
>
> **1 to 2 teaspoons pumpkin pie spice**

1 Combine all of the ingredients in a large bowl, whisking just until blended and lumps barely disappear, 10 to 15 seconds.

2 Proceed with pancake cooking instructions on page 36.

APPLE CINNAMON PANCAKES

> **3 cups Whole Grain Master Mix (page 33)**
>
> **1½ cups water, or slightly more for a thinner batter**
>
> **1 egg**
>
> **1¼ teaspoons cinnamon**
>
> **1–2 Granny Smith apples, peeled, cored, and chopped into ¼-inch pieces**

1 Combine the master mix, water, egg, and cinnamon in a large bowl, whisking just until blended and lumps barely disappear, 10 to 15 seconds.

2 Gently fold the apples into the batter.

3 Proceed with pancake cooking instructions on page 36.

CHOCOLATE CHIP PECAN PANCAKES

These pancakes are a hit with the teenage girls when they sleep over. A fun recipe to eat for breakfast, as a snack, or even for dessert with a scoop of vanilla ice cream and chocolate sauce.

> **3 cups Whole Grain Master Mix (page 33)**
>
> **1½ cups water, or slightly more for a thinner batter**
>
> **1 egg**
>
> **¾ cup chocolate chips**
>
> **¼ cup chopped pecans**

1 Combine the master mix, water, and egg in a large bowl, whisking just until blended and lumps barely disappear, 10 to 15 seconds.

2 Gently fold chocolate chips and pecans into the batter.

3 Proceed with pancake cooking instructions on page 36.

MASTER-MIX
PANCAKE VARIATIONS

BANANA NUT PANCAKES

Kids love these pancakes. Add 2 tablespoons of peanut butter for a real treat.

> 3 **cups Whole Grain Master Mix (page 33)**
> 1½ **cups water, or slightly more for a thinner batter**
> 1 **egg**
> 1 **teaspoon vanilla extract**
> 2 **ripe bananas, mashed**
> ½ **cup chopped walnuts**

1. Combine master mix, water, egg, and vanilla in a large bowl, whisking just until blended and lumps barely disappear, 10 to 15 seconds.

2. Gently fold bananas and walnuts into the batter.

3. Proceed with pancake cooking instructions on page 36.

MORNING GLORY PANCAKES

An exceptionally hearty pancake. Perfect before a morning of cross-country or downhill skiing.

> 3 **cups Whole Grain Master Mix (page 33)**
> 1½ **cups water, or slightly more for a thinner batter**
> 1 **egg**
> ½ **Granny Smith apple, diced**
> ½ **carrot grated and finely chopped, about 2–3 tablespoons**
> ½ **cup shredded coconut**
> ½ **cup chopped pecans**

1. Combine master mix, water, and egg in a large bowl, whisking just until blended and lumps barely disappear, 10 to 15 seconds.

2. Gently fold apple, carrot, coconut, and pecans into the batter.

3. Proceed with pancake cooking instructions on page 36.

KITCHEN 411: **When making pancakes or waffles, err on the side of too many, as you can save the extras for later. Cool leftovers completely, stack between waxed paper, and transfer to a ziplock freezer bag before freezing. Then, the next time you're in a time crunch but have a taste for a syrupy, sticky breakfast, simply pop 'em into the toaster.**

CINNAMON STICKY BUNS

Even though I cut back on the butter and use a low-fat dough, this recipe still makes an incredibly soft and chewy cinnamon bun, complete with the sticky stuff. They are still not an everyday breakfast food, but for a special treat these sticky buns are always a crowd pleaser. Serve with a big bowl of fresh fruit.

Prep time 5 minutes   **Cook time** 20 minutes   **Yield** 8 servings

- 4 **tablespoons butter, melted**
- ½ **cup firmly packed brown sugar**
- 1½ **teaspoons cinnamon**
- 1 **(11-ounce) container reduced-fat breadstick dough**

1. Preheat the oven to 350°F.

2. Pour the butter into an 8- or 9-inch round baking pan.

3. Combine the brown sugar and cinnamon on a shallow plate.

4. Separate the breadsticks and dredge them, one at a time, in the sugar mixture, without shaking off the excess. Roll up each stick and transfer it to the buttered baking pan, leaving some room between the rolls to allow for expansion while baking. Top them with the remaining sugar mixture.

5. Bake for 20 minutes, or until golden brown. Remove from the oven and quickly invert onto a serving platter. Serve immediately.

FOR KEEPS: The leftovers (if any) will keep for 1 day in a resealable container.

After School and at the Game

We're an active family, and as long as we're not oversched-uled, the whole family functions pretty well. I try to keep up my level of physical activity, which sets a perfect example for my kids.

By using the recipes in this chapter you can help bridge the gap between school and dinner as well as give your family some great hearty and healthy snacks that can tide them over even beyond the dinner hour. Check out the Game Time section for great ideas to take to the soccer field or wherever your kids are playing their hearts out.

Most of these recipes are teen-friendly *and* great for times other than after school. Your teens can take advantage of the freedom they so desperately want by making some of these great snacks themselves.

SMOOTHIES, FLOATS, FREEZES, AND SHAKES

Try these sweet, easy, and refreshing beverages on sticky, hot summer days.

SUPER SNACKS

RAINBOW FREEZE

Prep time 2 minutes
Yield 2 servings

- 4 scoops rainbow sherbet
- 1 banana, sliced
- ½ cup strawberries, sliced
- ½ cup blueberries or raspberries, fresh or frozen, optional
- 1 (12-ounce) can or bottle ginger ale

Put 2 scoops of sherbet in each glass. Divide the fruit evenly among the glasses. Add ginger ale to fill the glasses and serve.

THICK AND CREAMY MILK SHAKE

Prep time 5 minutes
Yield 4 servings

- 3 cups cold milk
- 1 (3.9-ounce) package instant pudding (any flavor)
- 2 cups vanilla ice cream

Combine all of the ingredients in a blender, in the order listed; blend for 30 seconds. Pour into tall glasses and serve with straws and spoons.

PINK LADY

Prep time 5 minutes
Yield 4 servings

- 1 (12-ounce) can low-fat evaporated milk
- 1 (14.5-ounce) can unsweetened pitted tart cherries, drained
- 2 tablespoons chocolate syrup
- 1½ teaspoons almond extract
- ⅓ cup confectioners' sugar
- 10–12 ice cubes

Combine all of the ingredients in a blender; blend until smooth and frothy. Serve in tall glasses.

KITCHEN 411: Pitted tart cherries can also be found in the frozen-foods section of the grocery store. Sometimes they are sweetened. If that is the case, cut down on the sugar by 1 tablespoon.

BERRY FRUIT SMOOTHIE

Prep time 5 minutes
Yield 2 servings

1 (8-ounce) container low-fat yogurt,
    any flavor
1 cup frozen low-fat whipped
    topping, thawed
1 cup berries (if using strawberries,
    cut into 1-inch chunks)

Combine all of the ingredients in a
blender; puree. Serve in tall glasses.

QUICK TIP: Try these smoothie
combinations: strawberries with
blueberry yogurt; strawberries with lemon
yogurt; raspberries with vanilla yogurt;
blackberries with lemon yogurt.

FROZEN FLOAT

Prep time 5 minutes
Yield About 8 servings

1 (12-ounce) can light Concord
    grape juice frozen concentrate,
    thawed
½ gallon reduced-fat vanilla ice
    cream or low-fat vanilla frozen
    yogurt

Prepare the grape juice in a pitcher,
using only half of the water called for
in the instructions on the can.

Cut the ice cream into large chunks
and distribute among eight large
glasses (12 ounces or more). Divide
the prepared juice among the glasses
with ice cream and serve immediately.

SUPER SNACKS

FRUIT ROCKS

My mother made this healthy frozen fruit treat on hot, humid summer days; try it on that steamy July afternoon after you mow the lawn, wash the car, or paint the garage. You can use whatever fruit you have on hand and make as much or as little as you like.

Prep time **5 to 10 minutes** **Freeze time** **30 minutes** **Yield** **Varies**

Seedless grapes, stems removed

Apples

Bananas

Oranges

Nectarines

Plums

1 Slice the fruit into ¼- to ½-inch-thick slices. Slice the oranges in half lengthwise (through the stem), and then slice each half crosswise into ¼-inch-thick slices. Use paper towels to pat the fruit very dry.

2 Line a baking sheet with waxed paper. Transfer the fruit to the prepared baking sheet and freeze for 30 minutes.

3 Transfer the fruit to an airtight container and return it to the freezer until you're ready to serve.

QUICK TIP: **For an adult gathering, float a few slices of this frozen fruit in a chilled glass of sangria or sparkling rosé.**

FOR KEEPS: **Store fruit in an airtight container in the freezer for up to 1 month.**

WHAT ARE *YOU* MADE OF?

Sport drinks are intended for a very active person performing a minimum of 45 minutes of strenuous exercise — not for someone casually consuming the salty, day-glo liquid as a beverage with a sandwich at lunch, or with a high-calorie candy bar snack.

My beverage of choice is water; my snack of choice is fresh fruit. When the teens get together, I think these are *the* options for drinks and eats. Our bodies consist of approximately 65 percent water, and it takes an average of eight to ten cups to replenish the water we lose each day, not including what's lost during strenuous exercise. Fruits consist of 85 to 90 percent water. Why not put back into your body what it loses?

SUPER SNACKS

FRUIT KABOBS WITH YOGURT DIP

A fresh-fruit recipe you can serve for breakfast, at a party, at a game, or as a snack.

Prep time 10 minutes   **Yield** 20 kabobs

10 cups fresh fruit (strawberries, oranges, apples, bananas, pears, peaches, pineapple, blueberries, kiwi, mandarin oranges, seedless grapes, watermelon), cut into large cubes

Juice of 1 lemon

20 bamboo skewers

DIP

1 (16-ounce) container frozen low-fat whipped topping, thawed

1 (16-ounce) container low-fat strawberry yogurt

1 Thread the fruit onto skewers. Lightly brush the bananas, apples, peaches, and pears with lemon juice to prevent browning.

2 Make the dip: Combine the whipped topping and yogurt in a medium bowl, stirring to blend. Serve immediately.

QUICK TIPS:

- Add a gumdrop or marshmallow to the end of each skewer to keep the fruit from falling off or shifting.

- Use 4-inch mini-skewers for this recipe when you're serving a crowd. You can find them in the housewares section of the grocery store. With smaller skewers, this recipe will yield twice as many kabobs.

RIGATONI DIPPERS

You can use pasta as a dipper! I drummed up this idea when my kids wore braces and couldn't eat much for lunch after appointments with the orthodontist. These dippers are soft enough to chew, but sturdy enough to dip in pizza sauce, salad dressing, or even ketchup. Try them with Crazy Dipping Sauce (page 47).

Prep time 5 minutes **Cook time** About 9 minutes
Drying time 30 minutes **Yield** 4–6 servings

1 pound rigatoni noodles, regular or whole wheat

1. Cook the rigatoni in a large pot of salted boiling water until al dente. Drain and rinse under cold water, tossing several times with your fingers until the noodles have cooled to room temperature.

2. Leave the rigatoni in the colander set over a bowl or the sink for at least 30 minutes and up to 2 hours, until it's dry. Toss it occasionally with your fingers.

3. Store the rigatoni in ziplock bags in the refrigerator.

QUICK TIP: Allowing the excess water to evaporate gradually will keep the noodles from sticking together. Whatever you do, *do not* toss with oil. Dips and sauces will not stick to oiled pasta.

LET'S TALK: You can pack this pasta in smaller bags and grab a handful of bags before running out the door to pick up the kids after school or practice. The result? A quick energy snack before they run off to their next activity.

FOR KEEPS: Store the rigatoni in the refrigerator for up to 5 days.

DIPS, SAUCES, AND SPREADS
FOR GOOD-FOR-YOU SNACKS

FAVORITE FRUIT DIP

Prep time 10 minutes
Yield 2 servings

Kids and adults love the sweetness of this dip. For a bit more protein and crunch, add nuts.

> 1 (8-ounce) package low-fat cream cheese, at room temperature
> 1 cup firmly packed brown sugar
> 1 teaspoon vanilla extract
> ½ cup chopped nuts, optional
> Sliced apples, pears, strawberries, and/or bananas

1. Combine cream cheese, brown sugar, and vanilla in a medium bowl; mix well. Add the chopped nuts, if desired, stirring to combine.

2. Serve immediately with fruit or store in the refrigerator until ready to serve.

KITCHEN 411: Do not soften the cream cheese in the microwave unless you really know what you are doing. Instead, unwrap the package and let it sit on the kitchen counter for 30 to 40 minutes. If you are short on time, press the cream cheese against the side of a bowl with a wooden spoon until it softens.

FOR KEEPS: You can prepare this dip up to 4 days in advance. Add nuts if desired just before serving.

CRAZY DIPPING SAUCE

Prep time 5 minutes
Yield 1½ cups

Try this dip with egg rolls, fried wontons, Rigatoni Dippers (page 46), cheese ravioli, potatoes, celery, carrots, or cucumbers.

> ½ cup low-sodium soy sauce
> ¼ cup rice wine vinegar
> 3 scallions (white and tender green parts), thinly sliced
> 2 tablespoons fresh lemon juice
> 2 teaspoons sesame oil
> 1 tablespoon chopped garlic

Combine all of the ingredients in a small bowl, stirring to blend. Let stand for at least 15 minutes before serving.

QUICK TIP: If you have leftover dip, toss it with cut-up raw chicken and marinate in the refrigerator for 30 minutes or up to 1 day. Sauté, grill, or bake the chicken for a quick, tasty dinner. Serve with sautéed onions, carrots, and steamed rice.

DIPS, SAUCES, AND SPREADS
FOR GOOD-FOR-YOU SNACKS

CARAMEL APPLE DIP

Prep time 5 minutes
Cook time 2 minutes
Yield 2 cups

With fresh apples, this rich, creamy, and easy recipe makes for a tasty fall treat!

> 1 (14-ounce) package caramels
> 1 (8-ounce) package low-fat cream cheese, at room temperature
> Apple and pear slices

1. Unwrap the caramels and transfer to a medium microwave-safe bowl.

2. Cook on high heat for 1 to 2 minutes, stopping the microwave to stir the caramels every 30 seconds, until melted.

3. Add the cream cheese, stirring until smooth.

4. Serve warm with the sliced fruit.

QUICK TIP: Pour over French vanilla ice cream for a luscious variation.

FOR KEEPS: Prepare the dip up to 4 days in advance and chill; it keeps in the refrigerator for up to 2 weeks.

CREAM CHEESE SPREAD

Prep time 5 minutes
Yield About 2 cups

A colorful selection of vegetables adds texture, color, and crunch to this tasty spread. If you would like to spice things up, add a dash of chili powder, onion powder, and/or dried oregano to the finished spread.

> 1 (8-ounce) container light whipped cream cheese (chive or onion flavor works well), at room temperature
> ½ carrot, peeled and grated
> ¼ cup finely chopped broccoli
> ¼ cup finely chopped green bell pepper

Combine the cream cheese, carrot, broccoli, and bell pepper in a small bowl; mix well.

QUICK TIPS:

- Spread on pita bread, flour or corn tortillas, or mini bagels.

- Serve this spread as a dip for celery sticks, Seasoned Pita Chips (page 66), or Rigatoni Dippers (page 46).

- Toss the leftovers with boiled red potatoes or add a dollop to a baked potato for lunch.

SUPER SNACKS

QUICK BEAN DIP

Prep time 5 minutes
Yield 1¼ cups

An easy, slightly spicy, Mexican-inspired dip. Serve it with vegetables, crackers, tortilla chips, or Seasoned Pita Chips (page 66).

> 1 (15.5-ounce) can kidney beans, drained
> 1 tablespoon vinegar
> 1 teaspoon chili powder
> ⅛ teaspoon cumin
> 1 tablespoon finely chopped onion

1 Combine all of the ingredients in a food processor. Process for 30 seconds, scraping down the sides of the bowl every 10 seconds.

2 Serve at room temperature or chilled.

FOR KEEPS: This dip keeps well for up to 5 days in the refrigerator.

JAZZY CHEESE DIP

Prep time 5 minutes
Yield About 12 servings

This spicy dip is very flexible — feel free to change or modify the flavors in the recipe. Make a Mediterranean version with 1 teaspoon crushed rosemary and a pinch of sage instead of the Mexican chiles and spices. Serve with pretzel sticks, crackers, Rigatoni Dippers (page 46), or Seasoned Pita Chips (page 66).

> 1 cup small-curd cottage cheese
> 1 (8-ounce) package low-fat cream cheese, softened
> 1 cup reduced-fat sour cream
> 1 (4-ounce) can green chiles, drained and chopped
> 1 small jalapeño pepper, chopped
> 1 teaspoon chili powder
> ½ teaspoon garlic powder
> 2–3 scallions (white and tender green parts), sliced

1 Combine all of the ingredients in a food processor. Process for 30 seconds, scraping down the sides of the bowl every 10 seconds.

2 Refrigerate until ready to serve.

FOR KEEPS: Prepare up to 3 days in advance and chill.

DIPS, SAUCES, AND SPREADS
FOR GOOD-FOR-YOU SNACKS

HUMMUS DIP

Prep time 5 minutes
Yield About 2 cups

This is a quick twist on hummus. Kids love it, especially when they don't know what's in it! If your family likes more garlic flavor, use 1 to 2 cloves of fresh garlic instead of the garlic powder.

> 2 (15-ounce) cans garbanzo beans, drained
> 6 tablespoons fresh lemon juice
> 2 tablespoons sesame oil
> ½ teaspoon garlic powder
> Pinch of salt

1 Combine all of the ingredients in a food processor. Process until smooth, pulsing for the first 10 seconds.

2 Serve with pita wedges, celery and carrot sticks, Rigatoni Dippers (page 46), or Seasoned Pita Chips (page 66).

QUICK TIP: Fresh lemon juice makes a big difference in this recipe. To extract the juice more easily, roll the lemon firmly under your palm on the counter for a minute.

FOR KEEPS: This dip will last for up to 4 days in the refrigerator.

GREAT GUACAMOLE

Prep time 5 minutes
Yield About 2½ cups

> 3 large avocados, peeled, pitted, and coarsely chopped
> 1 teaspoon lemon juice
> ¼ teaspoon dill
> ½ teaspoon garlic salt
> 2–4 tablespoons salsa
> 1 cup plain low-fat yogurt

1 Combine all of the ingredients in a medium bowl; mash with a fork and mix to desired consistency.

2 Serve chilled or at room temperature with tortilla chips, pita wedges, or Seasoned Pita Chips (page 66).

QUICK TIP: What to do with leftover fresh lemon juice? Squeeze it on a salad tossed with olive oil and garlic, on grilled fish or sautéed shrimp, or over oven-roasted potatoes. A sprinkle of coarse sea salt and some freshly ground black pepper over all of these suggestions takes a simple meal into the gourmet category.

SAUSAGE CON QUESO DIP

Prep time 10 minutes
Cook time 8 minutes
Yield 4 cups

- 1 pound spicy breakfast sausage
- 1 pound low-fat processed cheese, such as Velveeta, cut into ½-inch cubes
- 1 medium tomato, diced
- 1 (4-ounce) can green chiles, drained and chopped
- Tortilla chips

1. Cook the sausage in a large skillet over medium heat, stirring to break it up until crumbled and browned. Transfer the sausage to paper towels to drain.

2. Return the sausage to the skillet and add the cheese. Cook over low heat for about 5 minutes, stirring often, until the cheese melts. Stir in the tomato and chiles.

3. Serve warm with tortilla chips.

QUICK TIP: You can melt the cheese in the microwave and add it to the cooked sausage to speed up the process.

FOR KEEPS: Can be made and refrigerated up to 4 days in advance. Reheat in the microwave.

PEANUT DIP

Prep time 5 minutes
Yield About 1½ cups

This is one of my favorite recipes and it's very versatile — it can be sweet or savory. Many people are fooled by the taste; they think it is a caramel dipping sauce. It's a great substitute and a lot healthier than any prepared version. Serve with pretzels, Rigatoni Dippers (page 46), celery or carrot sticks, banana slices, or apple slices.

- 1 cup crunchy or creamy peanut butter
- 5 tablespoons light maple syrup
- 2 tablespoons low-sodium soy sauce

Combine all of the ingredients in a small bowl, whisking to blend. Serve or store in the refrigerator.

QUICK TIP: Leftover dip (approximately ½ cup) can be mixed with 1 cup of chicken broth and simmered on the stove with sautéed onions, green peppers, garlic, and chicken slices. Serve over elbow macaroni with a green salad.

FOR KEEPS: You can make this dip in advance and refrigerate for up 2 weeks, or freeze for up to 2 months.

DIPS, SAUCES, AND SPREADS
FOR GOOD-FOR-YOU SNACKS

SUPER SNACKS

PIZZA DIP

Prep time 15 minutes
Cook time 15 minutes
Yield 12 servings

This ingredient list looks long but the recipe is quite easy and delicious. The dip is easily doubled for a large crowd.

- **1 (8-ounce) package low-fat cream cheese, at room temperature**
- **½ cup reduced-fat sour cream**
- **⅛ teaspoon garlic powder**
- **⅛ teaspoon ground cayenne pepper**
- **½ cup 5-Minute Pizza sauce (page 62) or prepared pizza sauce**
- **¼ cup chopped red bell pepper**
- **¼ cup black olives, sliced**
- **½ cup chopped artichoke hearts, optional**
- **½ cup grated mozzarella cheese**
- **½ teaspoon dried Italian seasoning**
- **1 bunch scallions (white and tender green parts), thinly sliced**

1. Preheat the oven to 350°F. Coat a 9-inch pie plate with cooking spray.

2. Combine the cream cheese, sour cream, garlic powder, and cayenne in a small bowl, mixing until smooth. Spread the cream cheese mixture evenly into the prepared pan.

3. Top the cheese with the pizza sauce, then the bell pepper, olives, artichoke hearts, if desired, mozzarella, and the seasoning.

4. Bake for 15 to 20 minutes, or until the cheese is browned and bubbly.

5. Sprinkle with scallions and serve with crackers, pita chips, or tortilla chips.

QUICK TIP: **If you don't have scallions handy, use 1 or 2 tablespoons of finely chopped sweet or red onion.**

ASIAN HOT SAUCE

Prep time 5 minutes
Yield About 1½ cups

- **1 (10-ounce) jar sweet and sour sauce, such as La Choy**
- **2 tablespoons hot mustard**

Combine the ingredients in a small bowl and mix well.

FOR KEEPS: **Stores well in the refrigerator, tightly sealed, for up to 2 weeks.**

AUNT MARG'S CHEESE BALL

My very good friend's great-aunt developed this recipe, and no one would *ever* change the name to anything else because everyone loved Aunt Marg. This recipe is a variation of the original. It is easy, can be made at least one week in advance, and is much more delicious and less expensive than the prepared version. The key is having the cream cheese at room temperature before mixing.

Prep time 15 minutes   **Chill Time** 30 minutes–1 week
Yield Serves 12–16 as an hors d'oeuvre

- 1 (8-ounce) package low-fat cream cheese, at room temperature
- 3-4 scallions (white and tender green parts), thinly sliced
- 2 ounces smoked deli ham, chopped
- ¼ teaspoon garlic powder
  Salt and pepper
- ½ cup grated sharp cheddar cheese (about 2 ounces)

1 Combine the cream cheese, scallions, ham, and garlic powder in a large bowl; mix with a wooden spoon until well blended. Season with salt and pepper to taste.

2 Transfer the cheese mixture to a piece of waxed paper. Using the waxed paper as a rolling tool, roll the cream cheese mixture into a ball and chill for at least 30 minutes or up to 1 week.

3 Transfer the grated cheese to a shallow bowl larger than the cheese ball.

4 Remove the ball from the refrigerator and roll it in the cheddar, using your hands to press the cheese evenly onto the surface.

5 Serve with crackers, pretzels, celery, or carrots.

QUICK TIPS:

- Before chilling, divide the cheese mixture into mini-balls for individual servings.
- Try adding different ingredients to the ones listed above — for example, ½ cup shredded crabmeat, ¼ cup finely chopped jalapeño pepper, or ¼ cup chopped pimiento, in any combination.
- Chopped walnuts can replace the cheddar cheese.

teen-friendly

POWER BALLS

Very easy, very quick, very good — and very nutritious!

Prep time **5 minutes**   **Cook time** **none**   **Yield** **24–30 balls**

½ **cup crushed cereal, preferably more**
   nutritious than sweet
1 **cup peanut butter**
½ **cup honey**
1 **cup nonfat dry milk powder**

1 Pour the cereal into a wide, shallow bowl. Line a baking sheet with waxed paper.

2 Blend the peanut butter and honey in a small bowl using the back of a wooden spoon; gradually add the nonfat dry milk until the mixture is stiff, but still easy to handle.

3 Using your hands, form balls the size of walnuts. Roll the balls in the crushed cereal.

4 Transfer the balls to the prepared baking sheet and refrigerate until ready to serve.

FOR KEEPS: **This recipe freezes well.**

SOCCER BUTTER

This is a great, sweet treat for the soccer player to make with the soccer dad.

Prep time **20 minutes** **Yield** **10 servings**

½ **cup peanut butter**

2 **tablespoons honey**

2½ **tablespoons nonfat dry milk powder**

½ **cup raisins**

¼ **cup shredded coconut**

1 Blend the peanut butter and honey in a small bowl using the back of a wooden spoon; gradually add the nonfat dry milk until the mixture is stiff, but still easy to handle.

2 Transfer the mixture to a work surface and knead in the raisins.

3 Using a rolling pin, roll out to a ¼-inch thickness. Sprinkle with coconut, roll into a 1-inch-diameter log, and chill.

4 Slice into 10 pieces. Serve.

QUICK TIP: **Chocolate chips can be substituted for the coconut in this recipe.**

SUPER SNACKS

brown-bag special

HANNA'S CAJUN TRASH

My father-in-law makes this recipe every New Year's Eve, when the family gets together, plays games, and eats snacks for hours.

Prep time 5 minutes **Cook time** 24 minutes **Yield** 6–8 cups

4	tablespoons butter, melted
1½	tablespoons salt-free seasoning blend
4–6	dashes hot sauce, such as Tabasco
6	cups of corn, rice, and/or wheat Chex-type cereal
1½	cups mini-pretzels
1	(2.8-ounce) can french-fried onions, optional
1–1½	cups lightly salted dry-roasted peanuts, optional

1   Preheat the oven to 350°F.

2   Whisk the butter, seasoning blend, and hot sauce together in a large bowl. Add the cereal, pretzels, and onions and peanuts if desired, tossing to coat evenly.

3   Transfer to 2 large baking sheets and bake for 24 minutes, stirring every 8 minutes.

4   Spread on paper towels to cool.

QUICK TIP: If you don't have the correct seasoning on hand, you can speed up the prep process with some tasty results by using your favorite "all-in-one" seasoning.

FOR KEEPS: You can store this snack in an airtight container in the pantry for up to 4 days.

MACHO NACHOS

This is the easiest way to make nachos — so easy that the kids can do it themselves.

teen-friendly

1 (16-ounce) can refried beans
1 (4-ounce) can green chiles, drained and chopped
2 cups grated sharp cheddar cheese (about 8 ounces)
1 package whole grain tortilla chips

1. Spread the refried beans on a large, ovenproof serving platter. Top with the chiles and cheese.

2. Broil about 4 inches from the heat source for 1 to 2 minutes, or until the cheese is melted.

3. Serve with the tortilla chips for dipping.

QUICK TIPS:

- Add any combination of the following to this recipe: sliced black olives, sliced scallions, chopped red or green bell pepper, shredded chicken, chopped jalapeños, shredded pork, kidney beans, sliced avocado, guacamole, sesame seeds, sautéed onions and zucchini, steamed green beans.

- Snyder's of Hanover makes good whole-grain tortilla chips.

- Make a dip for these nachos by mixing 1 to 2 tablespoons of reduced-fat sour cream into a small bowl of guacamole.

SUPER SNACKS

teen-friendly

QUICK QUESADILLAS

Here's a real quick kid-pleaser that uses food items that you may already have in your refrigerator. These are good ingredients to have around for many quick recipes.

Prep time **2 minutes**   **Cook time** **3 minutes**   **Yield** **4 servings**

4 **(6-inch) flour tortillas**
½ **cup grated sharp cheddar or Monterey Jack
     cheese (about 2 ounces)**
1 **tomato, chopped**
½ **head lettuce, chopped**
1 **bunch scallions (white and tender green
     parts), sliced**

1   Preheat the broiler.

2   Lay the tortillas on a baking sheet. Spray one side of each
    tortilla lightly with cooking spray.

3   Top each tortilla with 2 tablespoons of the cheese. Transfer
    to the broiler and broil until the cheese is melted. Remove
    immediately and top with the tomato, lettuce, and scallion.

4   Roll up and serve.

QUICK TIPS:

• **You can substitute 1 tablespoon of finely chopped yellow onion for
  the scallions.**

• **For a heartier snack or a meal, add diced red or green bell pepper,
  guacamole, refried beans, or chopped, cooked chicken, beef, or
  pork.**

SALSA TURKEY MEATBALLS

Make sure that you use spicy salsa so the meatballs have some kick.

Prep time 10 minutes   **Cook time** 20 minutes   **Yield** 24 (1½-inch) meatballs

MEATBALLS

- 1 **pound lean ground turkey**
- ⅓ **cup spicy salsa**
- ¼ **cup Italian seasoned breadcrumbs**
- ¼ **cup grated Monterey Jack cheese**
- 1 **bunch scallions (white and tender green parts), finely chopped**
- 1–2 **teaspoons chopped garlic**

SAUCE

- ¼ **cup spicy salsa**
- ¾ **cup reduced-fat sour cream**

1 Preheat the oven to 400°F. Coat a baking sheet with cooking spray.

2 Combine the turkey, salsa, breadcrumbs, cheese, scallions, and garlic in a large bowl; mix well.

3 Using your hands, roll the mixture into 24 meatballs, each about the size of a ping-pong ball, and transfer them to the prepared baking sheet. Bake for 20 to 25 minutes, or until golden brown.

4 Make the sauce: Combine the salsa and the sour cream in a small bowl. Mix well and serve with the meatballs.

QUICK TIP: Use bottled chopped or minced garlic for convenience.

FOR KEEPS: The meatballs freeze well before or after baking. To freeze before baking, place uncooked meatballs on a baking sheet and freeze until solid. Transfer to a ziplock freezer bag and store in the freezer for up to 2 months. To serve, transfer the frozen meatballs to a greased baking sheet and proceed as directed above, increasing the baking time by 5 to 8 minutes.

To freeze after baking, cool the meatballs completely; transfer to a ziplock plastic bag and store in the freezer for up to 2 months. To serve, thaw the meatballs in the refrigerator, then reheat in a 275°F oven for 10 minutes.

SUPER SNACKS

EASY PIZZA SQUARES

While testing this recipe I had a heck of a time trying to fine-tune it, so I brought a few samples to my neighbors to get some help. When they had a high-school graduation party for their daughter, they asked me to make up a big batch. More than 100 pieces were devoured in a matter of minutes!

1 (10-ounce) container refrigerated pizza dough

2 cups grated mozzarella cheese (about 8 ounces)

2 large tomatoes, thinly sliced

⅓ cup grated Parmesan cheese

1 tablespoon dried basil

⅔ cup light mayonnaise

1 teaspoon chopped garlic

1. Preheat the oven to 375°F. Lightly coat a 10- by 15-inch pan with cooking spray.

2. Press the dough into the prepared pan, sealing the perforations with your fingers.

3. Sprinkle the dough with 1 cup of the mozzarella; top with a layer of tomatoes.

4. Combine the remaining 1 cup of mozzarella with the Parmesan, basil, mayonnaise, and garlic in a small bowl; mix well. Spoon the cheese mixture over the tomato, spreading evenly with a butter knife.

5. Bake for 15 to 20 minutes, or until browned and bubbly. The crust will be soft. Cut into small squares and serve warm.

FOR KEEPS: These pizza squares can be made 1 day in advance or can be frozen for up to 1 month. They won't be as crisp when reheated, but they'll taste just as good.

VEGGIE GARDEN PIZZA

vegetarian

This is a great recipe for cleaning out the veggie drawer before things start looking a bit fuzzy. Use the vegetables listed below, or experiment with whatever is in your fridge; the recipe is very flexible.

Prep time 10 minutes   **Cook Time** 15 minutes   **Yield** 8–10 servings

- 2 (8-ounce) containers reduced-fat crescent dinner rolls
- 1 (8-ounce) container reduced-fat sour cream
- 1 tablespoon fresh ground horseradish
- ¼ teaspoon salt
- ⅛ teaspoon black pepper
- 2 cups chopped raw mushrooms
- 2 cups chopped raw vegetables, such as broccoli, green bell peppers, and tomatoes
- 1 bunch scallions (white and tender green parts), thinly sliced
- ½ large carrot, grated

1   Preheat the oven to 375°F.

2   Unroll the dough onto a work surface. Press it into the bottom of a 10- by 15- by 1-inch pan or onto a large baking sheet with 1-inch sides. Using your fingers, seal all perforations. Bake 15 minutes or until the crust is golden brown; cool completely.

3   Meanwhile, combine the sour cream, horseradish, salt, and pepper in a small bowl, mixing until smooth. Spread the horseradish mixture over the cooled crust and top with the mushrooms, chopped vegetables, scallions, and carrot.

4   Serve immediately or store in the refrigerator for up to 2 days before serving (crust will soften slightly).

QUICK TIP: **Fresh ground horseradish can be found in jars in the cheese or dairy section of the grocery store.**

vegetarian

MINI OLIVE PIZZAS

This is an olive-lover's snack that your teens can put together themselves. This dish can also work as a quick dinner with a salad and fresh fruit slices.

Prep time 5 minutes **Cook time** 1–2 minutes **Yield** 6 servings

6 **English muffins, halved**

1 **(15-ounce) can pizza sauce or 2 cups 5-Minute Pizza Sauce (see below)**

2 **cups grated mozzarella cheese (about 8 ounces)**

1 **(6-ounce) can pitted black olives, drained and sliced**

1 Preheat the broiler.

2 Place muffins, cut sides facing up, on a baking sheet. Top with pizza sauce and sprinkle with cheese and olives.

3 Broil for 1 to 2 minutes, or until the cheese is melted and bubbly.

4 Let cool slightly and serve.

QUICK TIPS:

• If you're in a hurry, use a sheet of aluminum foil in place of the baking sheet. When the pizza is cool enough to handle, simply wrap it up in the foil, throw the kids in the minivan, and you're off.

• Add some cooked, shredded chicken for a bit of protein.

5-MINUTE PIZZA SAUCE

Here's a pizza sauce recipe that you can make in — you guessed it — five minutes. It makes enough sauce for two 12-inch pizzas.

1 **can (28-ounce) crushed tomatoes in puree**

1 **tablespoon dried oregano**

2 **teaspoons chopped garlic**

1 **tablespoon dried basil**

1 **teaspoon onion flakes**

½ **teaspoon salt**

¼ **teaspoon black pepper**

¼ **teaspoon garlic powder**

¼ **teaspoon sugar**

Combine all the above ingredients and let stand for 5 minutes.

FOR KEEPS: **This sauce will keep in the refrigerator for one week. It also freezes beautifully for up to two months.**

PEPPER & ONION BISCUIT PIZZA

vegetarian

An easy dish to whip together, this pizza is a favorite with the kids. You can even make it ahead of time, and store it in the refrigerator up to eight hours. I have taken this to many functions as an appetizer and it is always the first thing to disappear!

Prep time 5 minutes **Cook time** 13 minutes **Yield** 6 servings

- 1 (10-ounce) container reduced-fat biscuits
- 1½ tablespoons olive oil
- 2 teaspoons Italian seasoning
- ½ teaspoon garlic salt
- ½ large green bell pepper, stemmed, seeded, and chopped
- ½ large red bell pepper, stemmed, seeded, and chopped
- ½ small onion, chopped
- 1 cup grated mozzarella cheese (about 4 ounces)

1. Preheat the oven to 400°F.

2. In the center of a 12-inch round pizza pan, arrange the biscuits in a circle with the edges just touching. Using your fingers, press the biscuits down to a ½-inch thickness.

3. Brush the biscuits with olive oil and top with the remaining ingredients, in the order specified above.

4. Bake for 13 to 15 minutes or until the edges of the biscuits are golden brown. Serve immediately.

> **QUICK TIP:** Let the kids add their own toppings: Suggest fresh tomato, fresh herbs, diced ham, pepperoni, cheddar cheese, or pineapple — it's up to them.

GAME TIME

Here are four quick tips for simple food to take right to the game. The remaining recipes in this chapter provide great energy boosts for the athletes in your house. When you choose one of these recipes, feeding the entire team between tournaments is always a slam-dunk!

SUPER SNACKS

PEANUT BUTTER JAM SQUARES

All you need is 1 loaf of whole-grain bread, a jar of natural peanut butter, and a jar of 100-percent fruit spread. Spread a healthy dose of peanut butter on each slice of bread, and add a tablespoon of fruit spread to half the slices. Slice each sandwich into 4 squares and pack in a crushproof, resealable container. If you have the time, slice off the crust for a more uniform look, and to please the picky eaters.

CHILLED FRUIT BOWL

Cut navel oranges in half lengthwise. Place each half on a cutting board and slice crosswise. This makes for easy-to-eat orange slices. Combine them with red and green seedless grapes in a crushproof resealable container. Chill for at least 4 hours for a super-refreshing snack after a hot soccer game.

DIAL-A-PIZZA

Yes, the wheels fall off of my cart once in a while and I forget to pull together a snack for the team. This is when one needs the local pizza joint's number programmed into the cell phone. Order a few plain pizzas and a few with vegetables. Skip the greasy pepperoni, sausage, ground meat, and bacon. Have the pizzas delivered to the field by the end of the game and you'll see some very happy kids!

WATER, WATER, WATER

No matter how boring it may look, water is the best thing for kids to drink during and after a game. Juice boxes and sports drinks, by contrast, are loaded with sugar and sodium. Take along a case of 8-ounce mini-bottles of water in an ice-filled cooler or a big jug with a tap and plenty of paper cups, and you're set for the day.

WARM DRINK FOR A COLD SOCCER GAME

A great recipe for watching games on cold Saturday mornings.

Prep time 2 minutes   **Cook time** 5 minutes   **Yield** 4 cups

2 **cups cranberry juice**

2 **cups pineapple juice**

1 **cinnamon stick**

Combine all of the ingredients in a medium saucepan over low heat and simmer for about 10 minutes, until hot and steaming (the longer the simmer, the better the flavor). Remove the cinnamon stick and pour into a thermos or mugs. Serve hot.

QUICK TIP: You can also warm up the juice in the microwave. Remember to remove the cinnamon stick before serving or storing.

SUPER SNACKS

teen-friendly

brown-bag special

SEASONED PITA CHIPS

This is one of my favorite crunchy snacks, and you will find endless possibilities for these simple chips. Easy, quick, and tasty, they are a great substitute for greasy potato chips.

Prep time **10 minutes**   **Cook time** **15 minutes**   **Yield** **About 40 chips**

1 **package whole-wheat or white pitas, cut in half crosswise and then split open**
Butter or olive oil, at room temperature
Garlic salt
Dried parsley

1   Preheat the oven to 350°F.

2   Spread each pita lightly with butter or olive oil and transfer to a baking sheet. Sprinkle them lightly with garlic salt and parsley.

3   Bake the pitas for about 15 minutes or until browned, watching carefully so that they don't burn.

4   Cool the pitas completely on the baking sheet and then break apart into tortilla chip-size pieces; store in an airtight container for up to 5 days.

QUICK TIPS:

• **Crumble on top of your favorite casserole before baking.**

• **Great with Cream Cheese Spread (page 48).**

• **Serve with a creamy soup and a salad on a brisk fall day.**

• **Perfect with a hot crab dip during the holidays.**

SEASONED SOUP CRACKERS

Quick to make, perfect to take!

Prep time 5 minutes   **Cook time** 20 minutes   **Yield** About 3 cups

1 **(1-ounce) package ranch salad dressing and seasoning mix**
¾ **cup vegetable oil**
1 **teaspoon dill weed**
¼ **teaspoon lemon pepper seasoning**
¼ **teaspoon garlic powder**
1½ **(12-ounce) packages oyster crackers**

1   Preheat the oven to 250°F.

2   Combine the salad dressing mix, oil, dill, lemon pepper, and garlic powder in a large bowl. Add the crackers to the oil mixture, tossing to coat.

3   Pour the crackers into a large baking pan and bake, stirring twice, for 20 minutes.

4   Remove the crackers from the oven and let them cool. Store in an airtight container or a ziplock freezer bag for up to 2 weeks.

QUICK TIP: Serve with a creamy soup like High-Protein Tomato Soup (page 98).

2000 NUTS 'N' BOLTS (AKA CHEX PARTY MIX)

This is a new and easier way to make an old-fashioned snack favorite. My friend Lauren knows how lousy I am at making this snack in the oven — I always burn it. The microwave was an easy solution, but my daughter still thinks that the oven-baked version is the best.

Prep time 5 minutes   **Cook time** 8 minutes   **Yield** 8 servings (about 12 cups)

- 2 cups Rice Chex cereal
- 2 cups Wheat Chex cereal
- 2 cups Corn Chex cereal
- 2 cups Cheerios
- 2 cups roasted, salted peanuts
- 2 cups mini-pretzels
- ½ cup (1 stick) butter, melted
- ¼ cup Worcestershire sauce
- ½ teaspoon garlic powder
- ½ teaspoon onion powder

1 Combine the cereals, peanuts, and pretzels in a large microwave-safe bowl.

2 Stir the butter, Worcestershire, garlic powder, and onion powder together in a small bowl. Add the seasoned butter to the cereal mixture; toss well.

3 Heat the mixture in the microwave on high for 6 to 8 minutes, stirring well every 2 minutes.

4 Transfer the party mix to paper towels to cool completely. Serve or store in an airtight container.

GREAT GRANOLA CRUMBLE

Although you can buy granola bars and cereal in the grocery store, nothing beats this recipe for true, nutty granola taste. The bars are breakable, so consider eating them in chunks or by the handful, crumbled in yogurt, on top of ice cream, or sprinkled on your cereal in the morning.

vegetarian

Prep time **20 minutes**   Cook time **20 minutes**   Yield **About 5 cups**

3½ **cups old-fashioned rolled oats**
1 **stick plus 3 tablespoons butter, melted and cooled slightly**
¼ **cup firmly packed brown sugar**
¼ **cup honey**
1 **egg, beaten slightly**
1 **teaspoon vanilla extract**
½ **teaspoon salt**
1 **cup raisins**
½ **cup walnuts, chopped**

1. Preheat the oven to 350°F.
2. Spread the oats in a 9- by 13-inch pan, and bake for 12 minutes. Let them cool for about 5 minutes; remove the oats from the pan and set aside. When the pan is cool, coat it with cooking spray.
3. Whisk the butter, sugar, honey, egg, vanilla, and salt together in a large bowl. Add the oats, raisins, and walnuts; mix well. Pour oat mixture into the prepared pan. Press it firmly into the pan, and bake for 20 minutes.
4. Remove from oven. When cooled completely, slice into bars.

QUICK TIP: **Spray the measuring cup with cooking spray before measuring honey. The honey will slip right out of the cup, making cleanup a snap.**

FOR KEEPS: **Store in an airtight container for up to 5 days or in the freezer for up to 2 months.**

QUICK COCOA MUFFIN CAKES

This recipe delivers rich cocoa taste with a firm texture — handy for snacks at home, in the car, or after a game.

Prep time 8 minutes   Cook time 16 minutes   Yield 12 muffins

1½ cups all-purpose flour
¾ cup firmly packed brown sugar
¼ cup unsweetened cocoa
1 teaspoon baking soda
½ teaspoon salt
1 cup water
¼ cup vegetable oil
1 tablespoon white vinegar
1 teaspoon vanilla extract

1 Preheat the oven to 375°F and fill 12 muffin tins with paper liners.

2 Sift together the flour, sugar, cocoa, baking soda, and salt in a medium bowl.

3 Add the water, oil, vinegar, and vanilla, whisking just until the batter is smooth and well blended.

4 Fill the muffin cups two-thirds full. Bake for 16 to 18 minutes, or until a toothpick inserted into the center comes out clean.

5 Let the muffins cool for 10 minutes in the pan and then remove them from the pan and cool them completely on a wire rack.

LET'S TALK: **These cakes are so good by themselves that I do not recommend frosting them. My teenage daughter has some friends who are lactose intolerant, so she makes this recipe for them when she knows that they'll be visiting.**

SUPER SNACKS

POPCORN SNACKS

Using convenient microwave popcorn and simple seasonings, you can create better-than-movie-theater popcorn at home and offer your family a healthy snack at the same time.

POWER-PACKED POPCORN

Prep time 5 minutes
Cook time 15 minutes
Yield About 10 cups

- 1 (3.5-ounce) package light microwave popcorn, popped
- 2 cups unsweetened dry cereal, such as Cheerios or Chex
- 1 cup croutons (seasoned, if desired)
- 1 cup pretzel sticks
- ½ cup lightly salted dry-roasted peanuts
- 2 tablespoons butter, melted
- 2 teaspoons Worcestershire sauce
- ½ teaspoon garlic powder
- ½ teaspoon chili powder
- ½ teaspoon onion powder
- ½ cup raisins, optional

1. Preheat the oven to 300°F.

2. Combine the popcorn, cereal, croutons, pretzels, and peanuts in a large bowl.

3. Whisk together the butter, Worcestershire, garlic powder, chili powder, and onion powder in a small bowl; add to the popcorn mix, stirring to coat.

4. Spread the mixture onto a large baking sheet and bake, stirring once or twice, for 15 minutes, just long enough for the seasoned butter to infuse the mixture.

5. Remove from the oven and add raisins, if desired. Let the popcorn cool on the baking sheet and serve.

QUICK TIP: For a milder flavor, use 2 packages of popcorn.

FOR KEEPS: This recipe stores well for 4 days in an airtight container.

POPCORN SNACKS

SPICY CHILI POPPERS

Prep time 3 minutes
Cook time 1 minute
Yield About 10 cups

¼ cup vegetable oil
1½ tablespoons chili powder
½ teaspoon salt
Pinch of sugar
1 (3.5-ounce) package light
microwave popcorn

1 Combine the oil, chili powder, salt, and sugar in a small microwave-safe bowl. Microwave for 30 seconds; stir to blend.

2 Pop the popcorn in the microwave according to the package instructions, and then transfer to a large bowl.

3 While the popcorn is still hot, drizzle it with the seasoned oil, tossing to coat; serve immediately.

MACHO NACHO MEXICAN-STYLE POPCORN

Prep time 5 minutes
Cook time 3 minutes
Yield About 10 cups

½ teaspoon paprika
½ teaspoon cumin
⅛ teaspoon ground cayenne pepper
Pinch of sugar
4 tablespoons butter, melted
1 (3.5-ounce) package light
microwave popcorn
½ cup grated Parmesan cheese

1 Combine the paprika, cumin, and cayenne in a small bowl; add the sugar and butter, and mix well.

2 Pop the popcorn in the microwave according to package instructions; transfer to a large bowl.

3 While the popcorn is still hot, drizzle with the butter mixture and the Parmesan, tossing quickly to coat; serve immediately.

QUICK TIP: For a milder flavor, use two packages of popcorn.

ZESTY ITALIAN POPCORN

Prep time 2 minutes
Cook time 3 minutes
Yield About 18 cups

   4 tablespoons butter, melted
   1 envelope dry Italian salad dressing
     mix, such as Good Seasons
   2 (3.5-ounce) packages light
     microwave popcorn

1 Combine the butter with the salad dressing mix in a small microwave-safe bowl; microwave 10 to 20 seconds.

2 Pop the popcorn in the microwave according to the package instructions and transfer it to a large bowl.

3 While the popcorn is still hot, drizzle with the butter mixture, tossing quickly to coat; serve immediately.

POPCORN SALLY

This lightly seasoned snack is a recipe from my good friend, Sally Dishaw.

Prep time 5 minutes
Cook time 3 minutes
Yield About 10 cups

   4 tablespoons butter, melted
   ¼ teaspoon garlic powder
   ¼ teaspoon onion powder
   ¼ cup grated Parmesan cheese
   1 (3.5-ounce) package light
     microwave popcorn
   ⅛ teaspoon salt

1 Combine the butter, garlic powder, onion powder, and Parmesan in a small microwave-safe bowl; microwave for 30 seconds.

2 Pop the popcorn in the microwave according to the package instructions and transfer it to a large bowl.

3 While the popcorn is still hot, drizzle with the butter mixture, tossing quickly to coat; serve immediately.

SUPER SNACKS

On-the-Run Snacks and Meals

Okay, so you have five minutes to gather everything and everyone, pile into the car, and make it to the practice in fifteen minutes — *and* everyone is hungry. Go!

The recipes in this chapter will help you in exactly this kind of situation. They were created for, tested on, and fed to kids on the go (in my minivan, to be exact). Some can be prepared in five minutes; others can be prepared in advance, stored in the freezer, and grabbed when needed. These recipes are fun, tasty, nutritious, and convenient.

When it comes time to pack the food, always have on hand a small, insulated, lightweight cooler that you can sling over your shoulder. This will hold the juice boxes, yogurt cups, cheese sticks, and whatever else you grab. It can also be used as a trash receptacle when everyone has finished eating. Have the kids put all unwanted food items and trash back into the cooler and you'll need to remove only a single item from your vehicle rather than clean up tons of wrappers and half-empty juice boxes. The cooler will also help guard against "exploding juice box" syndrome (you know: when a juice box left in the trunk of the car explodes from the heat — yuck, what a mess).

These recipes have been lifesavers for me. I hope you enjoy them as much as I do!

QUICK SNACK TIPS

Here are some inventive approaches to finding healthy, quick snacks and meals when you're short on time.

FROM THE PANTRY

- In a ziplock bag, mix equal amounts of Life or Cheerios cereal, raisins, and dry-roasted, lightly salted peanuts; it's a great combination of flavors and easy to take anywhere.

- Open a can of refried beans (the kind with no lard). Spread 2 to 3 tablespoons on a whole-wheat flour tortilla, splash a bit of salsa on top, then unwrap a cheddar cheese stick and place in the middle of the tortilla. Roll up and eat.

- Open and drain a can of tuna. Add to the can 1 tablespoon of light mayonnaise, ¼ teaspoon of Italian seasoning, and a sprinkle of salt. Mix with a fork and eat over the sink. (Not a habit I would necessarily suggest mentioning to your mother.)

THE SANDWICH SOLUTION

- Keep a bag of mini-bagels in the freezer. A sliced-open bagel spread with horseradish sauce and topped with slices of turkey and cheese is a great mini-sandwich.

- A peanut butter sandwich can be a quick, healthy meal, especially when paired with nutritious toppings. Make sure that you have whole-wheat bread and natural peanut butter on hand, as well as some of the following toppings within easy reach, so that the kids can create their own sandwich combinations (and consider one for breakfast when you're on the go): raisins, fruit spread, wheat germ, shredded carrots, dried fruit, sunflower seeds, coconut, granola, banana slices, apple slices, or pretzel sticks.

MYSTERY ROLL-UPS

Whenever I have dinner leftovers, I chop them up together and put them in the middle of a whole-wheat flour tortilla. I sprinkle a bit of shredded cheese and salsa on top. Then I roll up the tortilla, wrap it in waxed paper, put it into a large ziplock freezer bag, and throw it into the freezer. When I'm in a hurry, I grab one of these mystery roll-ups, warm it in the microwave, and eat on the run. I've used leftovers like grilled steak, baked chicken, rice, eggs, pasta, potatoes, peas, broccoli, beans, and more for past roll-ups. With salsa and cheese, it's amazing how good they can taste.

SOCCER FUEL WRAPS

With a flour tortilla and an assortment of fillings, you have endless options. Try:

- Deli meat and a stick of mozzarella string cheese.
- Tuna and Swiss with a swipe of mayo, sprinkled with dill.
- Fried egg with salami slices.
- Leftover slices of beef with Havarti cheese and a swipe of horseradish sauce.
- Diced cucumber, tomato, cheese, and chopped lettuce, with a dollop of ranch dressing.

HELPFUL ITEMS FOR THE GRAB-AND-GO PANTRY:

- ☑ aluminum foil
- ☑ ziplock bags of assorted sizes
- ☑ waxed paper
- ☑ plastic wrap
- ☑ napkins, napkins, and more napkins
- ☑ travel-size moist wipes
- ☑ reuseable ice packs
- ☑ coolers of assorted sizes

A backpack containing:

- ☑ sharpened pencils
- ☑ pens
- ☑ a spiral notebook (for lists, ideas, etc.)
- ☑ a good book to read (maybe this one!)
- ☑ more napkins

TOM'S TURKEY ROLLS

Almost everyone has a version of this recipe, but I've found that the ingredients below make for the perfect combination.

Prep time 2 minutes   Yield 4 servings

4 (10-inch) flour tortillas

¼ cup light mayonnaise

2 teaspoons horseradish

12 ounces smoked turkey, thinly sliced

4 large romaine lettuce leaves, washed and dried

1 Warm the tortillas for a few seconds in the microwave.

2 Combine the mayonnaise and horseradish in a small bowl.

3 Spread a thin layer of the mayonnaise mixture on each tortilla and divide the turkey and lettuce evenly among the 4 tortillas. Roll up the tortilla tightly around the filling and wrap in foil or plastic wrap.

4 Serve immediately, refrigerate, or pack in a cooler until ready to eat.

KITCHEN 411: Jarred horseradish can be found near the cheese or dairy section of the supermarket. For this recipe, you can also use prepared horseradish sauce, which can be found in the condiments aisle (it's usually a mayonnaise and horseradish blend).

FOR KEEPS: Turkey rolls can be stored in the refrigerator for up to 2 days. To serve, transfer the rolls to a plate and cover with a damp paper towel; microwave on high for 6 to 10 seconds to soften.

GRAB AND GO

CHICKEN CAESAR PITAS

teen-friendly

This recipe is easy to make and can be wrapped and carried just about anywhere.

Prep time 5 minutes   **Yield** 4–6 servings

- 2 cooked chicken breast halves, thinly sliced
- 3 cups finely chopped salad greens
- ¼ cup grated Parmesan cheese
- ¼ cup light mayonnaise
- 2 tablespoons Caesar salad dressing
- 1 handful grape tomatoes
- 2–3 pita breads, halved

1 Combine the chicken, salad greens, Parmesan, mayonnaise, salad dressing, and tomatoes in a large bowl; toss to coat all of the ingredients.

2 Fill the pita halves and go.

QUICK TIPS:

- Italian salad dressing may be used in place of the Caesar salad dressing.
- See pages 10 and 11 for easy ways to prepare chicken for recipes such as this one.
- To make this a vegetarian main dish, replace the chicken with a can of drained garbanzo beans and serve with baby carrot sticks and Seasoned Pita Chips (page 66).

GRAB AND GO

FIVE-MINUTE
ON-THE-GO SNACKS

When you only have a few minutes and need just a little something to tide you over, try these snacks.

APPLE STACK

> 1 apple
> 2 slices sharp cheddar cheese, ¼-inch thick

Slice apple crosswise into 3 equal pieces (no need to core). Place slices of cheese between each layer, making a stack. Wrap and go.

KITCHEN 411: Nobody likes slices of brown apple. In this clever snack the cheese naturally stops the apples from browning when stuck firmly together.

SPARTAN ROUNDBALLERS TRAIL MIX

Yield About 4 cups

> 1 cup salted Spanish peanuts
> 1 cup raisins
> ½ cup dried coconut flakes
> ½ cup dried banana chips
> ½ cup dried pineapple
> ¼ cup chocolate chips

Combine all ingredients and store the mix in an airtight container.

QUICK CRACKERS

> **Crackers:** Wheat, sesame, saltines, cheddar, etc.
> **Cheese:** Slices of cheddar, mozzarella, Muenster, Swiss, reduced-fat cream cheese, etc.
> **Toppings:** Ham, turkey, bologna, peanut butter, green olives, black olives, pineapple chunks, bananas, apples, low-sodium bacon bits, tomato slices, etc.

Assemble the crackers, cheese, and toppings as desired. Wrap and go.

HAM POCKETS

Wonderful as a snack, as a quick meal, or in a lunch box. Take the time to make several batches at once and you'll be happy when it comes time to grab and go.

Prep time 30 minutes   **Cook time** 15 minutes
Yield 4 dinner or 8 snack servings

1 (10-ounce) package frozen chopped broccoli, thawed and drained

4 ounces deli ham, finely chopped

1 bunch scallions (white and tender green parts), thinly sliced

⅓ cup stuffed green olives, chopped

1½ cups grated Swiss or cheddar cheese (about 6 ounces)

1½ teaspoons savory or oregano

¼ teaspoon salt

¼ teaspoon black pepper

1 pound frozen bread dough, thawed

1 Preheat the oven to 375°F. Coat 2 baking sheets with cooking spray.

2 Combine the broccoli, ham, scallions, olives, cheese, and spices in a large bowl; mix well.

3 Cut the dough into 8 equal pieces. On a lightly floured surface, roll out each piece of dough to a 6-inch square. Top each square with ⅓ cup of the ham mixture. Fold one corner over the filling to form a triangle, pinching the edges with your fingers to seal. Make 2 small slits in the top of each pocket to allow steam to escape.

4 Transfer the pockets to the prepared baking sheets. Bake for 15 to 20 minutes, or until golden brown.

5 Cool completely on a wire rack.

FOR KEEPS: **When cool, wrap the pockets in aluminum foil and refrigerate up to 3 days or freeze up to 2 months. Reheat them uncovered in a 350°F oven for 10 to 15 minutes.**

vegetarian

KID'S BURRITO

It can't get much easier than this. Beans, cheese, and tortillas. It really is a perfect combination — as simple as it sounds. We all have these essential ingredients in the fridge and pantry and if you don't, add them to your shopping list. They're lifesavers when all else fails and you're on the go.

Prep time 5 minutes **Cook time** 10 minutes **Yield** 10 servings

1 (16-ounce) can refried beans
10 (6-inch) flour tortillas
3 cups grated sharp cheddar cheese
(about 12 ounces)

1 Preheat the oven to 350°F.

2 Divide the beans evenly among the tortillas, spreading them down one side. Sprinkle with cheese, and roll up. Transfer to a baking sheet, seam-side down. Bake for 8 to 10 minutes.

3 Cool slightly, grab, and go!

QUICK TIPS:

• Find refried beans that are made without lard — they're a lot healthier for the whole family.

• Add a little salsa to the refried beans for a twist.

• Burritos can be topped with lettuce, tomato, onion, sour cream, and/or salsa. These toppings may make the burritos a little harder to eat in the car, but they also make for a great after-school snack or quick dinner.

LET'S TALK: I don't always have refried beans when I need them, so I figured out how to make an emergency batch. In a small saucepan, sauté ½ teaspoon of prepared chopped garlic in 2 teaspoons of olive oil for 30 seconds over medium heat. Add one well-drained can of pinto beans and stir. Mash the beans with a potato masher to desired consistency, adding water to thin out the mixture as needed. Remove from heat and voilà!

JJ'S PIZZA SNACK

My daughter makes this recipe when she comes home from school: one serving each for her brother and her. She sandwiches together the remaining two servings, wraps them in foil, and places them in the refrigerator for lunch the next day. Hot from the oven, at room temperature, or cold, this snack works great on the go.

Prep time 8 minutes   **Cook time** 13 minutes   **Yield** 4 servings

  4 **whole English muffins**
  1 **(12-ounce) can tomato sauce**
  ½ **teaspoon basil**
  ½ **teaspoon oregano**
  ¼ **teaspoon salt**
  ⅛ **teaspoon black pepper**
  1 **cup grated mozzarella or Monterey Jack cheese (about 4 ounces)**
 24 **slices pepperoni**

1 Preheat the oven to 400°F.

2 Split the muffins open and lay on a baking sheet, cut sides up.

3 Combine the tomato sauce, basil, oregano, salt, and pepper in a small bowl; mix well with a whisk or fork. Spread 1 to 2 tablespoons of the sauce mixture onto each muffin; top with grated cheese and 2 pieces of pepperoni.

4 Transfer to the oven and bake until the cheese is melted, 13 to 15 minutes.

vegetarian

PIZZA POCKETS

These pockets are easy to make and they freeze well. Just microwave when needed, pack, and eat on the road.

Prep time **10 minutes** **Cook time** **15 minutes** **Yield** **4 servings**

1 (10-ounce) container refrigerated pizza
    dough

¼ cup 5-Minute Pizza Sauce (page 62) or
    ¼ cup canned pizza sauce

1 cup grated mozzarella cheese
    (about 4 ounces)

Finely chopped olives, chopped mushrooms,
    finely chopped green bell pepper, or finely
    chopped onion, optional

½ pound thinly sliced deli ham or salami,
    optional

Italian seasoning

1   Preheat the oven to 400°F.

2   On a work surface, unroll the dough and cut into 4 equal pieces. Transfer to a large baking sheet.

3   Spread 1 tablespoon of sauce on each piece of dough to within 1 inch of the edge; top with cheese and any optional ingredients, as desired. Sprinkle with Italian seasoning.

4   Fold the short side of the dough in half over the filling, pinching the edges together to seal.

5   Bake for 15 to 20 minutes, or until golden brown.

6   Let them stand for 5 minutes to cool. Serve or cool completely before storing in the refrigerator or freezer.

GRAB AND GO

STUFFED CHICKEN CRESCENTS

Great to serve as an appetizer at home, or to grab and go.

Prep time   **10 minutes**   Cook time   **20 minutes**   Yield   **4 servings**

3 ounces low-fat cream cheese, at room temperature

2 tablespoons butter, melted

2 tablespoons milk

2 cups cubed cooked chicken

¼ teaspoon salt

⅛ teaspoon black pepper

1–2 scallions (white and tender green parts), thinly sliced

1 (8-ounce) container reduced-fat crescent dinner rolls

1 Preheat the oven to 350°F.

2 Combine the cream cheese, butter, and milk in a medium bowl, mixing until smooth. Add the chicken, salt, pepper, and scallions; mix well.

3 On a work surface, separate the crescent dough into 4 rectangles; firmly press perforations to seal. Flatten the dough slightly with your fingers.

4 Divide the chicken mixture evenly among the dough rectangles, mounding the mixture in the center of each. Gather the 4 corners of each dough rectangle at the top of its mound of mixture, twisting gently to seal.

5 Transfer them to a baking sheet and bake for 20 to 25 minutes, or until golden brown. Serve.

QUICK TIPS:

• See pages 10 and 11 for easy ways to prepare chicken for recipes like this one.

• You can make the filling for this recipe up to 1 day in advance. For a luncheon, assemble the crescents and pop them in the oven just before your guests arrive. Then serve with a tossed green salad and slices of tropical fruit.

GRAB AND GO

SAUSAGE ROLL

Dense, rich, and chock-full of goodies, this snack is great to take to practice during the dinner hour. Or serve with salad for a meal at home.

½ pound Italian sausage, hot or mild, casing removed

1¼ cup grated sharp cheddar cheese (about 5 ounces)

¼ cup finely chopped onion

2 tablespoons finely chopped green bell pepper

2 tablespoons finely chopped celery

1 jalapeño pepper, finely chopped, optional

1 pound frozen bread dough, thawed

1 Cook the sausage in a medium skillet over medium-high heat for 5 minutes, breaking up the sausage as it browns. Use a slotted spoon to transfer it to paper towels to drain.

2 Combine the sausage, cheese, onion, bell pepper, celery, and jalapeño, if desired, in a medium bowl.

3 Roll out the dough on a work surface to a 9- by 16-inch rectangle. Spread sausage mixture evenly over the dough, leaving a ½-inch border. Starting with one long side, tightly roll up the dough, pinching the seam closed.

4 Line a baking sheet with parchment. Place the roll on the parchment, seam-side down. Let it rest for 30 minutes in a warm draft-free place.

5 While the roll is resting, preheat the oven to 350°F.

6 Bake until golden brown, 30 to 35 minutes. Let the roll stand to cool and serve at room temperature.

QUICK TIPS:

• Finely chopped carrots, zucchini, red bell peppers, scallions, and Polish sausage would all be delicious options for this recipe.

• Use a meat substitute to create a vegetarian dish.

GRAB AND GO

BEEF CORNER POCKETS

Fantastic flavor that takes a bit of up-front time, but well worth it.

Prep time 30 minutes   **Cook time** 15 minutes   **Yield** 6–8 servings

⅔ pound lean ground beef or turkey

2 tablespoons finely chopped onion

2 tablespoons finely chopped green bell pepper

1 medium tomato, seeded and finely chopped

½ teaspoon salt

¼ teaspoon black pepper

1 tablespoon cornstarch

½ cup low-sodium beef broth

2 tablespoons raisins, chopped

1 tablespoon chopped, slivered almonds, optional

2 (9-inch) prepared refrigerator piecrusts

1 Preheat the oven to 400°F.

2 Sauté the meat in a medium skillet over medium heat for about 8 minutes, breaking up the meat as it browns. Drain.

3 Return the pan to the heat and add the onion, bell pepper, tomato, salt, pepper, cornstarch, and broth. Stir for 3 to 4 minutes, until the mixture begins to thicken. Remove from the heat; add raisins and almonds, if desired, stirring to combine. Add the meat to the vegetable mixture.

4 Roll out 1 piecrust slightly on a floured surface. Using a biscuit cutter or a drinking glass, cut 3-inch circles from the dough. Repeat with the other piecrust. Spoon 1 teaspoon of the meat mixture onto the center of each dough circle.

5 Fold each circle in half over the filling to form a crescent shape, and press the edges with your fingers to seal. Make a slit in the top of each crescent to allow steam to escape. Transfer to an ungreased baking sheet.

6 Bake for about 15 minutes, or until golden brown. Serve warm.

QUICK TIP: Freeze the cooled pockets. Warm them in the microwave for another great grab-and-go snack!

GRAB AND GO

PIGGY IN A BLANKET

Picky eaters tend to like this recipe. It's perfect for the lunch box; round it out with carrot sticks for crunch and grapes for sweetness.

Prep time 15 minutes   **Cook time** 14 minutes   **Yield** Serves 10–12

1 (11-ounce) container reduced-fat breadstick dough
1 (16-ounce) package cocktail frankfurters
Ketchup, mustard, and barbecue sauce for dipping

1 Preheat the oven to 375°F.

2 Unroll the dough onto a work surface and separate the breadsticks. Cut each piece into 4 equal sections; you should have 48 small rectangles. Using your fingers, press out each piece of dough slightly.

3 Transfer 1 frankfurter to each piece of dough; roll the dough around the frankfurter, carefully stretching the dough to fit all the way around. Press the seam to seal. Transfer them, seam-side down, to a large baking sheet.

4 Bake for about 14 minutes, until golden brown.

QUICK TIP: Ketchup, mustard, barbecue sauce, light mayonnaise, salsa, cheese dip, relish — the dip options for these little snacks are limited only by what's in your pantry and refrigerator.

SOUTHWEST-STYLE CHEESY BREAD

This recipe works great as an on-the-go snack. It also makes a quick and easy companion to a bowl of soup. Add a salad and you've got yourself a meal.

Prep time 5 minutes   **Cook time** 18 minutes   **Yield** 4–6 servings

- 1 (10-ounce) container refrigerated pizza dough
- 1 (4-ounce) can green chiles, drained and chopped
- ¾ cup grated sharp cheddar cheese (about 3 ounces)
- ½ cup grated Monterey Jack cheese (about 2 ounces)
- ½ teaspoon garlic powder

1. Preheat the oven to 375°F. Coat a large baking sheet with cooking spray.
2. Unroll the dough onto the prepared baking sheet. Using your fingers, press out the dough into a 10-inch square.
3. Top with the chiles and both cheeses, leaving a ½-inch border.
4. Starting at one side, fold in the dough, just past the middle. Fold the opposite side just past the middle to form a pocket. Pinch closed at the seam formed by the second fold to form a pillow. Dust with garlic powder.
5. Bake for 18 to 20 minutes, until golden brown. Let cool for about 10 minutes and serve.

GRAB AND GO

QUICK TIPS:

- Add thin slices of tomato, red or green bell pepper, or red onion to turn this simple snack into a quick adult appetizer.
- Add cooked, shredded chicken to the filling for added protein.

FOR KEEPS: This bread freezes well before baking. Increase the baking time by 10 minutes if it's frozen.

brown-bag special

HURRICANE TWISTERS

Packed with carbohydrates and flavor!

Prep time 8 minutes   **Cook time** 16 minutes   **Yield** 6 servings

- 2 **tablespoons olive oil**
- 2 **tablespoons grated Parmesan cheese**
- 2 **tablespoons poppy seeds**
- 2 **tablespoons sesame seeds**
- 2 **teaspoons chopped garlic**
- 1 **(11-ounce) container reduced-fat breadstick dough**

1   Preheat the oven to 375°F. Coat a large baking sheet with cooking spray.

2   Combine the olive oil, Parmesan, poppy seeds, sesame seeds, and garlic in a small bowl.

3   Separate the dough into 12 breadsticks. Stretch and twist each one to a 10-inch length and transfer to the baking sheet. Divide the seed mixture evenly over the dough twists, spreading it out with your fingers.

4   Bake for 16 to 18 minutes, until golden. Serve warm or at room temperature.

QUICK TIP: Baking parchment can be expensive, so use it sparingly. When you're in a hurry, use it for this recipe to make cleanup a snap.

GRAB AND GO

RASCAL NUTS

Grab a few handfuls of this tasty, high-protein, vegetarian snack, throw them into a ziplock bag, and go.

Prep time **5 minutes** **Cook time** **60 minutes** **Yield** **About 1½ cups**

> 1 **teaspoon garlic powder**
> 1 **teaspoon onion powder**
> ¾ **teaspoon salt**
> 1 **(15-ounce) can garbanzo beans, drained but still moist**

1 Preheat the oven to 300°F. Lightly coat a baking sheet with cooking spray.

2 Combine the garlic powder, onion powder, and salt in a medium bowl. Add the beans; toss well. Spread the beans out in a single layer on the prepared baking sheet.

3 Bake the beans, stirring every 15 minutes, for about 60 minutes, until browned and crisp.

4 Cool the beans completely on the baking sheet. Transfer them to an airtight container and store in the refrigerator for up to 2 weeks or in a cool dark place for 4 days.

Soups, Salads, and Sandwiches

Lunches in our house are often prepared and packed in brown paper bags at 5:30 in the morning for the school or work day. At other times they are packed in a cooler and eaten in periodic spurts depending on what athletic event is being held on a Saturday. And sometimes lunch is actually a leisurely event (typically on Sunday afternoons) when we can sit together, grab a salad, sandwich, or cup of soup, and catch up on what everyone's schedules are for the rest of the day. Lunch can be leftover chicken stuffed into a quick chicken salad sandwich, or it can be a hot bowl of tomato soup with cheese and a heel of bread. Whatever the case, our lunches are always interesting, hearty, easy, and quick to make.

Soups, salads, sandwiches, and miscellaneous goodies that are great for lunch (or dinner), and are also convenient and nutritious, were what I had in mind when creating these recipes. Like the recipes in the other chapters, a lot of the ingredients are already in your pantry or refrigerator.

The soups in this chapter have wonderful flavors and warm the soul on a cool day. Also included are a lot of great salad choices to help round out any meal and satisfy many different needs — potluck dinners, group dinners, brown-bag specials, or quick eating on the run.

vegetarian

TEXAS CORN CHOWDER

If you can use a can opener, you can make this soup.

Prep time **5 minutes**   **Cook time** **5 minutes**   **Yield** **4–6 servings**

1 **(15-ounce) can whole kernel corn, drained**

1 **(15-ounce) can cream style corn**

1 **(14.5-ounce) can diced tomatoes with garlic and onions**

1 **(15-ounce) can black beans, drained and rinsed**

½ **cup low-sodium chicken broth**

Combine all of the ingredients in a medium pot over medium heat; simmer for 5 minutes and serve.

QUICK TIPS:

• Top this chowder with cheddar cheese, fresh chopped green pepper, chopped jalapeño, or a dollop of reduced-fat sour cream.

• You can also add ½ pound of Italian or Polish sausage, or a chunk of ham. I slice it up and sauté it with a coarsely chopped onion until the onion is limp, about 8 minutes. Then follow the recipe.

FOR KEEPS: This soup keeps in the refrigerator for 2 days and freezes well for up to 2 months.

SOME THINGS I'VE LEARNED ABOUT MAKING DELICIOUS SOUP:

• Leftovers are the best starters for soup.

• Always sauté your vegetables in a bit of oil in the soup pot before you add the broth.

• Use low sodium broth so you can control the salt.

• Leftover pan juices, gravy, or spaghetti sauce will give the soup a lot of depth.

• Use beans, pasta, barley, or potatoes to thicken the soup instead of cream.

• Don't follow a recipe word for word; follow your instincts.

BLT SOUP

My kids love this soup. Eaten with a big hunk of crusty bread, it tastes just like a BLT sandwich.

Prep time **10 minutes**   Cook time **15 minutes**   Yield **4–6 servings**

- 8 slices bacon, cut into 2-inch pieces
- 1 medium onion, chopped
- 1–2 stalks celery, chopped
- 3 cups low-sodium beef broth
- 1 (14.5-ounce) can diced tomatoes
- 1 tablespoon Worcestershire sauce
- ¼–½ teaspoon garlic powder
- 1 teaspoon dried parsley
- ½ teaspoon dried thyme
- ½ teaspoon freshly ground black pepper
- Dash of hot sauce, optional
- 2 cups shredded lettuce

1. In a large pot over medium heat, cook the bacon until crisp.

2. Transfer the bacon to paper towels to drain. When cool enough to handle, crumble the bacon. Discard all but 2 tablespoons of the pan drippings. Sauté the onion and celery in the pan drippings over medium heat, stirring frequently, until soft, about 8 minutes.

3. Add the broth, tomatoes, Worcestershire, garlic powder, parsley, thyme, pepper, and hot sauce, if desired; bring the soup to a boil. Reduce the heat to low and simmer for 15 to 20 minutes.

4. Serve immediately, topped with shredded lettuce and the reserved crumbled bacon.

QUICK TIP: **Adding a sprinkle of sharp cheddar cheese and a slice of avocado with the lettuce adds a nice twist. You can also add shredded beef, chicken, or pork.**

FOR KEEPS: **Make this soup up to 2 days in advance. When ready to serve, just reheat and top with bacon and lettuce.**

KITCHEN SINK SOUP

Rummaging through my vegetable crisper drawer one day, I came across enough slightly neglected vegetables to build a delicious soup. I dumped everything into the sink, carefully washed each piece, and got to work. When you're worried about items in your vegetable drawer going to waste, build your own kitchen sink soup! This one is quick, light, and delightful.

Prep time 5 minutes   **Cook time** 15 minutes   **Yield** 4–6 servings

7	cups low-sodium chicken broth
2	large carrots, grated or finely chopped
2-3	stalks celery, chopped
1	small onion, chopped
2	(15-ounce) cans great northern beans, drained and rinsed
½	teaspoon black pepper
1	(10-ounce) package frozen chopped spinach (see note on fresh greens on the following page)

1. Combine the broth, carrots, celery, and onion in a large pot over medium-high heat; bring to a boil.

2. Reduce the heat and simmer until the celery is tender, about 10 minutes; add the beans, pepper, and spinach.

3. Simmer for 3 to 5 minutes, until spinach has thawed and broken up. Serve.

QUICK TIP: A sprinkle of Parmesan cheese and a few croutons will dress this soup up for an elegant dinner starter. Serve with French bread and cheese.

LET'S TALK: In the dead of winter, fresh spinach is not always easy to come by. Even the stems in the produce section look pretty sick, so opt for frozen spinach. But in the middle of the summer when greens are at their peak, use fresh spinach as often as you can.

KITCHEN 411: **WORKING WITH FRESH GREENS**

My general rule of thumb is:

1 pound fresh = 1 cup cooked = 5 ounces frozen

To wash fresh greens, cut off all but 1 inch of stem. Stack 5 leaves on top of each other and cut into 1-inch slices. Place in a large bowl and fill with cool water. Soak for 5 to 10 minutes, occasionally stirring greens vigorously with your hands to loosen any dirt, grit, or sand attached to the leaves and stems. Gently lift the greens from the surface of the soaking water, which allows the dirt to stay in the bottom of the bowl. Discard the water, rinse the bowl, and repeat.

Store washed and drained greens in a ziplock bag for up to 2 days in the refrigerator. You can keep the stems and steam them a bit longer than you would the leaves. Then sprinkle them with olive oil and sea salt and serve with grilled sirloin steak.

THE LUNCH CRUNCH

teen-friendly

HIGH-PROTEIN TOMATO SOUP

This canned-soup recipe will supply kids with plenty of the calcium and protein needed for growing bodies.

Prep time **3 minutes**   **Cook time** **5 minutes**   **Yield** **4 servings**

1 **(10.5-ounce) can condensed low-sodium tomato soup**
10½ **ounces milk (enough to fill the soup can)**
½ **cup grated sharp cheddar cheese (about 2 ounces)**

Combine the soup, milk, and cheese in a medium microwave-safe bowl; microwave to heat it through, stirring occasionally, until the cheese melts. Serve immediately.

QUICK TIPS:

• **Serve with Seasoned Pita Chips (page 66).**

• **For a more filling soup, add 1 cup of cooked rice.**

• **For a chunky tomato soup, add 1 (14.5-ounce) can seasoned diced tomatoes.**

• **Nothing goes together better than tomato soup and a grilled cheese sandwich. Serve this soup with the Best-Ever Grilled Cheese Sandwich (page 123).**

THE LUNCH CRUNCH

MIDWESTERN CORN CHOWDER

In the late fall, the weather in the Midwest can be described as sharp, brisk, biting, crisp, or downright cold. This calls for a hot bowl of hearty soup. This chowder is quick and easy, and it seals in the essence of that crisp November day. In the words of Clementine Paddleford, "Chowder breathes reassurance. It steams consolation."

Prep time 15 minutes **Cook time** 15 minutes **Yield** 4–6 servings

2 tablespoons vegetable oil
3 cups good quality country ham, cubed
1 medium onion, finely chopped
1 stalk celery, finely chopped
4 cups low-sodium chicken broth

2 large potatoes, scrubbed and diced
1 bay leaf
1 teaspoon salt
3½ cups milk
2½ tablespoons all-purpose flour
1 (15-ounce) can whole kernel corn, drained

1 Heat the oil in a large pot over medium-high heat; add the ham, onion, and celery, and sauté for 5 minutes.

2 Add the broth, potatoes, bay leaf, and salt; bring to a simmer. When the potatoes are just tender, about 8 minutes, remove the pot from the heat.

3 Whisk together 1½ cups of the milk and the flour in a medium bowl; add to pot. Simmer over medium-low heat until thickened, about 10 minutes. Add the corn and the remaining 2 cups of milk.

4 Heat the chowder through and serve.

QUICK TIPS:

- **Look for sliced or cubed ham in vacuum packages near other cured meats in the refrigerator case of your local grocery store.**
- **This soup can be prepared up to 2 days in advance. Heat and serve.**

PEANUT SOUP

Peanut soup is popular on the coast of Virginia and is typically served with slices of French bread and a simple green salad. The ground peanuts or peanut butter create a thick, rich, soup, satisfying enough for a meal.

Some of my daughter's girlfriends were a little hesitant when I served this lunch to celebrate the end of their high school finals. They ended up asking for seconds and thirds, and two of their parents called later that day asking for the recipe.

Prep time **10 minutes**   **Cook time** **10 minutes**   **Yield** **4–6 servings**

4	cups low-sodium chicken broth
1	(14.25-ounce) can stewed chopped tomatoes
2–3	carrots, chopped
2	bunches scallions (white and tender green parts), thinly sliced
1	cup peanut butter
1	cup milk
¼	cup instant mashed potato flakes

1 Bring the broth, tomatoes, carrots, and scallions to a boil in a large pot. Reduce the heat to medium-low; simmer until the carrots are tender, about 5 minutes.

2 Stir in the peanut butter until well blended.

3 Add the milk and potato flakes; simmer 2 minutes. Serve immediately.

QUICK TIP: When you know you've got picky eaters around, use an immersion blender to puree all of the vegetables into the soup — they'll have no idea what may be in the mix.

FOR KEEPS: Store the soup in the refrigerator for up to 2 days. It also freezes well for up to 2 months.

THE LUNCH CRUNCH

BLUE CHEESE AND WALNUT SALAD (FOR SOCCER PARENTS)

A grown-up salad with a light dressing and the sophisticated flavor combination of blue cheese, walnuts, and dried apricots.

Prep time 5 minutes   Marinate time 30 minutes   Yield 6–8 servings

¾ **cup olive oil**

¼ **cup rice vinegar**

½ **cup dried apricots, cut in quarters**

2 **(16-ounce) bags salad greens**

¾ **cup crumbled blue cheese (about 3 ounces)**

½ **cup chopped walnuts**

1 **cup croutons, plain or seasoned**

1   Whisk together the oil and vinegar in a small bowl. Add the apricots and marinate for 30 minutes.

2   Put the salad greens in a salad bowl; sprinkle with cheese and walnuts.

3   Pour the dressing over salad and toss gently to coat. Add the croutons and serve.

QUICK TIP: **Kitchen shears are a perfect tool for cutting dried fruit into smaller pieces.**

CUCUMBER TOMATO SALAD

Nothing tastes better than a crisp, cool salad on a hot summer evening. Serve this one with steaks or burgers from the grill and a large loaf of country Italian bread. Because you can make the salad in advance, it leaves you time to relax with friends.

Prep time 5 minutes   **Yield** 6–8 servings

- 6 tablespoons olive oil
- ¼ cup fresh lemon juice
- ½ teaspoon salt
- ⅛ teaspoon black pepper, plus more for seasoning
- ¼ teaspoon crushed red pepper flakes
- 3 large cucumbers, seeded and peeled
- 4 pints grape tomatoes
- ¼ small red onion, thinly sliced

1 Whisk together the oil, lemon juice, salt, black pepper, and pepper flakes in a large serving bowl.

2 Cut the cucumber in half lengthwise and then slice into ½-inch pieces. Add the cucumber, tomatoes, and red onion to the bowl, tossing to coat with dressing. Season with more pepper to taste.

3 Let the salad stand at room temperature for 30 minutes to 4 hours, tossing occasionally. Serve at room temperature.

QUICK TIPS:

- **Add a little crumbled feta cheese for a Mediterranean flair.**
- **Scoop out the cucumber seeds with a spoon if the salad will be sitting for a few hours. This step will prevent the cucumbers from watering down the dressing.**
- **Toss leftovers with chilled pasta. Add diced chicken and a can of drained garbanzo beans for an instant pasta salad.**

FOR KEEPS: Because there are no salad greens that will wilt, you can keep the leftovers in the refrigerator for up to 3 days.

THE LUNCH CRUNCH

MAKE-YOUR-OWN ANTIPASTO PASTA SALAD

This pasta recipe is like a deli counter. Some people like ham and some people like salami. You can pick and choose your own ingredients.

Prep time **5 minutes**   **Cook time** **10 minutes**   **Yield** **4–6 servings**

1 **pound pasta**
  Your favorite antipasto ingredients
  Italian, Caesar, or Greek salad
    dressing

1 Bring salted water to a boil for the pasta.

2 Meanwhile, choose desired ingredients from the Menu Board Options and toss gently in a serving bowl.

3 Cook the pasta al dente in the boiling water. Drain and rinse briefly under cool water; drain well. Add to the serving bowl with the antipasto ingredients; drizzle with enough dressing to coat everything well, but not so much that the dressing pools in the bottom of the bowl.

4 Serve warm or chilled.

MENU BOARD OPTIONS

1 **(6-ounce) jar marinated artichoke hearts, drained and quartered**

1 **(4-ounce) jar roasted red peppers, drained and sliced**

⅓ **pound thinly sliced salami**

⅓ **pound thinly sliced deli ham**

1 **(6-ounce) can white albacore tuna in vegetable oil, drained and flaked**

¼ **red onion, thinly sliced**

1 **large tomato, chopped**
  Broccoli florets

¼ **cup pitted green or black olives**

¼ **pound provolone cheese, cubed**

¼ **cup grated Parmesan cheese**

Vegetarian

MANDARIN SALAD

This is not the quickest salad in the West, but I believe that it's the tastiest. The candied almonds set this salad apart — they add crunch, texture, and flavor.

Prep time 15 minutes   Cook time 3 minutes   Yield 4–6 servings

CANDIED NUTS

½ **cup sliced almonds**

3 **tablespoons sugar**

DRESSING

¼ **cup vegetable oil**

2 **tablespoons vinegar (preferably red wine vinegar)**

1 **tablespoon chopped fresh parsley**

2 **tablespoons sugar**

1-2 **dashes hot sauce**

½ **teaspoon salt, plus more for seasoning**

⅛ **teaspoon black pepper, plus more for seasoning**

SALAD

1 **(16-ounce) bag salad greens**

2 **stalks celery, chopped**

2 **scallions (white and tender green parts), sliced**

1 **(11-ounce) can mandarin oranges, drained**

Salt and pepper

1 Heat the almonds and sugar in a small nonstick skillet over medium-high heat, stirring constantly to prevent burning, until the almonds are coated and the sugar has dissolved, 3 to 5 minutes. Transfer the almonds to paper towels to cool.

2   Make the dressing: Combine the oil, vinegar, parsley, sugar, hot sauce, salt, and pepper in a jar. Shake well to blend.

3   Combine the lettuces, celery, and scallions in a salad bowl. Add the oranges and the candied almonds. Shake the dressing, add it to the salad, and toss to coat.

4   Season with salt and pepper to taste; serve.

QUICK TIP: To enliven the flavor of nuts before topping a salad or any other dish, heat ¼ cup of nuts in a small skillet over medium heat, shaking the pan vigorously a few times and keeping a close eye on the nuts. Within 1 to 2 minutes you will see the nuts brown slightly, and they will become more fragrant. Remove them from the heat immediately and let them cool in the pan for a few minutes before sprinkling them on your salad.

FOR KEEPS: You can make the almonds ahead of time and store in an airtight container for up to 1 week. The dressing will keep in the refrigerator for up to 1 week.

LET'S TALK: Nuts (and seeds) are a nutritious alternative to croutons, and their texture, crunch, appearance, and flavor all work together to help tie together almost any salad. Try using almonds, walnuts, pecans, peanuts, macadamias, sunflower seeds, cashews, or pistachios. Just a sprinkle goes a long way.

UNTOSSED SALAD

If you are not aware of this type of salad, you must try this recipe. The idea is similar to that of a layered dip. You don't toss it so that you get some of everything in equal amounts. This is a great salad to make in advance when you're having a crowd over for the weekend.

| Prep time | 15 minutes | Chill time | 8 hours or overnight | Yield | 8–10 servings |

- 1 large head of lettuce, shredded
- 2 bunches scallions (white and tender green parts), thinly sliced, (or ½ red onion, finely chopped)
- 1 (10-ounce) bag frozen peas, thawed
- 3–4 strips cooked, crumbled bacon or 2 tablespoons prepared bacon bits
- 5 hard-cooked eggs, peeled and chopped
- 1 cup whipped salad dressing, such as Miracle Whip
- 2 tablespoons sugar
- 1 cup shredded sharp cheddar or Swiss cheese (about 4 ounces)

In a 9- by 13-inch glass casserole dish, layer the lettuce, scallions, peas, bacon, and egg; spread with the salad dressing. Top with the sugar and cheese. Cover and refrigerate for 8 hours, overnight, or up to 3 days.

QUICK TIP: **Pair this easy side dish with garlic bread and grilled pork chops.**

THE LUNCH CRUNCH

GREEK SALAD

Serve this assertive salad with simple grilled chicken on a summer evening.

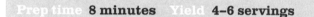

2-3 **medium cucumbers, diced (peel and seed if desired)**
1 **cup plain low-fat yogurt**
1 **teaspoon chopped garlic**
1½ **teaspoons dried dill**
2 **teaspoons cider vinegar**
¾ **teaspoon salt**
Black pepper

1 Combine all of the ingredients in a serving bowl; toss well. Add pepper to taste.

2 Cover and chill until ready to serve.

THE LUNCH CRUNCH

GREEN SALAD WITH BACON AND CREAMY GARLIC DRESSING

This quick and easy salad is perfect for a potluck or summer side dish. The water chestnuts give it a pleasant crunch.

Prep time 5 minutes   **Chill time** 10 minutes   **Yield** 4–6 servings

- ½ cup reduced-fat sour cream
- 3 tablespoons red wine or cider vinegar
- 1 tablespoon milk
- 2 teaspoons sugar
- ½ teaspoon salt
- ¼ teaspoon garlic powder
- 1 (10-ounce) package frozen peas, thawed and patted dry
- 1 (8-ounce) can sliced water chestnuts, drained
- 1 bunch scallions (white and tender green parts), thinly sliced
- 6 slices cooked, crumbled bacon or 4 tablespoons prepared bacon bits

1. Whisk together the sour cream, vinegar, milk, sugar, salt, and garlic powder in a serving bowl. Chill for 10 minutes or up to 2 days.

2. Add the peas, water chestnuts, scallions, and bacon to the bowl; toss to coat. Serve.

QUICK TIP: Add ½ cup dry roasted peanuts or cashews.

MAKIN' BACON

I buy a couple of packages of bacon at a time when it's on sale. I throw one into the freezer and chop the other into small chunks — I usually get four to six chunks from a 1-pound package. I wrap the chunks individually in foil and then store them in a ziplock freezer bag. Whenever a recipe needs some extra flavor and crunch, I grab a chunk and add it, still frozen, to the skillet or soup pot.

SIMPLE SLAW

Cole slaw is easy to make — even easier now that prepackaged slaw mixes are available in produce sections across the nation. What's nice about this recipe is its ease of preparation and that it lasts for a good week in the fridge.

vegetarian

Prep time **10 minutes** **Yield** **6–8 servings**

- ½ **cup light mayonnaise**
- ¼ **cup reduced-fat sour cream**
- 2 **tablespoons vinegar**
- 2 **teaspoons Dijon mustard**
- ¼ **teaspoon sugar**
- ¼ **teaspoon salt**
- ⅛ **teaspoon black pepper**
- 1 **(16-ounce) bag packaged cole slaw mix**
- 1 **small onion, thinly sliced**
- 2 **tablespoons caraway seeds, optional**

1. Whisk together the mayonnaise, sour cream, vinegar, mustard, sugar, salt, and pepper in a large bowl with a lid.

2. Add the cole slaw mix, onion, and caraway seeds, if desired; toss well to coat.

3. Refrigerate for at least 1 hour to allow the flavors to develop. Serve cold.

QUICK TIP: You can also use a broccoli slaw mix if you prefer.

CHICKEN AND CHERRY SALAD

Michigan dried cherries are outstanding and are now available all across the United States. This recipe features this chewy little fruit, bursting with flavor. This is a perfect salad to take in a cooler and stuff into pita pockets to serve to the kids between tournament games. Add some raspberry iced tea and some celery and carrot sticks to your cooler, and off you go!

Prep time 15 minutes **Yield** 4 servings

- ½ cup dried tart cherries
- 2 cooked boneless, skinless chicken breast halves, cubed
- 2 stalks celery, finely chopped
- 1 large Granny Smith apple, peeled, cored, and finely chopped
- ½ cup chopped walnuts
- 1 cup light mayonnaise
- 2 tablespoons finely chopped fresh parsley
  Salt and pepper

1 Combine the cherries with ¼ cup of boiling water in a medium sealable bowl. Let the cherries stand for 5 minutes or until they have plumped; drain well and pat dry. Return the cherries to the bowl.

2 Add the chicken, celery, apple, walnuts, mayonnaise, and parsley; mix well. Add salt and pepper to taste.

3 Cover and chill before serving.

QUICK TIPS:
- **You will need cooked chicken for this recipe. Check out the quick chicken recipes on pages 10 and 11.**
- **Serve the salad on a bed of lettuce or stuffed into a pita.**

FOR KEEPS: This salad keeps well in the refrigerator for up to 3 days.

SEVEN-LAYER CHICKEN SALAD

An excellent dish to take to a potluck cookout.

brown-bag special

Prep time	10 minutes	Chill time	1 hour	Yield	4–6 servings

1 large head romaine lettuce, torn into bite-size pieces

1 (3-ounce) package ramen noodle soup mix, any flavor

2 cups diced cooked chicken

1 (15-ounce) can whole kernel corn, drained

1 large tomato, chopped

1 bunch scallions (white and tender green parts), thinly sliced

½ cup chopped walnuts, pecans, or dry roasted peanuts

Salad dressing of your choice — you can try an Asian dressing or a basil vinaigrette; both produce good results

1. Put the lettuce in a serving bowl.

2. Discard the noodle seasoning packet; crush the noodles with the palm of your hand and add them to the serving bowl.

3. Layer the chicken, corn, tomato, scallions, and walnuts over the noodles; chill for 1 hour or up to 1 day.

4. When you're ready to serve, toss with your favorite salad dressing.

QUICK TIPS:

• **You will need cooked chicken for this recipe. Check out the quick chicken recipes on pages 10 and 11.**

• **A light vinaigrette or ranch dressing is also perfect for this salad.**

FOR KEEPS: Make 4 mini-versions of this salad and store them in the refrigerator in small, resealable containers for up to 4 days. Toss with your favorite dressing for a quick, light meal.

THE LUNCH CRUNCH

QUICK ASIAN CHICKEN SALAD

The sesame dressing brings together the chips, chicken, and sesame seeds in a salad that is simple, light, and pleasantly salty. Don't be tempted to make this salad if you're missing any of the ingredients. You will need every item to really make it special.

Prep time 5 minutes **Yield** 6–8 servings

1 (16-ounce) bag tortilla chips, crushed lightly

1 large head of lettuce, torn

4 cups shredded or diced cooked chicken

1–2 bunches scallions (white and tender green parts), finely sliced

2 tablespoons sesame seeds, toasted

DRESSING

½ cup vegetable oil

¼ cup vinegar (rice or cider)

3 tablespoons sugar

1 tablespoon sesame oil

½ teaspoon salt

½ teaspoon black pepper

1 Layer the chips, lettuce, chicken, scallions, and sesame seeds in the bottom of a large serving bowl.

2 To make the dressing, combine the oil, vinegar, sugar, sesame oil, salt, and pepper in a small jar. Cover and shake well. Pour the dressing over the salad, tossing gently to coat.

3 Serve immediately.

QUICK TIPS:

• Add a dash of soy sauce or ginger powder to the dressing for a new and interesting taste.

• Use unsalted tortilla chips for less sodium.

• Substitute fresh spinach for some of the lettuce.

KITCHEN 411: To toast seeds, place them in a small skillet over medium heat, keeping a *very* close eye on them so that they don't burn, for 2 to 3 minutes or until golden; remove them from the heat immediately. My favorite seeds and nuts to roast include sesame seeds, sunflower seeds, almonds, pecans, and pumpkin seeds.

MEXICAN SALAD

Here is a fresher and lighter version of a typical Mexican salad. The chips add a nice crunchy topping, and you won't even miss the costly deep-fried tortilla basket.

1 **pound lean ground meat (beef or turkey)**
1 **small onion, chopped**
1 **tablespoon chili powder**
½ **teaspoon salt**
¼ **teaspoon black pepper**
1 **large head lettuce, chopped**

2 **large tomatoes, diced**
½ **cup Italian salad dressing**
1 **cup grated sharp cheddar cheese (about 4 ounces)**
1 **cup crumbled tortilla chips (plain or seasoned)**

1 Cook the meat and onion in a medium skillet over medium heat until browned, 8 to 10 minutes. Drain off any fat. Add the chili powder, salt, and pepper; heat for 2 minutes, stirring well. Cool slightly.

2 Combine the lettuce and tomatoes in a serving bowl; add the meat, salad dressing, and cheese; toss well.

3 Transfer to individual plates, sprinkle with chips, and serve.

QUICK TIPS:

- For a variation, slice a green bell pepper lengthwise, fill with seasoned meat, sprinkle with cheese, and eat right from your hand.

- Roll up this salad in flour tortillas, wrap it in foil, and take it to go. Or fill whole romaine leaves with the seasoned meat and cheese.

FOR KEEPS: Seasoned and cooked meat can be made in advance and stored in the refrigerator for up to 2 days or frozen for up to 2 months.

THE LUNCH CRUNCH

DRESSED-UP TUNA

The curry makes this dish unique, and because it's made without mayonnaise, it makes a good low-fat recipe.

Prep time **5 minutes**   Yield **4 servings**

  1 **(6-ounce) can chunk light tuna in water,
     drained and flaked**
⅓–½ **cup plain, low-fat yogurt**
  1 **stalk celery, finely chopped**
  ½ **teaspoon dried dill**
  ⅛ **teaspoon garlic powder**
  ¼ **teaspoon curry powder**
  ¼ **teaspoon salt**
  ⅛ **teaspoon black pepper**
  2 **pita breads, halved**
  8 **lettuce leaves**
    Tomato slices, optional

1 Combine the tuna, yogurt, celery, dill, garlic powder, curry powder, salt, and pepper in a medium bowl.

2 Line the pita pockets with lettuce leaves. Divide the tuna mixture evenly among the 4 pockets and top with tomato, if desired. Serve immediately.

QUICK TIP: **A handful of currants or toasted nuts is delicious in this tuna salad.**

FOR KEEPS: **The tuna salad can be made up to 2 days in advance and stored in the refrigerator.**

THE LUNCH CRUNCH

COUNTRY RANCH POTATO SALAD

Kids love this potato salad.

Prep time 10 minutes   **Cook time** 20 minutes   **Yield** 12–16 servings

10-12 medium russet potatoes, scrubbed and cubed

1 (1-ounce) package ranch salad dressing mix

1 cup light mayonnaise

1 tablespoon dehydrated onion flakes

½ tablespoon dried dill

2 teaspoons vinegar, any kind

½ cup water

3 stalks celery, chopped

½ red onion, finely chopped

Salt and pepper

1   Boil the potatoes in a large pot of salted water. When the potatoes are just fork tender, drain, rinse in cold water, and drain again.

2   While potatoes are cooking, combine the dressing mix, mayonnaise, dehydrated onions, dill, vinegar, and water in a large resealable serving bowl.

3   Add the potatoes, celery, and onion to the dressing; toss until well coated. Season with salt and pepper to taste. Cover and chill until ready to serve.

QUICK TIP: **Packaged precooked potatoes will do in a pinch.**

FOR KEEPS: **This salad actually tastes better the next day. It will keep in the refrigerator for up to 4 days. Serve chilled.**

KITCHEN 411: **Dehydrated onion flakes (also called minced or dried onion) can be found in the spice aisle of the grocery store.**

LET'S TALK: **I hate peeling potatoes and carrots, so I opt to scrub them instead. You can use a firm vegetable brush or a disinfected pan scrubber (designated strictly for vegetable use) and firmly scrub the vegetables' skin under warm tap water. Guess what? A ton of nutrition lies within the skins of vegetables like potatoes and carrots, so you can feel pretty good about balancing any lack of peeling with the nutrition your family gains.**

THE LUNCH CRUNCH

vegetarian

TEX-MEX POTATO SALAD

Crunchy and rich with a lot of Southwest flavor — a great dish to take to a picnic.

Prep time 5 minutes   **Cook time** 15 minutes   **Yield** 6–8 servings

5–6	large russet potatoes, scrubbed and diced
½–1	cup light whipped salad dressing, such as Miracle Whip
2	teaspoons chili powder
1	teaspoon onion powder
1	(15-ounce) can whole kernel corn, drained
1	(4-ounce) can green chiles, drained and chopped
1	large stalk celery, chopped
1	red bell pepper, stemmed, seeded, and chopped
	Salt and pepper

1. Boil the potatoes in a large pot of salted water until fork-tender, about 15 minutes. Drain and cool slightly.

2. Meanwhile, whisk the dressing, chili powder, and onion powder together in a serving bowl.

3. Add the potatoes, corn, chiles, celery, and bell pepper to the dressing, tossing to coat. Season with salt and pepper to taste.

4. Serve warm or refrigerate for up to 1 week.

QUICK TIP: For a variation, use 5 to 6 cups of diced sweet potatoes in place of the russets. Sweet potatoes should be peeled as the skins are often too thick and fibrous to eat.

KITCHEN 411: Salt the water when boiling potatoes; you need to add only ½ teaspoon of salt to the water to evenly season the potatoes, drawing out a lot of hidden flavor. It also means that less salt is needed in the dish later.

FOR KEEPS: This salad can be made up to 2 days in advance. Keep chilled.

SPRING SALAD

A great side dish to take to your mother-in-law's house for the holidays. Even if she is the more experienced cook, she will be impressed with this dish, and only you will know how easy it was to prepare. It has a creamy texture and the mild flavors blend nicely.

Prep time 10 minutes   **Cook time** 8 minutes   **Yield** 4–6 servings

2 cups cooked white rice (instant is fine), cooled slightly

1 (15-ounce) can mandarin oranges, drained

¼ cup plain low-fat yogurt

¼ cup light mayonnaise

1–2 teaspoons fresh lemon juice

1 teaspoon honey

¼ cup sliced toasted almonds

⅓ cup toasted coconut

Salt and pepper

Combine all of the ingredients; season with salt and pepper. Chill and serve.

QUICK TIP: For a variation, add cooked chicken to create a main dish; use red grapes or fresh strawberries instead of mandarin oranges.

KITCHEN 411: To toast nuts and coconut, place them in a small skillet over medium heat for 2 to 3 minutes, or until lightly browned, and remove them from the heat immediately. Keep a *very* close eye on them as they burn easily. This step is well worth the small investment of time and cleanup, as the flavors released through roasting add an extraordinary depth of flavor.

Vegetarian

PITA ANTIPASTO

Don't be concerned by the number of ingredients here; this recipe is quick, easy, packed with flavor and crunch, and loaded with nutrition.

Prep time 15 minutes   **Cook time** 15 minutes   **Chill time** 2 hours
Yield 4–6 servings

2 cups Italian salad dressing (the zestier the better)

¼ cup water

½ teaspoon dry mustard

3–4 carrots, scrubbed and thinly sliced

½ head cauliflower, broken into small florets

4 ounces button mushrooms, sliced

½ cup sliced black olives

⅓ pound salami, sliced

½ cup diced provolone cheese (about 2 ounces)

1 (2-ounce) jar pimientos, drained and chopped

1 (6-ounce) can chunk light tuna in water, drained and flaked

3 pita breads, halved

1 Bring the salad dressing, water, and mustard to a boil in a medium saucepan. Add the carrots and cauliflower, boiling gently until the vegetables are tender crisp, about 10 minutes. Using a slotted spoon, transfer the vegetables to a large bowl, leaving the liquid in the pan.

2 Add the mushrooms to the dressing and boil gently for 3 minutes. Using a slotted spoon, transfer the mushrooms to the bowl.

3 Discard all but ½ cup of the cooking liquid; set it aside in the refrigerator.

4 Add the olives, salami, cheese, pimiento, and tuna to the vegetables; mix gently with a spoon. Refrigerate the salad mixture until well chilled, about 2 hours.

5 Divide the vegetables evenly among the pita pockets and drizzle with the reserved chilled cooking liquid.

CHICKEN WRAPS

A Mexican-inspired dish that you can take to go.

brown-bag special

Prep time 5 minutes **Cook time** 15 minutes **Yield** 4–6 servings

- **1** tablespoon vegetable oil
- **2–3** boneless, skinless chicken breasts halves, cut into thin strips
- **2** cups water
- **1** cup salsa
- **1** (1.25-ounce) package low-sodium taco seasoning mix
- **2** cups instant rice, uncooked
- **8–12** (6-inch) flour tortillas

1. Heat the oil over medium-high heat in a large skillet. Add the chicken and sauté until cooked through, 6 to 8 minutes.

2. Add the water, salsa, and seasoning mix to the skillet, stirring to combine. Bring to a boil.

3. Stir in the rice; reduce the heat to low and cover. Cook for 5 minutes.

4. Serve immediately with tortillas that you have warmed in the microwave.

QUICK TIPS:

- Serve with grated cheddar cheese, lettuce, and/or tomato.
- You can use 1 pound of top sirloin steak cut into thin strips instead of chicken.
- Add a can of drained black beans, a chopped green bell pepper, and some sliced onion to the skillet after the chicken is cooked. Sauté for 5 minutes and continue with the recipe.

teen-friendly

CHICKEN SALAD LISA

My daughter, Lisa, will eat anything as long as it has ranch dressing in or on it. She created this recipe one day in the kitchen and loves to make it with leftover rotisserie chicken.

Prep time **5 minutes**   **Yield** **4–6 servings**

1 **(1-ounce) package ranch salad dressing mix**

½ **cup light mayonnaise**

1 **(20-ounce) can pineapple chunks in natural juice, drained (reserve ¼ cup of juice)**

4 **cups cubed cooked chicken (about 1 rotisserie chicken or 4 chicken breast halves)**

2 **stalks celery, chopped**

4–6 **hard rolls or pita pockets**

1   Whisk together the dressing mix, mayonnaise, and the reserved pineapple juice in a medium bowl.

2   Add the chicken, celery, and pineapple chunks, tossing to coat.

3   Serve on hard rolls or in pita pockets, or refrigerate for up to 2 days.

QUICK TIPS:

- **You will need cooked chicken for this recipe. Check out the quick chicken recipes on pages 10 and 11.**
- **You can add chopped nuts and/or sliced apples to this recipe.**
- **Serve the dish with sliced veggies or on a bed of greens with sliced fruit on the side.**

ITALIAN COUNTRY SANDWICH

brown-bag special

A versatile sandwich you can serve for lunch, for dinner, as an appetizer, or at a picnic. Perfect, too, for brown-bagging it. You can use any type of deli meat and cheese in place of the ingredients listed below. *And* you can cook it anywhere — from the microwave to a campfire grate. This is a wonderful recipe that I make often for my family. Everyone I have shared it with reports great success too.

Prep time	5 minutes	Cook time	Varies; see below	Yield	4–6 servings

- 2 **(8-inch) precooked pizza shells, such as Boboli, which come 2 per package**
- 4 **ounces seasoned cream cheese (vegetable cream cheese works well)**
- 3–4 **thin slices tomato**
- 3–4 **thin slices green bell pepper**
- 3–4 **thin slices pastrami**
- 3–4 **thin slices salami**
- 2 **thin slices red onion**
- 4 **slices provolone cheese (smoked, if available)**

Lay the pizza shells on a work surface. Spread 1 pizza shell with cream cheese. Top with even layers of tomato, green pepper, pastrami, salami, and red onion, and end with provolone. Top with the remaining pizza shell. See the chart below for cooking options. Cut the hot sandwich into wedges and serve.

Cook Method	Time	Preparation
Microwave	1 minute, 30 seconds	on paper plate covered with plastic wrap or waxed paper
Oven	25 minutes at 350°F	wrapped in foil set on baking sheet
Grill	20 minutes on a medium-hot grill	wrapped in heavy-duty foil
Skillet	8 to 10 minutes per side	wrapped in heavy-duty foil
Campfire	8 minutes per side	wrapped in heavy-duty foil

THE LUNCH CRUNCH

THE ULTIMATE SALAMI SANDWICH

The title describes it; nothing more needs to be said. I have made this so many times I can do it in my sleep. It is always on the top of the list for a weekend lunch.

Prep time 30 minutes   **Cook time** 35 minutes   **Yield** 6 servings

- 1 pound frozen bread dough, thawed
- 1 tablespoon olive oil
- 1 teaspoon chopped garlic
- ¼ pound thinly sliced salami (15–20 slices)

- ¼ pound sliced provolone cheese (about 6 slices)
- 1 (7-ounce) jar roasted red peppers, drained, sliced in 4-inch strips
- 2 scallions (white and tender green parts), sliced

1. Preheat the oven to 350°F.

2. Stretch the bread dough out into 12-inch square and place on a parchment-lined baking sheet. Brush the oil over the dough and sprinkle with garlic.

3. Spread the salami and cheese slices down the middle third of the dough with a slight overlap; top with the roasted red peppers and scallions.

4. Slice the bread dough with kitchen shears or a sharp knife by making eight 3-inch cuts along both sides of the filling. Bring dough strips up across the filling at a slight angle, alternating sides to create a braided effect; seal the ends with a pinch.

5. Let the sandwich sit for 20 to 30 minutes in a warm area of the kitchen. Bake for 35 minutes or until golden brown. Cool for 5 minutes. Serve warm or chilled.

QUICK TIP: You can use smoked ham or pastrami in place of the salami.

BEST-EVER GRILLED CHEESE SANDWICH

Sharp cheddar cheese makes all the difference in this sandwich.

Prep time **3 minutes**   Cook time **5 minutes**   Yield **1 sandwich**

2 **teaspoons butter, at room temperature**
2 **slices whole grain bread**
2–3 **ounces sharp cheddar cheese, thickly sliced**
2 **thin slices tomato**
Worcestershire sauce

1 Preheat a nonstick griddle.

2 Spread butter on one side of each slice of bread.

3 Place 1 bread slice, butter-side down, on a work surface; top with 1 slice of cheese, tomato, a few dashes of Worcestershire and the remaining cheese. Top with the second piece of bread, butter-side up.

4 Grill until the sandwich is browned on both sides and the cheese is melted.

QUICK TIP: **You can add thin slices of salami, ham, turkey, shredded chicken, or pork to this sandwich.**

brown-bag special

REUBEN LOAF

A good friend from Texas gave me this recipe. I have yet to meet a woman from Texas without a fantastic recipe to share — especially a margarita recipe, but I'll leave the margaritas for a different book.

Prep time 20 minutes   **Cook time** 22 minutes   **Yield** 4–6 servings

- **1 pound frozen bread dough, thawed**
- **¼ cup Thousand Island dressing**
- **6 ounces thinly sliced lean corned beef**
- **¼ pound sliced Swiss cheese (about 6 slices)**
- **1 cup sauerkraut, drained well**

1. Preheat the oven to 400°F. Coat a large baking sheet with cooking spray.

2. On a work surface, roll out the bread dough to a 10- by 14-inch rectangle. Transfer it to the baking sheet.

3. Spread the dressing down the middle of the dough; top with the corned beef, Swiss cheese, and sauerkraut, leaving the outside edges of the dough uncovered.

4. Make cuts in the dough at 1-inch intervals, starting at the filling and cutting out to the dough edges.

5. Fold the cut dough over the filling at an angle (at about 45 degrees), alternating sides to create a latticed or braided look.

6. Let the sandwich stand for 20 to 30 minutes on a warm counter. Transfer the baking sheet to the oven and bake for 22 to 24 minutes.

7. Cool slightly; slice and serve.

THE LUNCH CRUNCH

ULTIMATE TRAVEL SANDWICH

Winters in Michigan are long, cold, and cloudy, so by the end of March we try to take a vacation someplace warm and sunny. We pack up the minivan with swim gear, shorts, and sandals. We also take breakfast, lunch, and dinner to keep the travel fast and the food costs low. This recipe has been our "travel sandwich" over the last ten years. It keeps well in the cooler. With some fresh fruit and carrot sticks we have a healthy lunch on the road that satisfies everyone.

Prep time 5 minutes   **Yield** 4 servings

- 1 (1-pound) loaf French bread
- 4 tablespoons light mayonnaise
- 4 slices provolone cheese, plain or smoked (about 2 ounces)
- 12 very thin slices hard salami (about 2 ounces)
- 6 medium-thick slices deli ham (about 4 ounces)
- 1 small tomato, thinly sliced
- 1 tablespoon zesty Italian salad dressing
- 2 cups shredded iceberg or Romaine lettuce

1   Slice the bread in half, lengthwise. Remove some of the bread from the bottom half, creating a trough in the center. (You can reserve this bread for another use, such as crumbs or a quick dipper with pizza sauce and shredded mozzarella cheese.)

2   Spread each bread half with mayonnaise. Layer the cheese, salami, and ham on the bottom half of the bread. Top with the tomato; sprinkle dressing over the tomatoes. Top the tomato with lettuce and the top half of the bread. Wrap tightly in aluminum foil and refrigerate until ready to serve.

QUICK TIPS:
- **You can use any deli meat in this recipe.**
- **Cutting the loaf into 2 equal pieces crosswise makes it more manageable to construct, wrap, and refrigerate.**

FOR KEEPS: Sandwiches can be made in the morning and refrigerated until later in the day.

OPEN-FACED PIZZA HOAGIES

This has a tart, zesty flavor that complements the pork. Because most of this recipe can be made in advance, it is perfect for nights when the kids have a sleepover.

Prep time	10 minutes	Marinate time	2–24 hours
Cook time	10 minutes	Yield	4–6 servings

½ cup Italian salad dressing

1½ pounds boneless pork loin chops, cut into thin strips

4 hoagie or hero buns

1 cup 5-Minute Pizza Sauce (page 62), or prepared pizza sauce

1 cup grated mozzarella or provolone cheese (about 4 ounces)

1 Preheat the oven to 350°F.

2 Pour the dressing into a medium bowl and add the pork, stirring to coat. Cover and transfer to the refrigerator to marinate for at least 2 and up to 24 hours.

3 Heat a skillet over high heat. Add the meat and marinade, and bring to a boil for 1 minute. Reduce the heat to medium-high and cook for 5 to 7 minutes longer, or until the meat is slightly browned.

4 Meanwhile, slice the buns lengthwise and transfer them to a baking sheet. Spread pizza sauce evenly over the buns; top with the pork and sprinkle with cheese.

5 Bake for 10 minutes; serve immediately.

QUICK TIP: **You can substitute cooked chicken for the pork.**

THE LUNCH CRUNCH

CHICKEN PIZZA

So easy and yet so sophisticated. Serve this dish with a green salad and you've got a meal.

Prep time 5 minutes   Cook time 8 minutes   Yield 4 servings

3 tablespoons olive oil

1 large yellow, green, or red bell pepper, stemmed, seeded, and thinly sliced

4 whole pita breads
    Garlic salt

2-3 medium tomatoes, sliced

2 cooked chicken breast halves, cut into ¼-inch slices

8 black olives, pitted and sliced
    Crushed red pepper flakes, optional

1¼ cups grated mozzarella cheese (about 5 ounces)

1. Preheat the oven to 425°F.

2. Heat 1½ tablespoons of the oil in a medium skillet over medium-high heat. Sauté the bell pepper for 5 minutes, stirring frequently. Remove from the heat.

3. Rub the remaining 1½ tablespoons of the oil over the pitas; sprinkle both sides lightly with garlic salt.

4. Place the pitas on a baking sheet and top with the sautéed peppers, tomato, chicken, olives, and pepper flakes, if using. Sprinkle with cheese.

5. Bake for 8 minutes or until the cheese is melted and the bottoms of the pitas are crispy.

6. Serve hot, at room temperature, or chilled.

QUICK TIPS:

- **You will need cooked chicken for this recipe. Check out the quick chicken recipes on pages 10 and 11.**

- **For the greens lover in the family, top with torn pieces of spinach before serving.**

- **For a more sophisticated taste, sprinkle with Gorgonzola cheese and a few fresh herbs in place of the mozzarella cheese.**

THE LUNCH CRUNCH

15-MINUTE *Dishes*

Super-Quick, Nutritious Meals in Fifteen Minutes or Less

The recipes in this chapter make enough for a main course and are easy to double when you have more folks to feed. I like these recipes because they are conveniently quick, and their ingredients are typically already in my pantry, refrigerator, or freezer.

If you have cooked chicken in your freezer or fridge, you can really expand your fifteen-minute menu repertoire. See pages 9 through 12 for tips on cooking and storing chicken.

Whether we work from home, work out of the home, or stay at home, we all have days so busy that we just want to stop the world and jump off. These are the recipes for times like those — recipes that can bring the family together even on your most hectic days.

SALMON BURGERS

Canned salmon has come a long way in recent years. The options available and the taste and texture of the fish have all improved tremendously. Pass cocktail, tartar, and/or barbecue sauce at the table. Ranch dressing works well too. Shredded lettuce, tomato, and slices of Swiss cheese would not go amiss on these burgers.

Prep time 5 minutes	Cook time 10 minutes	Yield 4 servings

1 (6-ounce) can skinless, boneless salmon, drained
¼ cup breadcrumbs
¼ cup onion, finely chopped
2 tablespoons light mayonnaise
1 egg, beaten
1 teaspoon fresh lemon juice

1 teaspoon dried parsley flakes
¼ teaspoon garlic salt
1 tablespoon vegetable oil
4 hamburger buns
Cocktail, tartar, or barbecue sauce

1. Combine the salmon, breadcrumbs, onion, mayonnaise, egg, lemon juice, parsley, and garlic salt in a medium bowl. Using your hands, shape the mixture into 4 patties.

2. Heat the oil over medium-high heat in a large nonstick skillet. Add the patties to the skillet and cook until browned on both sides, about 5 minutes per side. Meanwhile heat the buns in the toaster or under the broiler.

3. Serve the burgers immediately on the buns with sauce.

FOR KEEPS: These burgers freeze well, uncooked, for up to 2 months; thaw completely before cooking.

LET'S TALK: If you don't have a nonstick skillet large enough for all 4 burgers, cook them in stages and keep them warm in a 250°F oven, covered loosely with aluminum foil. If you don't have a nonstick skillet, increase the vegetable oil to 3 tablespoons.

COBB SALAD PITAS

I fell in love with the Cobb salad when I had my first real job out of college and had enough money to go out to lunch once a week. It is still my favorite; its mixture of flavors and textures work perfectly together. This recipe makes it easy to take your Cobb salad along when you're on the go.

Prep time 5 minutes **Yield** 4 servings

- 1 cup grated Monterey Jack or cheddar cheese (about 4 ounces)
- 1 tomato, chopped
- 1 large avocado, pitted, peeled, and diced
- 1 (5-ounce) can chicken, drained and flaked
- ⅓ cup bacon bits or 7–8 slices of cooked, crumbled bacon
- ⅓ cup Italian dressing
- 2–3 cups finely chopped lettuce
- 4 pitas, halved

1 Combine the cheese, tomato, avocado, chicken, bacon, dressing, and lettuce in a medium bowl; toss gently to coat.

2 Fill the pita pockets with the salad mixture.

3 Serve immediately.

QUICK TIP: Combine everything but the lettuce, dressing, and pitas in the morning and chill. Add the lettuce and dressing just before stuffing your pita pockets.

vegetarian

VEGGIE MIX SALAD

A favorite main-dish salad. The creamy dressing complements the flavors of the broccoli and cauliflower. Quick and easy to eat by itself or on a bed of lettuce.

Prep time 15 minutes   **Marinate time** 4 hours to 4 days   **Yield** 6–8 servings

1¾ cups light mayonnaise

¾ cup sugar

½ cup cider vinegar

2 bunches broccoli florets, chopped into bite-size pieces

1 head cauliflower, chopped into bite-size pieces

6 hard-cooked eggs, chopped into bite-size pieces

1 small onion, minced

1 (12-ounce) package bacon, cooked and crumbled

1 Whisk the mayonnaise, sugar, and vinegar in a large container with a tight fitting lid. Add the broccoli, cauliflower, eggs, onion, and bacon to the dressing; toss to coat.

2 Cover tightly and marinate for at least 4 hours and up to 4 days in the refrigerator.

3 Toss gently before serving.

QUICK TIPS:

• Buy precut veggies at the store for convenience.

• You can use bacon bits in place of the cooked bacon.

• You can use almost any vegetable in this recipe (bell peppers, radishes, cucumber, or other crisp, raw vegetables).

FRESH HERB TURKEY BURGERS

Even my husband, who is not a turkey lover, thought that these burgers were the best he'd ever had! Pan-fry these tender patties — they are too fragile for the grill.

Prep time 8 minutes **Cook time** 8 minutes **Yield** 4 servings

1	**pound lean ground turkey**
¼	**cup chopped fresh mint**
1	**bunch scallions (white and tender green parts), minced**
¼	**cup Parmesan cheese**
2	**teaspoons chopped garlic**
2	**tablespoons olive oil**
	Salt and pepper
4	**hamburger buns**

1 Combine the turkey, mint, onion, Parmesan, and garlic in a medium bowl. Using your hands, form into four patties.

2 Heat the oil over medium-high heat in a large skillet; add the patties and cook for 5 minutes per side, or until the meat is cooked through. Add salt and pepper to taste and serve on hamburger buns.

QUICK TIP: These meat patties can be made and refrigerated 1 day in advance, or frozen for up to 2 months. Thaw before cooking.

KITCHEN 411: Mint can be found in prepackaged containers in the produce section of the grocery store, trimmed, washed, and ready to use. Of course, if you have it growing in your garden, by all means use that instead.

TASTY SEASONED BURGERS

This is a quick and easy way to make the perfect burger even better. You can grill, broil, or pan-fry these burgers.

Prep time 5 minutes   **Cook time** 10 minutes   **Yield** 4–6 burgers

1½ pounds lean ground beef or turkey
2 tablespoons Italian breadcrumbs
¾ teaspoon garlic powder
2 teaspoons Worcestershire sauce

2 teaspoons A-1 steak sauce
½ teaspoon salt
¼ teaspoon black pepper
4–6 buns or rolls

1. For grilling, prepare a hot fire in a gas or charcoal grill. For broiling, preheat the broiler.

2. Combine the meat, breadcrumbs, garlic powder, Worcestershire, A-1, salt, and pepper in a large bowl; mix with your hands just until the seasonings are incorporated. Form the meat mixture into 4 to 6 patties.

3. Grill, broil, or pan fry for 4 minutes per side for a burger cooked medium. Serve immediately on buns (you don't even need ketchup!).

QUICK TIPS:

- Remember: when you're working with ground meat, the less you handle it, the more tender the outcome.

- For an even simpler recipe, combine the meat with 1 (1-ounce) package of ranch salad dressing mix in place of all of the seasonings.

LET'S TALK: If you feel compelled to form your burgers into the absolute perfect shape and thickness — molding, shaping, slapping the meat into submission — I recommend that you hand the job over to your eight-year-old, who will be less exacting about the shape. The burgers will be lumpy and half falling apart, but I guarantee that they'll be a lot more tender!

OPEN-FACED ROAST BEEF SANDWICH

Serve this comforting sandwich with mashed potatoes, applesauce, and a big glass of milk to complete a heartwarming meal.

Prep time **5 minutes** **Cook time** **10 minutes** **Yield** **2–3 servings**

- ¼ cup low-sodium soy sauce
- 1 (.87-ounce) package brown gravy mix
- 1½ cups water
- 8 ounces sliced roast beef
- 1 baguette, sliced in half lengthwise, each half cut into halves or thirds

1 Combine the soy sauce, gravy mix, and water in a medium skillet, whisking to blend. Cook the gravy according to the package directions. Add the beef and cook until it's heated through.

2 Serve over slices of French bread. Eat with a fork and knife!

HAMBURGER CRUMBLE

Another great idea for ground beef. The meat is so tender that it crumbles in the pan. Serve with rice or buttered noodles and the kids will invariably ask for seconds. I suggest that you make a double batch — one to eat and one to freeze.

Prep time **5 minutes** **Cook time** **10 minutes** **Yield** **4–6 servings**

- 1½ **pounds lean ground beef**
- ½ **cup light mayonnaise**
- 4–6 **tablespoons chopped onion**
- 2 **teaspoons chili powder**
- ½ **teaspoon salt**

Mix the beef, mayonnaise, onion, chili powder, and salt in a large bowl.

Cook the mixture in a skillet over medium-high heat until the meat is no longer pink and the onions are tender, 10 to 12 minutes. Serve with rice or potatoes.

QUICK TIP **Add 1 (15-ounce) can of seasoned chopped tomatoes and simmer for 15 minutes. Serve over toasted hamburger buns with a side of sandwich pickles. Vlasic makes a style called Stackers that is great.**

FOR KEEPS **Make this up to 1 day in advance or freeze for up to 2 months.**

QUICK TUNA-NOODLE CASSEROLE

teen-friendly

My mother would make this dish when she was in a pinch. She sent the recipe with me when I went off to college, and I was able to feed all my roommates with it on several occasions.

Prep time 5 minutes   **Cook time** 10 minutes   **Yield** 4 servings

- 2 **cups water**
- 1 **(3-ounce) package Ramen noodles, any flavor**
- 1 **(6-ounce) can chunk light tuna in water, drained and flaked**
- 1 **(10-ounce) package frozen mixed vegetables**
- 3 **tablespoons all-purpose flour**
- 1 **cup half-and-half**
  Salt and pepper

Bring the water to a boil in a large skillet. Break up the noodles and add them to the water with the contents of the enclosed seasoning packet. Add the tuna and vegetables; stir; return to a boil. Reduce the heat to medium; cover and simmer for 5 minutes.

Whisk the flour and cream in a small bowl until combined and add it to the tuna mixture. Simmer, uncovered, until the sauce thickens, stirring constantly for 2 to 3 minutes. Season with salt and pepper to taste. Serve hot.

QUICK TIPS:

- If you are a tuna lover, try this recipe with two cans of tuna.
- Instead of half-and-half, you can combine ½ cup of cream with ½ cup of 2 percent milk. You can also use whole milk in this recipe. The flavor is still great; it will just be a bit more soupy.

GREEK PORK PITA POCKETS WITH CUCUMBER SAUCE

Start the meat marinating before you leave for work or as soon as you get home from the office. Either way, this tasty meal will be ready to cook in a flash.

Prep time 10 minutes **Marinate time** 1–8 hours
Cook time 6–8 minutes **Yield** 4 servings

4 tablespoons olive oil
4 tablespoons fresh lemon juice
1 tablespoon prepared mustard
2 teaspoons chopped garlic
1 teaspoon dried oregano
1 pound boneless pork loin chops, cut into ¼-inch-thick strips

SAUCE

1 cup plain, low-fat yogurt
1 cucumber, peeled and diced
½ teaspoon garlic powder
½ teaspoon dill

2 pita rounds, cut in half
Shredded lettuce
Chopped red onion

1 Combine 3 tablespoons of the oil, the lemon juice, mustard, garlic, and oregano in a non-reactive bowl (stainless steel, glass, or ceramic), whisking to blend. Add the meat and toss to coat. Refrigerate for at least 1 and up to 8 hours.

2 Heat the remaining 1 tablespoon of olive oil over medium-high heat in a large nonstick skillet. Add the meat and marinade to the skillet and cook for 6 to 8 minutes, being sure to bring the mixture to a boil for at least 1 full minute.

3 To make the sauce, combine the yogurt, cucumber, garlic powder, and dill in a small bowl, mixing well to blend.

4 Serve the pork in the pita pockets with lettuce, red onion, and cucumber sauce.

KITCHEN 411: Certain metals, such as aluminum and copper, react chemically with acidic ingredients like lemon juice and can add off-tastes to your food.

MODERN MAMMA'S PIEROGI

You can find pierogi in the frozen food section of most grocery stores. They are *very* easy to make. I always keep a stash in the freezer.

Prep time 2 minutes   **Cook time** 8 minutes   **Yield** 4 servings

- **1 box frozen pierogi, any flavor**
- **2 large onions**
- **4 tablespoons butter**

1. Add the frozen pierogi to a large pot of boiling water; boil for 3 to 5 minutes; drain.

2. Meanwhile, heat the butter in a large skillet over medium heat; add the onion and cook until translucent, about 8 minutes.

3. Add the pierogi to the skillet and toss to coat; serve immediately.

QUICK TIPS:

- You can top pierogi with stir-fried vegetables or add the boiled pierogi to the stir-fry pan to brown them.
- Sautéed bell peppers and zucchini are a good addition to help stretch the meal. If you are looking for some protein, add 2 boneless skinless chicken breasts cut into bite-size chunks and sautéed with the onion.

BARBECUED SALMON FILLETS

This recipe's pleasant barbecue flavor doesn't overpower the flavor of the fish. These fillets are on my short list of favorites.

Prep time 2 minutes **Cook time** 10 minutes **Yield** 4 servings

2 tablespoons light mayonnaise

¼ cup barbecue sauce

1 teaspoon Worcestershire sauce

⅛ teaspoon hot sauce

1 teaspoon fresh lemon juice

1 tablespoon brown sugar or honey

1 pound salmon fillets, at room temperature

1 Preheat the broiler or prepare a medium-hot fire in a gas or charcoal grill.

2 Combine the mayonnaise, barbecue sauce, Worcestershire, hot sauce, lemon juice, and sugar in a small bowl, whisking to blend.

3 Brush the fish with the mayonnaise mixture and broil or grill, basting occasionally, for about 10 minutes, or until the salmon is tender and cooked through. Serve immediately.

QUICK TIPS:

- Remember to baste the fish occasionally during broiling or grilling.
- A good rule of thumb for cooking fish is 10 minutes per every inch of thickness.

KITCHEN 411: You cannot compare the taste of wild and farm-raised salmon. Wild salmon is far superior in taste but not always available (especially at a good price). If you are able to find wild salmon at a decent price, buy a few extra fillets. Portion them out, wrap them tightly in plastic, and transfer them to a ziplock freezer bag. You can freeze the fillets for up to 2 months. When you're ready to use them, unwrap and thaw in a bowl of cold water in the refrigerator on the day that you plan to serve.

SWEET AND SPICY GLAZED CHICKEN

A great dinner idea with simple ingredients. Serve it with a fresh fruit salad and garlic bread or over rice or couscous. Stick a toothpick into each chicken morsel for a quick and elegant hors d'oeuvre.

Prep time 2 minutes   **Cook time** 10 minutes   **Yield** 4 servings

- ⅓ cup Dijon mustard
- ¼ cup apricot preserves
- 2 teaspoons ground ginger
- 1 teaspoon dry mustard
- 1 tablespoon vegetable oil
- 4 boneless, skinless chicken breast halves, cut into 1-inch pieces

1 Combine the Dijon, preserves, ginger, and dry mustard in a medium bowl; mix well. Add the chicken, tossing to coat.

2 Heat the oil in a medium nonstick skillet over medium-high heat. Reduce the heat to medium and add chicken. Cook, stirring frequently, until browned, about 10 minutes. Serve immediately.

FOR KEEPS: This recipe can be made up to 2 days in advance and reheated for a quick dinner.

teen-friendly

15-MINUTE CHICKEN AND RICE

You may have a recipe similar to this one, but this is a keeper — simple, easy, and mild.

Prep time 5 minutes   **Cook time** 15 minutes   **Yield** 4 servings

2 tablespoons vegetable oil

4 boneless, skinless chicken breast halves, cut into 1-inch chunks

Salt and pepper

1 head of broccoli, chopped (about 2 cups)

1 (10¾-ounce) can low-sodium cream of chicken soup

1 cup water

¼ teaspoon black pepper

¼ teaspoon paprika

1½ cups instant rice (uncooked)

1 Heat the oil in a large skillet over medium-high heat. Season the chicken with salt and pepper and add it to the hot skillet. Cook the chicken until browned on all sides, 8 to 10 minutes. Transfer the chicken to a serving platter and cover it to keep warm.

2 Meanwhile, chop the broccoli and transfer it to a microwave-safe dish; cover with plastic wrap or waxed paper, securing the ends under the dish. Microwave on high for 2 to 3 minutes, checking for doneness. If needed, cook 1 minute longer.

3 Add the soup, water, pepper, and paprika to the skillet; bring to a boil over high heat. Stir in the rice, broccoli, and chicken. Reduce the heat to low, cover tightly, and cook for 2 minutes, or until the chicken is heated through and the rice is cooked.

QUICK TIPS:

• Add 1 to 2 tablespoons of water if you prefer a moister dish.

• Add a chopped green bell pepper with the onion for a twist.

FOR KEEPS: This dish can be stored in the refrigerator for up to 3 days and tastes great when reheated.

CHICKEN PESTO

An easy, summery dish.

Prep time **4 minutes**   **Cook time** **About 8 minutes**   **Yield** **4 servings**

   2 **tablespoons olive oil**
   4 **boneless, skinless chicken breast halves,
       8 thighs, or 12 chicken breast tenders
       (1–1½ pounds), cut into ½-inch-thick
       strips**
   ½ **cup prepared pesto**

1 Heat the oil in large nonstick skillet over medium-high heat.
   Add the chicken; cook and stir for 2 to 3 minutes.

2 Add the pesto; cook and stir for 3 to 4 minutes longer or until
   the chicken is cooked through.

RECIPE IDEAS

This chicken is delicious in the
following recipes:
- Quick Hot Pasta Salad (page 247)
- Better Buttered Noodles (page 240)

CHICKEN SALAD BARBECUE

Creamy and spicy, this is a delicious recipe for any kind of cooked chicken. I have made this dish many times with baked, roasted, or barbecued chicken, with each preparation lending a different taste. My family never knows whether it's a leftover. It is one of my many little secrets.

Prep time 10 minutes   **Yield** 4–6 servings

2	whole cooked chickens, 2–3 pounds each; or 3 pounds cooked, cubed chicken
⅓	cup spicy barbecue sauce
⅓	cup light mayonnaise
1–2	jalapeño peppers, finely chopped, optional
1	bunch scallions (white and tender green parts), sliced
1	red or green bell pepper, stemmed, seeded, and chopped
	Salt and pepper
	Pita bread
	Leaf lettuce

1 Remove the chicken meat from the bones and discard the bones; chop the meat into small cubes.

2 Combine the chicken with the barbecue sauce, mayonnaise, jalapeños, scallions, and bell pepper in a large bowl; mix well. Season with salt and pepper to taste.

3 Serve on the pita bread with leaf lettuce or on a bed of salad greens.

QUICK TIP: Combine the barbecue sauce, mayonnaise, peppers, and onions, and serve as a dip with hot skewers of grilled chicken.

SOUTHWEST CHICKEN

I love the combinations of these spices — an intense and flavorful fiesta in your mouth. I like to double the batch when I make this dish. My family eats their fill of a great main dish and then I have leftovers to serve with a salad of fresh greens for lunch the next day. Serve it for dinner with a green salad and roasted potatoes.

Prep time 5 minutes   **Cook time** About 10 minutes   **Yield** 4 servings

- 2 tablespoons olive oil
- 2 teaspoons chopped garlic
- 1 teaspoon ground cumin
- 1 teaspoon chili powder
- 1 teaspoon dried oregano leaves
- ¼ teaspoon salt
- ⅛ teaspoon black pepper
- 4 boneless, skinless chicken breast halves, 8 thighs, or 12 chicken breast tenders (1–1½ pounds)

RECIPE IDEAS

You can add this chicken to the following recipes in this book:
- Chicken Tacos (page 146)
- Fast Skillet Pasta (page 246)

1. Prepare a medium-hot fire in a gas or charcoal grill.
2. Combine the oil, garlic, cumin, chili powder, oregano, salt and pepper and brush over both sides of the chicken to coat.
3. Grill, turning once, for 4 to 5 minutes per side, or until the chicken is no longer pink in the center. Serve immediately.

QUICK TIP: Chicken tenders will cook in half the time needed for boneless, skinless chicken breast halves.

CHICKEN TACOS

The combination of onion, garlic, and taco seasoning makes for a zesty chicken dish that the whole family will enjoy.

Prep time 2 minutes   **Cook time** 15 minutes   **Yield** 4–6 servings

2 tablespoons vegetable oil
1 medium onion, finely chopped
1 teaspoon chopped garlic
2–3 cups chopped or shredded cooked chicken
1 (15-ounce) can tomato purée
1 (4.5-ounce) can chopped green chiles
1 (1.25-ounce) package low-sodium taco seasoning mix
Salt and pepper
6 corn tortilla shells

OPTIONAL TOPPINGS

Grated cheese
Guacamole
Shredded lettuce
Chopped green or red bell pepper
Jalapeño slices
Salsa

1   Heat the oil over medium heat in a large skillet; add onion and sauté until translucent, about 5 minutes. Add garlic, chicken, tomato puree, chiles, and taco seasoning to skillet. Simmer over medium-low heat for 10 minutes, stirring occasionally. Season with salt and pepper to taste.

2   Serve in tortilla shells with all the toppings.

QUICK TIP: **You will need cooked chicken for this recipe. Check out the quick chicken recipes on pages 10 and 11.**

FAST FAJITAS

A quick and easy Mexican-inspired chicken dish.

| Prep time | 5 minutes | Cook time | 8–10 minutes | Yield | 4–6 servings |

- 1 tablespoon vegetable oil
- 3 boneless, skinless chicken breast halves, cut into ½-inch strips
- ½ large green bell pepper, stemmed, seeded, and thinly sliced
- 1 small onion, thinly sliced
- 1 (4.5-ounce) can chopped green chiles
- ½ teaspoon crushed garlic
- 1 (1.25-ounce) package fajita seasoning mix
- 8–10 (10-inch) flour tortillas
- 1 cup grated sharp cheddar cheese (about 4 ounces)
- 1 head iceberg lettuce, shredded

1. Heat the oil over medium-high heat in a large skillet. Add the chicken, bell pepper, onion, chiles, garlic, and seasoning; cook, stirring frequently, for 8 to 10 minutes.

2. Fill the flour tortillas with the chicken mixture, top with the cheese and lettuce, and serve immediately.

QUICK TIPS:

- **Use chopped or minced prepared garlic for convenience.**
- **Use turkey or sirloin steak in place of chicken.**
- **To bulk up this dish, cut into bite-size pieces 3 summer squash, 3 zucchini, and 1 large red onion; add to the skillet with the chicken and 2 cups frozen sweet corn. Sauté until the vegetables are softened and lightly browned. Serve with guacamole (1 avocado mashed with 1 tablespoon spicy salsa) and a side of refried beans.**

30-MINUTE *Dishes*

Pretty Darn Quick and Nutritious Meals in Thirty Minutes or Less

In this chapter you'll find a great selection of recipes that you can use time after time: chicken, beef, vegetarian options, and more.

Thirty minutes and counting: I have lived my life by the clock since having kids. It actually started before they were born: to be specific, when the timed contractions started, then how long they slept, how long they nursed, and how long they were awake (especially in the middle of the night). Then came preschool, when I had two hours and fifteen minutes of "freedom" four days a week, and by golly I used every minute of it.

When elementary and middle school rolled around, times changed again to accommodate everyone's schedule — catering jobs, coffee house baking, dance recitals, viola lessons, softball, scouts, track, cross country, trumpet, piano, and oboe lessons. The clock was my guard, my dictator, my menace. I became known as the "queen of quick." My neighbors and friends listened to descriptions of my quick meals with curiosity and a quick jotting-down of ingredients and techniques. They marveled at how I kept so many balls in the air and still got dinner on the table. Perfection is not my forte, and I assured them the local pizza place was always a phone call away when the wheels fell off my cart.

I shared my quick ideas and also found myself talking to strangers in the grocery store, giving tips on which pizza sauce tastes great, how to select fresh produce, what to pair with it, and how to prepare it. Around this time I realized that my talent was not a talent, but a gift of giving and communicating what I do best. This was when I started writing this book. Enjoy the recipes in this chapter — I am probably making one of them tonight for my family.

PEANUT BUTTER CHICKEN

A mild nutty flavor gives this chicken versatility with any kind of side dish.

½ **cup peanut oil**

6–8 **boneless, skinless chicken thighs (about 1 pound), cut into 3 pieces each**

¼ **teaspoon garlic powder**

Salt and pepper

3 **medium onions, chopped**

½ **cup peanut butter, creamy or crunchy**

2 **cups low-sodium chicken broth**

¼ **teaspoon cayenne pepper**

Chopped peanuts, optional

1 Heat the oil in a large skillet over medium-high heat. Add the chicken; season with the garlic powder, salt, and pepper. Cook, turning occasionally, until the chicken is browned and tender on all sides, about 12 minutes. Transfer the chicken to a platter and keep it warm.

2 Pour off all but 2 tablespoons of oil from the skillet; add the onion and cook for 5 minutes.

3 Stir in the peanut butter, broth, and cayenne; whisk until combined. Return the chicken to the skillet and simmer until the sauce thickens slightly, 8 to 10 minutes.

4 Garnish with chopped peanuts, if desired, and serve.

QUICK TIP: **Serve over couscous or rice.**

GRILLED SPICY CHICKEN STIX

A spicy and sweet dish for the heat lovers in the house.

| Prep time | 10 minutes | Cook time | 8–10 minutes | Yield | 4 servings |

- **12 chicken breast tenders (1–1½ pounds)**
- **12 wooden skewers, soaked in water for 30 minutes**
- **½ cup barbecue sauce**
- **½ cup honey**
- **3 tablespoons hot sauce, such as Tabasco**

1. For grilling, prepare a medium-hot fire in a gas or charcoal grill. For broiling, preheat the broiler and coat a broiler pan with cooking spray.

2. Weave chicken tenders onto 12 skewers. Place skewers into a large baking dish; set aside.

3. Combine the barbecue sauce, honey, and hot sauce in a small bowl. Reserve ¼ cup sauce for basting. Pour the remaining mixture over the chicken, turning the skewers to coat.

4. Grill for 3 to 4 minutes on each side or until the chicken is no longer pink in the center; basting frequently.

5. If you are using the broiler, transfer the chicken to the prepared pan and broil, basting frequently, for about 5 minutes per side. Serve.

QUICK TIP: This sweet, sticky sauce tends to burn easily on a hot grill. Rub the grates with a small rag soaked in vegetable oil before grilling the skewers. The oil helps to eliminate burning.

CHILI CORN–CRUSTED CHICKEN TENDERS

Great cornmeal taste with a perfect crunch.

Prep time 8 minutes   **Cook time** About 8 minutes   **Yield** 4 servings

¼ **cup milk**
¾ **cup cornmeal (white or yellow)**
1 **tablespoon chili powder**
½ **teaspoon salt**
12 **chicken breast tenders (1–1½ pounds)**
2 **tablespoons vegetable oil**

1. Pour the milk into a shallow bowl. Combine the cornmeal, chili powder, and salt in a separate shallow bowl.

2. Dip the chicken, one piece at a time, in the milk, then in the cornmeal mixture, coating all sides.

3. Heat the oil in a large nonstick skillet over medium-high heat. Cook the chicken for 4 minutes per side, until no longer pink in the center.

KITCHEN 411: When cooking or browning chicken, do not put too many pieces in the skillet at one time. Cook in batches if necessary, leaving some space between the pieces to allow them to brown and cook more evenly.

CINNAMON CHICKEN

A sweet and savory seasoned dish that goes well with steamed rice and broccoli.

- 4 **boneless, skinless chicken breast halves (1–1½ pounds)**
- ¼ **teaspoon cinnamon**
- ¼ **teaspoon ground cloves**
- ¼ **teaspoon salt**
- ¼ **teaspoon black pepper**
- 3 **tablespoons vegetable oil**
- 1 **large onion, chopped**
- 2 **teaspoons crushed garlic**
- ¾ **cup orange juice**
- 2 **tablespoons raisins**

1. Pat the chicken dry with paper towels. Combine the cinnamon, cloves, salt, and pepper in a small bowl. Season the chicken on both sides with the spice mixture.

2. Heat the oil in a large skillet over medium heat. Add the chicken to the skillet and cook until browned on one side, about 6 minutes. Turn the chicken and add the onion and garlic. Brown the second side of the chicken while stirring the onion and garlic to prevent scorching, about 8 minutes.

3. Add the orange juice and raisins; reduce heat to low. Cover and cook for 10 minutes, or until the juices run clear when the chicken is pierced with a knife. Serve.

FOR KEEPS: This recipe can be assembled and cooked, cooled, and stored in the refrigerator 1 day in advance. It also freezes well for up to 2 months.

PAN-FRIED ITALIAN CHICKEN

When it's cloudy and cold outside, I like to cook this dish; it has a simple, fresh flavor that evokes the warm Mediterranean sun. Serve with steamed green beans tossed with almonds and Italian salad dressing, and a fresh loaf of bread.

Prep time 5 minutes **Cook time** 25 minutes **Yield** 4 servings

- 6 tablespoons butter, at room temperature
- 2 scallions (white and tender green part), sliced (or 2 tablespoons chopped red onion)
- 1–2 teaspoons minced garlic
- 1 teaspoon fresh lemon juice
- 1 teaspoon dried sage
- ¼ teaspoon salt
- ¼ teaspoon black pepper
- 4 boneless, skinless chicken breast halves (1–1½ pounds)

1 Combine the butter, scallion, garlic, lemon juice, sage, salt, and pepper in a food processor and process until smooth, about 10 seconds.

2 Heat a large skillet over medium heat. Pat the chicken breasts dry with paper towels; spread half of the butter mixture on one side of each chicken breast.

3 Transfer the chicken to the skillet, butter side down, and cook for 10 minutes. Spread the remaining butter mixture on top of the chicken in the skillet, dividing the mixture evenly among the pieces. Turn the chicken over and cook for 10 minutes longer, or until the juices run clear when pierced with a knife. Serve immediately.

FOR KEEPS: This recipe can be assembled and cooked in advance, cooled, and stored in the freezer for up to 2 months. When the chicken breasts have cooled, place them on a baking sheet and freeze. When they are frozen (after 2 to 4 hours), transfer them to a ziplock freezer bag and store them in the freezer. Now you have perfectly seasoned pieces of chicken for sandwiches and salads.

THAI GRILLED CHICKEN

A sweet and savory Thai-inspired dish.

Prep time 5 minutes	**Marinate time** 10 minutes		
Cook time About 10 minutes	**Yield** 4 servings		

4   **boneless, skinless chicken breast halves, 8 thighs, or 12 chicken breast tenders (1–1½ pounds)**

¼   **cup low-sodium soy sauce**

2   **teaspoons minced garlic**

½   **teaspoon crushed red pepper flakes**

2   **tablespoons honey**

1   **tablespoon fresh lemon juice**

1   Prepare a medium-hot fire in a gas or charcoal grill.

2   Place the chicken in a shallow baking dish.

3   Whisk together the soy sauce, garlic, pepper flakes, honey, and lemon juice in a measuring cup. Pour over the chicken, turning to coat. Let the chicken stand for 10 minutes.

4   Grill the chicken for 4 to 5 minutes on one side. Turn it over and grill 4 to 5 minutes longer or until the chicken is no longer pink in the center. Discard the marinade. Serve.

SUNSHINE CHICKEN KABOBS

I've found that both kids and adults like eating any kind of food on a kabob — so when you serve this fresh and light version of chicken kabobs, you can be sure that the whole family will enjoy the meal.

Prep time	10 minutes	Marinate time	30 minutes
Cook time	20 minutes	Yield	4–6 servings

½ cup fresh lemon juice

½ cup fresh lime juice

½ cup orange juice

¼ cup honey

1 teaspoon salt

8 boneless, skinless chicken thighs (about 1½ pounds), cut into 1½-inch cubes

2 green bell peppers, stemmed, seeded, and cut into 2-inch chunks

2 medium onions, cut into quarters

10 (8-inch) metal skewers

1 Combine the juices, honey, and salt in a medium bowl; whisk well.

2 Add the chicken to the marinade; coat well. Refrigerate for 30 minutes.

3 Prepare a medium-hot fire in a gas or charcoal grill. Drain the chicken and discard the marinade.

4 Thread a combination of the chicken, bell peppers, and onions onto each skewer.

5 Grill, turning occasionally, until the meat is fully cooked and all sides of the chicken pieces are nicely marked by the grill, about 8 minutes. Serve immediately.

QUICK TIP: You can also skewer and grill mushrooms, zucchini, marinated artichoke hearts, and cocktail tomatoes with the chicken. These come in handy when you find that you have a few more mouths to feed than you anticipated.

HONEY MUSTARD-GLAZED CHICKEN

A great glaze to put together an hour or two before cooking. It will leave you enough time to take a bike ride with the kids, walk the dog, or do a load or two of laundry.

30-MINUTE DISHES

Prep time **5 minutes** **Marinate time** **1–2 hours**
Cook time **18 minutes** **Yield** **4 servings**

½ **cup honey mustard**
3 **tablespoons teriyaki sauce, any type**
4 **boneless, skinless chicken breast halves**
   (1–1½ pounds)

1 Combine the mustard and teriyaki sauce in a medium resealable container, whisking to blend. Set aside ⅓ cup of the marinade.

2 Add the chicken to the marinade, turning to coat. Seal and refrigerate for 1 to 2 hours, turning occasionally if possible.

3 Prepare a medium fire in a gas or charcoal grill. Drain the chicken and discard the marinade.

4 Grill the chicken, basting with the reserved marinade, for 8 minutes per side, or until the juices run clear when the meat is pierced with a knife.

5 Serve with steamed vegetables and rice.

FOR KEEPS: **You can freeze the chicken in the marinade; place in it the refrigerator in the morning to thaw and then grill it in the evening.**

GRILLED TEXAS
SPICE-RUBBED CHICKEN

A spicy and deeply flavored dish that can be made on the grill or stove top.

Prep time **4 minutes**   **Cook time** **8–16 minutes**   **Yield** **4 servings**

- 1 **tablespoon paprika**
- 1 **teaspoon seasoned salt**
- ½ **teaspoon sugar**
- ¼ **teaspoon garlic powder**
- ⅛ **teaspoon cayenne pepper**
- 2 **teaspoons vegetable oil**
- 4 **boneless, skinless chicken breast halves, 8 thighs, or 12 chicken breast tenders (1–1½ pounds)**
- 1 **tablespoon vegetable oil, if pan-frying**

1. For grilling, prepare a medium fire in a gas or charcoal grill.
2. Combine the paprika, salt, sugar, garlic powder and cayenne; add the oil to make a paste. Rub it on the chicken to coat evenly.
3. Grill for 4 to 5 minutes on each side or until the chicken is no longer pink in the center.
4. For pan-frying, heat 1 tablespoon of oil in a large nonstick skillet over medium-high heat. Add the chicken and cook for 6 to 8 minutes per side, or until the juices run clear when pierced with a knife.

QUICK TIP: For more dry spice rub recipes, see page 209.

STIR-FRIED CHICKEN WITH ASIAN FLAVORS

A mildly spicy, fresh-tasting, healthy, flavorful dish, great in springtime when you can use fresh spring onions in place of the scallions.

- 2 **tablespoons vegetable oil**
- 4 **boneless, skinless chicken breast halves, 8 thighs, or 12 chicken breast tenders (1–1½ pounds), cut into ½-inch pieces**
- 2 **teaspoons fresh minced ginger root**
- 2 **teaspoons minced garlic**
- ½ **teaspoon crushed red pepper flakes**
- ½ **cup bottled teriyaki sauce**
- ¾ **cup prepared coleslaw mix**
- 2 **bunches scallions (white and tender green parts), sliced**

1. Heat the oil in a large nonstick skillet over medium-high heat. Sauté the chicken for 2 minutes. Add the ginger, garlic, and pepper flakes; sauté 2 minutes longer. Add the teriyaki sauce and mix well. Add 2 tablespoons of water if the sauce is too thick.

2. Add the coleslaw mix and scallions; stir-fry for 4 minutes or until the cabbage is tender crisp.

QUICK TIP: **Wrap this chicken in flour tortillas and drizzle with plum sauce or hoisin sauce for a quick meal.**

KITCHEN 411: **Plum sauce is sometimes called duck sauce and can typically be found in the Asian section of your grocery store.**

ASIAN GRILLED BEEF

This is a quick, easy, and wonderfully savory recipe. Be sure not to overcook the meat, as this cut gets tougher the longer you cook it.

Prep time	10 minutes	Marinate time	6–12 hours
Cook time	6 minutes	Yield	4 servings

- **2–3** bunches scallions (white and tender green parts), sliced
- **½** cup low-sodium soy sauce
- **½** cup water
- **½** cup sugar
- **⅓** cup sesame seeds
- **3–4** teaspoons minced garlic
- **½** teaspoon black pepper
- **1½–2** pounds bottom round beef, cut into ½-inch-thick slices

1. Combine scallions, soy sauce, water, sugar, sesame seeds, garlic, and pepper in a ziplock bag or a container with a tight-fitting lid; mix well.

2. Add the meat to the soy sauce mixture, shaking or stirring to coat, and refrigerate for 6 to 12 hours.

3. Prepare a medium fire in a gas or charcoal grill.

4. Grill the meat 3 minutes per side for medium doneness. Serve immediately.

QUICK TIPS:

- **Garnish with additional sliced scallions and serve with rice and steamed veggies.**
- **This marinade works well with pork and chicken, too. My mother used a whole top round roast, marinated overnight, for this recipe and grilled it on a spit, then sliced the meat before serving — it turned out great.**

PEPPER STEAK STIR-FRY

Make instant rice while cooking the stir-fry and you will have a meal in 30 minutes. This recipe is very quick; the key is to use high heat to sear in the flavor.

Prep time 10 minutes   **Marinate time** 1–12 hours
Cook time 20 minutes   **Yield** About 6 servings

MARINADE

- 2 tablespoons low-sodium soy sauce
- 2 tablespoons fresh lemon juice
- ½ teaspoon ground ginger
- ¼ teaspoon garlic powder
- ⅛ teaspoon black pepper

- 1 pound top round beef, cut into ⅛-inch-thick strips
- 1 tablespoon vegetable oil
- 3 bunches scallions (white and tender green parts), thinly sliced

- 2 green, red, yellow, or orange bell peppers, stemmed, seeded, and chopped
- 2 stalks celery, thinly sliced
- 1 (8-ounce) can sliced water chestnuts, drained, liquid reserved
- 1 (4-ounce) can sliced mushrooms, drained, liquid reserved
- 1 tablespoon cornstarch

1. To make the marinade, whisk the soy sauce, lemon juice, ginger, garlic powder, and pepper together in a medium non-reactive resealable bowl. Add the beef strips. Cover and refrigerate for 1 to 12 hours.

2. Heat the oil in a large skillet over medium-high heat. Remove the beef from the marinade; reserve marinade. Cook the beef in the skillet over high heat until it browns and any remaining liquid evaporates, about 8 minutes.

3. Add the scallions, peppers, celery, water chestnuts, and mushrooms to the skillet; cover and cook until the vegetables are cooked through but still tender crisp, about 5 minutes.

4. Combine the cornstarch with reserved juices from the water chestnuts and mushrooms and the reserved marinade; whisk. Add to the vegetable/beef mixture; bring to a boil then simmer until thickened, at least 5 minutes. Serve.

TEXAS RANCH STEAK

My husband prepared this for a family reunion where everyone brought a dish to share. The steak disappeared even before the lasagna; in my family, that's a big deal. My husband's grilling reputation rose a number of notches that day. He never told anyone that I gave him the recipe.

Prep time 5 minutes   **Cook time** 16 minutes   **Yield** 4 servings

1 (1-ounce) package ranch salad dressing mix
1½ tablespoons water
2 tablespoons olive oil
1½ pounds flank steak

1   Prepare a medium-hot fire in a gas or charcoal grill.

2   Combine the dressing mix, water, and olive oil in a small bowl. Mix with a wooden spoon to make a paste.

3   Coat 1 side of the steak with half of the paste. Transfer the meat, coated-side down, to the grill and cook for 7 to 8 minutes. Coat the top side of the meat with the remaining paste. Turn the meat and grill 7 to 8 minutes longer for medium-rare. Serve immediately.

QUICK TIP: For medium doneness, cook the meat about 1 minute longer per side. For well-done, cook about 2 minutes longer per side.

QUICKEST MEATLOAF IN THE WEST

Meatloaf is a classic and this recipe makes it faster than fast. The microwave is the key here, but this meatloaf tastes and looks like it came from the oven. This was my mother-in-law's favorite standby, and I have modified it over the years for our faster-paced lifestyle. Slice the leftovers for great sandwiches the next day.

Prep time 10 minutes   **Cook time** 20 minutes   **Yield** 4 servings

30-MINUTE DISHES

1 **pound lean ground beef (ground round or ground chuck both work well)**
1 **egg**
¼ **cup milk**
½ **cup old-fashioned rolled oats**
1 **small onion, chopped**
¼ **cup ketchup**

2 **teaspoons prepared mustard**
½ **teaspoon salt**
½ **teaspoon black pepper**

GLAZE
2 **tablespoons brown sugar**
2 **tablespoons ketchup**
2 **teaspoons prepared mustard**

1. Coat a microwave-safe baking dish with cooking spray.

2. For the meatloaf, combine the beef, egg, milk, oats, onion, ketchup, mustard, and salt and pepper to taste in a large bowl, mixing just until combined with your hands.

3. Pat the meat mixture into the baking dish, forming a loaf 2 to 3 inches high. Microwave uncovered on high for 14 minutes; drain any liquid that forms in the bottom of the baking dish.

4. For the glaze, combine the sugar, ketchup, and mustard in a small bowl and spread on top of the meat.

5. Microwave on high 5 minutes longer. Let stand for 5 minutes, slice, and serve.

QUICK TIPS:
- You can make this recipe with lean ground turkey.
- To double this recipe, use two separate baking dishes and microwave them separately.
- Times may vary depending on the wattage of the microwave used.

GRILLED GINGER-GARLIC PORK

Another foolproof marinade. Serve this tenderloin with a green salad and rice.

Prep time 2 minutes Marinate time 4–8 hours
Cook time 15–20 minutes Yield 4 servings

- ½ cup low-sodium soy sauce
- ½ cup orange juice
- 1 teaspoon ground ginger or 1 teaspoon minced fresh gingerroot
- 2 teaspoons minced garlic
- 2 (12-ounce) pork tenderloins

1. Combine the soy sauce, orange juice, ginger, and garlic in a ziplock bag. Add the meat, shaking to coat, and refrigerate for 4 to 8 hours, turning occasionally if possible.

2. Prepare a medium-hot fire in a charcoal or gas grill.

3. Remove the meat from the marinade, discarding the marinade, and transfer the meat to the grill.

4. Grill the meat, turning frequently, until the internal temperature reaches 160°F, 15 to 20 minutes.

5. Remove the meat from the grill, slice, and serve.

KITCHEN 411: **Pork is one of those meats that get along very well with strong seasonings, so don't be afraid to load up on the garlic or ginger in this recipe or in any pork recipe calling for such ingredients.**

30-MINUTE DISHES

SWEET AND SAVORY GRILLED PORK KABOBS

Pork kabobs are a great option if your family is tired of chicken and beef on the grill. Garlic, honey, and soy sauce blend nicely in this sweet and salty marinade.

30-MINUTE DISHES

Prep time 2 minutes **Marinate time** 2–24 hours
Cook time 20 minutes **Yield** 4–6 servings

   4 teaspoons minced garlic
   ½ cup low-sodium soy sauce
   2 tablespoons honey
   2 teaspoons chili powder
1–1½ pounds lean pork, cut into 2-inch cubes
     Skewers

1. Combine the garlic, soy sauce, honey, and chili powder in a small bowl. Put the pork and half of the marinade into a ziplock bag, shaking to coat. Transfer it to the refrigerator and marinate for at least 2 and up to 24 hours.

2. Store the other half of the marinade in the refrigerator to use for basting skewers on the grill.

3. Prepare a hot fire in a charcoal or gas grill.

4. Remove the pork from the bag; discard the marinade. Thread the pork cubes onto skewers and grill, basting with the reserved glaze and turning occasionally, for 15 minutes, or until browned and cooked through.

QUICK TIP: **Serve with fresh veggies, dip, and a loaf of French bread.**

FOR KEEPS: **Put the pork in the marinade directly into the freezer. It will keep for up to 2 months. Just thaw it in the refrigerator 24 hours before you are ready to grill. The meat thaws and marinates at the same time.**

SWEET AND SOUR PORK CHOPS

A microwave dish that no one will believe came out of the microwave. Its wonderful Asian flavor pairs well with rice or couscous.

Prep time 5 minutes	Cook time 15 minutes	Yield 4 servings

- 1 **tablespoon ground ginger**
- 2 **teaspoons minced garlic**
- ¼ **cup ketchup**
- 3 **tablespoons low-sodium soy sauce**
- 2 **teaspoons cornstarch**
  Dash crushed red pepper flakes
- 1 **(20-ounce) can pineapple chunks, drained, liquid reserved**
- 4 **boneless pork chops (about ½-inch thick)**
- 1 **bunch scallions (white and tender green parts), sliced**
- 2 **tablespoons toasted sesame seeds**
  Salt and pepper

1 Combine the ginger, garlic, ketchup, soy sauce, cornstarch, pepper flakes, and pineapple juice in a microwave-safe casserole dish; whisk until smooth.

2 Transfer the pork chops to the casserole dish, turning to coat. Cover with plastic wrap.

3 Microwave on high for 6 minutes; stir gently and add the pineapple chunks.

4 Cover and microwave for 5 minutes longer, rotating the dish halfway if your microwave does not have a turntable.

5 Let the meat stand, covered, for 2 to 3 minutes to cool. Sprinkle with scallions and sesame seeds, and season with salt and pepper to taste. Serve immediately.

SAVORY SAN ANTONIO PORK CUTLETS

I love the city of San Antonio — the sunshine, the lively atmosphere, the great food packed with color and flavor. This dish was given to me by a good friend who used to live in San Antonio. Don't let the list of ingredients scare you away; the recipe itself is very easy and the whole dish can be on the table in less than 30 minutes.

Prep time 10 minutes **Cook time** 10 minutes **Yield** 4 servings

- 4 boneless pork chops (about ½-inch thick)
- 1 teaspoon garlic salt
- 1 teaspoon ground cumin
- 2 tablespoons vegetable oil
- 1 red bell pepper, stemmed, seeded, and chopped into ½-inch pieces
- 1 bunch scallions (white and tender green parts), sliced
- 1 teaspoon minced garlic
- 1 cup frozen corn, thawed
- 1 avocado, pitted, peeled, and diced
- 1 tablespoon chopped cilantro, optional
- 1 teaspoon fresh lime juice

1 Rub both sides of the pork chops with the garlic salt and cumin.

2 Heat the oil in a large skillet over medium heat; add the meat and sauté for 5 minutes per side. Remove the meat from the skillet, place it on a serving platter, and keep it warm.

3 Increase the heat to medium-high. Add the bell pepper, scallions, garlic, and corn to the skillet; cook for 5 minutes.

4 Remove the skillet from the heat and stir in the avocado, cilantro, if desired, and lime juice; pour over the meat, and serve.

KITCHEN 411:

- Avocado complements many dishes. Try slices on top of grilled chicken or grilled portobello mushrooms.

- Avocado discolors quickly and does not do well if it's cooked for any length of time, so be sure to slice it and add it at the end of the preparation. A sprinkle of sea salt draws out the flavor.

vegetarian

SPEEDY GONZALES CHILI

Aside from opening a can, this is the quickest method for making chili that I've found. It can be made with meat or a vegetarian ground beef substitute; both turn out great.

Prep time **10 minutes**   **Cook time** **20 minutes**   **Yield** **4 servings**

2 tablespoons vegetable oil

1 pound ground beef substitute (or lean ground beef or turkey)

1 medium onion, chopped

1 (15-ounce) can red kidney beans, drained

½ teaspoon garlic powder

1 (10.75-ounce) can condensed low-sodium tomato soup

⅔ cup water

¾ teaspoon salt

1 tablespoon chili powder

1 Heat the oil in a large skillet over medium-high heat. Add the beef substitute and onion and cook until lightly browned, 6 to 8 minutes; drain any grease.

2 Add the beans, garlic powder, soup, water, salt, and chili powder; stir well.

3 Bring to a boil, then lower the heat, cover, and simmer for 20 minutes, stirring occasionally.

QUICK TIPS:

• Serve with crackers, grated sharp cheddar cheese, shredded lettuce, and sliced scallions.

• Add an extra can of beans, serve over brown rice or whole grain pasta, and this recipe can serve 6.

KITCHEN 411: There are several commercial brands of vegetarian ground beef substitute, sometimes called meat-free vegetable protein. They can be found in either the frozen foods section (with other vegetarian products) or in the refrigerator case near the tofu. Two products I like are the Lightlife Smart Ground Original and the Morningstar Farms Meal Starters, Grillers Recipe Crumbles.

CHILI CHEESE CASSEROLE

This dish is so quick and easy that you can trust your teen to put it together.

teen-friendly

3 handfuls corn chips (about 3 ounces)

1 (15-ounce) can chili

1 medium onion, chopped

1 cup grated sharp cheddar cheese
     (about 4 ounces)

1 Preheat the oven to 375°F.

2 Coat an 8-inch square baking pan with cooking spray. Arrange 2 handfuls of the chips on the bottom of the baking pan.

3 Combine the chili and onion in a bowl and spread over the chips. Top the chili mixture with the remaining handful of chips.

4 Bake for 20 to 25 minutes. Sprinkle the cheese on top of the chips and bake 5 minutes longer, or until the cheese melts. Serve.

QUICK TIP: To speed up the process, cook in the microwave instead. Use a microwave-safe baking dish and cook for 5 minutes, turning the dish occasionally. Finish by melting the cheese under the broiler for 2 minutes. Your chips may not be as crispy, but you will have one very quick meal.

LET'S TALK: Canned chili is one way to prepare this recipe, but if you are trying to reduce the number of processed foods in your kids' diets, keep some containers of homemade chili in the freezer; your teens can then use them for this dish. My Veggie Chili (page 218) is great in this recipe.

MACBURGER MEAL

This rich and satisfying meal is quick and quite a child-pleaser. Balance the richness of this meal with a fresh fruit salad. This recipe seems quite old-fashioned and outdated, but it is one of those great comfort-food meals that hit home.

| Prep time | 2 minutes | Cook time | 18 minutes | Yield | 4–6 servings |

1-1¼ pounds lean ground turkey or beef

2¾ cups water

⅓ cup ketchup

2 teaspoons onion powder

½ teaspoon salt

8 ounces elbow macaroni

12 ounces processed cheese, such as Velveeta, cut into small chunks

1 Cook the meat in a large skillet over medium-high heat, stirring to break it up, until browned, about 8 minutes. Drain.

2 Add the water, ketchup, onion powder, and salt. Bring to a boil. Add the pasta, stirring thoroughly to moisten the pasta.

3 Reduce the heat to medium-low, cover, and simmer for 20 minutes, or until the pasta is fully cooked.

4 Remove from the heat and add the cheese; stir until melted, 1 to 2 minutes. Serve immediately.

QUICK MAC CASSEROLE

This is a classic mac 'n' cheese dish, but with meat added for protein and flavor.

1 (7.5-ounce) package macaroni and cheese dinner

1 pound lean ground beef or turkey

1 stalk celery, sliced

½ green bell pepper, stemmed, seeded, and chopped

1 medium onion, chopped

1 (16-ounce) bag frozen whole kernel corn, or 1 (15.25-ounce) can corn, drained

1 (6-ounce) can tomato paste

1 cup water

1 teaspoon salt

¼ teaspoon black pepper

1. Preheat the oven to 350°F. Coat a 9- by 13-inch baking pan with cooking spray.

2. Prepare the macaroni and cheese dinner according to the package directions.

3. While the macaroni is cooking, combine the ground meat, celery, green pepper, and onion in a large skillet over medium-high heat. Cook until the vegetables are tender and the meat is browned, about 10 minutes.

4. Add the corn, tomato paste, water, salt, and pepper to the skillet; mix well. Add the prepared macaroni and cheese dinner to the skillet; mix well.

5. Pour the skillet contents into the prepared pan. Cover and bake for 15 to 20 minutes. Serve.

FOR KEEPS: This can be prepared a day in advance and chilled. Reheat it in the microwave until heated through. It may not be quite as creamy, but the taste is great.

FAST AND CHEESY TUNA AND NOODLES

After testing a lot of recipes for a tuna-noodle combination, I found that this dish was the easiest and had the best flavor.

Prep time 5 minutes   Cook time 15 minutes   Yield 4 servings

3 cups water

8 ounces wide egg noodles

12 ounces processed cheese, such as Velveeta, cut into ½-inch cubes

1 (16-ounce) bag frozen peas and carrots

1 (6-ounce) can chunk light tuna in water, drained and flaked

½ teaspoon salt

¼ teaspoon black pepper

1 Bring 2½ cups of the water to a boil in a large skillet. Reduce the heat to medium-low; add the noodles.

2 Cover and simmer for 8 minutes or until the noodles are tender, stirring occasionally.

3 Add the cheese, vegetables, tuna, ½ cup water, salt, and pepper to the skillet; stir until the cheese is melted.

4 Cover and cook for 3 minutes; serve.

SASSY HAWAIIAN PORK BURGERS

Pineapple slices add just the right amount of sweetness to these burgers, which are a great alternative to beef.

Prep time 8 minutes   **Cook time** 20 minutes   **Yield** 8 servings

1¼–1½ **pounds lean ground pork**

1 **(8-ounce) can water chestnuts, drained and finely chopped**

1 **large egg, beaten**

1 **bunch scallions (white and tender green parts), minced**

½ **teaspoon ground ginger**

½ **teaspoon salt**

¼ **teaspoon black pepper**

6 **tablespoons seasoned breadcrumbs**

4 **tablespoons teriyaki sauce**

1 **(8-ounce) can pineapple rings, drained**

8 **Kaiser rolls**

1 Combine the pork, water chestnuts, egg, scallions, ginger, salt, pepper, breadcrumbs, and 2 tablespoons of the teriyaki sauce; mix well.

2 Wet your hands and form the meat mixture into 8 patties.

3 Cook the patties in a large skillet over medium-high heat for about 10 minutes per side, basting occasionally with the remaining 2 tablespoons of the teriyaki sauce.

4 Top with the pineapple rings and serve on the rolls.

QUICK TIP: **Serve these burgers with lettuce, tomato, and red onion slices.**

BARBECUED TURKEY BURGERS

Serve these low-fat burgers with baked beans and cole slaw (see the Simple Slaw on page 109). My son likes to put the slaw right on the burger.

Prep time 10 minutes   **Cook time** 12 minutes   **Yield** 4–5 servings

1¼ **pounds lean ground turkey**
1 **small zucchini, grated and patted dry with paper towel (about ½ cup)**
1 **bunch scallions (white and tender green parts), sliced**
3 **tablespoons spicy barbecue sauce, plus more for basting**
2 **tablespoons seasoned breadcrumbs**
1 **teaspoon chili powder**
1 **teaspoon minced garlic**
1 **teaspoon salt**
1 **teaspoon black pepper**
3 **tablespoons vegetable oil**

1 Combine the turkey, zucchini, scallions, barbecue sauce, breadcrumbs, chili powder, garlic, salt, and pepper in a large bowl. Mix well and form into 4 to 5 patties.

2 Heat the vegetable oil in a large skillet over medium-high heat. Cook the patties in the skillet, basting occasionally with barbecue sauce, 7 to 8 minutes per side.

FOR KEEPS: **Freeze these burgers before cooking. Wrap tightly in plastic wrap and freeze in a ziplock freezer bag. To cook, place them frozen on a medium grill or in a skillet over medium heat. Starting with frozen burgers will prevent them from falling apart.**

RED BEAN BURGERS

These veggie burgers are hands-down better than any prepared variety — and easy, too.

vegetarian

Prep time 8 minutes   **Cook time** 15 minutes   **Yield** 6 servings

SPECIAL SAUCE

- ¼ **cup light mayonnaise**
- 1 **tablespoon horseradish**
- 1 **tablespoon minced scallions taken from the bunch minced for the burgers**
- 1 **teaspoon low-sodium soy sauce**

BURGERS

- 2 **(15-ounce) cans red kidney beans, rinsed and drained**
- ½ **cup seasoned breadcrumbs**
- 1 **bunch scallions (white and tender green parts), minced**
- 2 **eggs**
- 1 **tablespoon soy sauce**
- 1 **teaspoon ground ginger**
- 1 **teaspoon minced garlic**
- 2 **tablespoons vegetable oil**
- 6 **buns**

  Lettuce, sliced cucumber, and tomato

1   For the sauce, combine the mayonnaise, horseradish, scallions, and soy sauce in a small bowl; refrigerate until ready to serve.

2   For the burgers, mash the beans in a large bowl; add the breadcrumbs, scallions, eggs, soy sauce, ginger, and garlic. Mix thoroughly and form into 6 patties.

3   Heat the oil in a large skillet over medium heat. Cook the patties 6 to 8 minutes per side, or until dark brown and crisp.

4   Serve on the buns with the lettuce, cucumber, tomato, and the sauce.

FOR KEEPS: The sauce can be made up to 3 days in advance.

KITCHEN 411: When choosing scallions in the produce section of the grocery store, you'll notice that they're sometimes as thin as pencils, and at other times as fat as cigars. No matter what their size, scallions are very tender and mild — you won't ruin a recipe with a bit too much or too little.

RED BEANS AND RICE

Great for the vegetarian in the family or for any time you want a hearty meatless supper. Serve any leftovers the next day in flour tortillas or over a bed of greens.

Prep time 5 minutes   **Cook time** 30 minutes   **Yield** 4 servings

2 tablespoons olive oil

1 large onion, thinly sliced

2 teaspoons minced garlic

1 green, red, or yellow bell pepper, stemmed, seeded, and chopped

1 (32-ounce) can peeled whole tomatoes, chopped

1 medium tomato, chopped

2 teaspoon Tex-Mex-style seasoning

2 (15-ounce) cans pinto beans, drained

Salt and pepper

Cooked brown or white rice

1 Heat the oil in a large skillet over medium heat; add the onion and garlic and sauté for 5 minutes. Add the bell pepper and cook 5 minutes longer.

2 Add the canned and fresh tomatoes and seasonings; simmer for 15 minutes.

3 Stir the beans into the thickened tomato sauce; simmer 5 minutes longer to heat the beans. Season with salt and pepper to taste. Serve over rice.

QUICK TIPS:

• If you don't have Tex-Mex seasoning mix, substitute ½ teaspoon each of basil, oregano, thyme, and chili powder.

• For meat eaters, add 1 pound of precooked spicy sausage with the bell pepper.

• Brown rice adds a great flavor to this dish if you have a little extra time to prepare it.

TOMATO-CHEESE PIE

A rich, cheesy dish that is great for potlucks.

vegetarian

1 cup grated sharp cheddar
   cheese (about 4 ounces)
1 cup grated mozzarella cheese
   (about 4 ounces)
1 cup whole milk ricotta cheese
4 ounces mushrooms, sliced
½ small onion, chopped

1 (9-inch) prebaked piecrust
½ large tomato, thinly sliced
   (5–6 slices)
2 teaspoons Italian seasoning
1 bunch scallions (white and
   tender green parts), sliced
   Salt and pepper

1 Preheat the oven to 325°F.

2 Combine the cheddar, mozzarella, ricotta, mushrooms, and
   onion in a large bowl; mix well.

3 Spoon the cheese mixture into the piecrust; top with tomato
   and sprinkle with the Italian seasoning, scallions, and salt and
   pepper to taste.

4 Bake for 20 minutes. Let cool for 5 minutes, slice, and serve.

QUICK TIPS:

• For extra protein, add 1 (6-ounce) can of salmon or tuna to the
  cheeses.

• To speed up the prep time, use packaged grated or shredded
  cheese and presliced mushrooms.

• For a variation, you can add any of the following to the cheese
  mixture:

   ½   pound precooked and crumbled sweet Italian sausage
   6–8 slices cooked, crumbled bacon
   6–8 ounces cubed deli ham

FOR KEEPS: Bake this pie, wrap it tightly in plastic wrap, and
freeze for up to 2 months.

30-MINUTE DISHES

NO-CRUST CHEESE PIE

This pie makes a simple and satisfying meal. You can serve it for breakfast, brunch, lunch, or a light dinner with a side salad.

Prep time 5 minutes   **Cook time** 27 minutes   **Yield** 4–6 servings

1½ **cups milk**

3 **eggs**

1¼ **cups Whole Grain Master Mix (page 33), or low-fat baking mix, such as Bisquick**

⅓ **cup grated Parmesan cheese**

½ **teaspoon salt**

¼ **teaspoon black pepper**

¾ **cup cubed mozzarella cheese (about 3 ounces)**

1 **medium tomato, sliced**

½ **cup grated mozzarella cheese (about 2 ounces)**

1 Preheat the oven to 425°F. Coat a 10-inch pie pan with cooking spray.

2 Combine the milk, eggs, master mix, Parmesan, salt, and pepper in a large bowl; whisk for 1 minute. Pour the mixture into the pie pan and sprinkle with the mozzarella cubes.

3 Bake for 20 minutes or until puffy and golden brown.

4 Remove the pie from the oven and preheat the broiler. Top the pie with tomato slices (it will seem unstable, but the tomatoes won't fall off) and then with the grated mozzarella. Broil for 2 minutes, or until the cheese is melted and bubbly. Let cool for 5 minutes before slicing.

TOMATO TART

This recipe is very easy and the finished tart looks so professional that your family will think it came from a French bistro. Make several of these pies at once. They freeze and reheat beautifully and can be served for brunch, lunch, dinner, or snacks.

vegetarian

Prep time 8 minutes   **Cook time** 35 minutes   **Yield** 8 servings

- 2 medium tomatoes, cut into ¼-inch slices
- 1 (9-inch) prebaked piecrust
- 1 cup whole milk ricotta cheese
- ½ cup grated Monterey Jack cheese (about 2 ounces)
- ½ cup grated mozzarella cheese (about 2 ounces)
- 2 eggs, lightly beaten
- 1 tablespoon Italian seasoning mix
- ¼ teaspoon black pepper
- 2 tablespoons grated Parmesan cheese

1. Preheat the oven to 375°F.
2. Layer half of the tomatoes in the piecrust.
3. Combine the ricotta, Monterey Jack, mozzarella, eggs, seasoning mix, and pepper in a large bowl; whisk until well blended.
4. Spoon the cheese mixture on top of the tomatoes in the piecrust; top with the remaining tomato slices, and sprinkle with Parmesan.
5. Bake the pie until the filling is set and golden brown and a knife inserted in the center comes out clean, about 30 minutes. Let cool for 5 minutes; slice and serve.

QUICK TIP: If you don't have Italian seasoning, make your own by combining 1 teaspoon basil, 1 teaspoon oregano, ½ teaspoon garlic powder, and ½ teaspoon onion powder.

FOR KEEPS: Place the assembled pie on a tray and freeze. Wrap the frozen pie tightly with foil, and store in a ziplock freezer bag for up to 2 months. To bake, place the frozen pie on a tray in a preheated oven and bake for 1 hour and 10 minutes or until a knife inserted into the center comes out clean. Wrap the crust edges with foil so that it doesn't burn.

MA'S FRITTATA

I remember my mother making frittatas once or twice a month for dinner. She would serve them with bread and a large garden salad. When I finally asked her for the recipe, she confessed that she made frittatas only when leftovers were piling up in the refrigerator, as a way to stretch the food on hand to make one more meal. There's no need to run to the store for special ingredients. See the Quick Tip below for creative additions.

Prep time 5 minutes   **Cook time** 20 minutes   **Yield** 6 servings

- 4 **tablespoons olive oil**
- 3 **medium russet potatoes, peeled and cut into ¼-inch rounds**
- 3 **tablespoons all-purpose flour**
- ½ **teaspoon garlic powder**
- ½ **teaspoon Italian seasoning**
- 8 **eggs**
- ¼ **cup grated Parmesan cheese**
- **Salt and pepper**

1. Heat the oil in a large nonstick skillet over medium-high heat.

2. Toss the potato slices with flour, garlic powder, and Italian seasonings in a large bowl. Transfer the potatoes to the skillet and cook, covered, until they are tender, 10 to 12 minutes; stir often.

3. In the same large bowl, combine the eggs, Parmesan, and salt and pepper, whisking to blend.

4. Pour the egg mixture over the potatoes, quickly tipping the pan so that the egg flows under the potato. Cook uncovered for 1 minute.

5   With your spatula, gently move the potatoes and egg around to let the egg work its way to the bottom of the pan. Do not stir the eggs. Reduce the heat to medium and cover the skillet; cook until the eggs are set, 8 to 10 minutes.

6   Loosen the frittata from the pan with the spatula and slide gently onto a serving platter.

7   Serve immediately with toast and a fresh fruit salad.

QUICK TIP: **Here are some other ingredients you can add to this frittata: cooked asparagus, frozen peas, thawed, scallion, green bell pepper, mushrooms, sweet red onion (you can add these last three to the skillet with the potatoes to sauté, or sauté ahead of time and add later), a handful of chopped salami, pitted green or black olives, a few dollops of ricotta cheese, 1 tablespoon of capers, or sliced tomato.**

FAMILY MEALS
and
One-Pot Deals

Easy Recipes for When You Have a Little More Time to Eat Together

No matter how busy you are, there needs to be time when the whole family regroups and has a meal together. A family meal is a necessity so that you can count heads and make sure that you didn't forget to pick someone up after the last soccer match or piano lesson.

This chapter includes all kinds of recipes that take longer than 30 minutes to prepare but are still easy and fun to make. Most do not require a lot of complicated tasks or a lot of preparation time. They are just good ol' Sunday dinner recipes that maybe your mom used to make, but slightly modified for today's busier lifestyle.

Check out the great marinades and dry rubs on pages 208 and 209 of this chapter. And the one-pot meals for simple dinners with the family — just add a salad and bread. Afterwards, you'll have only one pot to clean!

NEIGHBORHOOD CHICKEN

When you want to make a dish that: 1) freezes well *before* baking; 2) serves a lot of people at once; 3) is suitable for a potluck or a family in need; 4) freezes well *after* baking; and 5) is versatile with any other dish — this recipe is it. I have made this chicken many times, and have given the recipe to friends who have called me back with their thanks and their variations.

Prep time 5 minutes   Cook time 1½ hours   Yield 8–10 servings

2 **(4–5 pound) chicken fryers, cut into 6 pieces**
1 **(16-ounce) bottle Russian salad dressing**
2 **(1.25-ounce) packages dry onion soup mix**
1 **(18-ounce) jar apricot preserves**

1   Preheat the oven to 350°F.

2   Coat 2 large casserole dishes with cooking spray. Arrange the chicken in one layer in the prepared dishes.

3   Combine the dressing, soup mix, and preserves in a medium bowl; pour over the chicken.

4   Cover the chicken and bake for 1 hour. Remove the cover and bake 30 minutes longer.

5   Serve over rice, noodles, or couscous.

QUICK TIPS:

- You can use precut chicken parts or assorted thighs and drumsticks instead of whole fryers. Remove the skin from the chicken if you prefer; you'll still have a tender piece of meat when you're ready to serve.

- Boneless, skinless chicken breasts cook too quickly for this recipe. You will end up with Rubber Chicken instead of Neighborhood Chicken if you use them.

- Add chopped green bell pepper, mushrooms, zucchini, or olives with the chicken to the casserole dish.

- Garnish with cherry tomatoes.

FAMILY MEALS AND ONE-POT DEALS

CHILI-BAKED CHICKEN

Great flavor with a crisp skin!

Prep time **10 minutes**   Cook time **1 hour**   Yield **6 servings**

1 **tablespoon vegetable oil**	1 **teaspoon salt**
½ **cup cornmeal**	½ **teaspoon cayenne pepper**
½ **cup all-purpose flour**	⅓ **cup buttermilk**
1 **tablespoon chili powder**	1 **whole chicken, cut into**
2 **teaspoons dried oregano**	**6 pieces**
1½ **teaspoons cumin**	2 **tablespoons butter, melted**

1 Preheat the oven to 375°F. Coat a large baking dish with the oil.

2 Combine the cornmeal, flour, chili powder, oregano, cumin, salt, and cayenne in a ziplock freezer bag and shake to combine; set aside.

3 Pour the buttermilk into a large shallow bowl. Pat the chicken dry with paper towels, then dip the chicken in the buttermilk. Shake off the excess buttermilk and add the chicken pieces to the bag with the dry ingredients.

4 Shake the bag until all of the pieces of chicken are coated. (Don't forget to close the bag tightly!)

5 Place the coated chicken in the baking dish and drizzle with the melted butter. Bake uncovered, turning the chicken once or twice, for 1 hour or until deep brown.

QUICK TIPS:

- If you don't want the hassle of cutting up a whole chicken, buy the parts already cut up.
- Buy spices in bulk rather than in jars — bulk spices are fresher and much less expensive. Store the spices in your freezer and refill kitchen jars as they run low.

FAMILY MEALS AND ONE-POT DEALS

BAKED STUFFED CHICKEN

A satisfying, soft stuffing with a Mexican flair.

Prep time 10 minutes   **Cook time** 1 hour   **Yield** 4 servings

1 whole chicken, cut into 6 pieces

3 cups stuffing (any flavor)

¾ cup low-sodium chicken broth

2 tablespoons butter

1 (.87-ounce) package chicken gravy mix

2 tablespoons fajita seasoning mix

1 cup cold water

1 Preheat the oven to 375°F.

2 Coat a large casserole dish with cooking spray and arrange the chicken pieces in the dish.

3 Combine the stuffing, chicken broth, and butter in a microwave-safe bowl. Heat on high in the microwave for 1 minute and fluff with a fork. Place the prepared stuffing around the chicken pieces.

4 In the same microwave-safe bowl, whisk together the chicken gravy mix, fajita seasoning mix and cold water; microwave for 1 minute. Pour over the chicken and stuffing mixture.

5 Cover and bake for 45 minutes. Remove the cover and bake 15 minutes longer. Serve.

QUICK TIP: You can use 4 skinless, bone-in chicken breast halves to reduce fat. Serve the chicken and stuffing with Tarragon Carrots (page 258) and dinner rolls.

FOR KEEPS: This chicken freezes well before or after baking. For uncooked frozen chicken, increase the cooking time by 50 to 60 minutes, or until the juices run clear when the chicken is pierced with a knife. Reheat the baked and frozen dish in a microwave or oven until heated through.

CAN-YOU-KEEP-A-SECRET CHICKEN

I got this recipe from a friend who refused to tell me who she got it from. Don't tell anyone how you made this dish, because they won't believe how easy it is.

Prep time 5 minutes   **Cook time** 35 minutes   **Yield** 4 servings

- 4 **boneless, skinless chicken breast halves (1–1½ pounds)**
- 1 **(1.4-ounce) package herb-vegetable soup mix**
- ⅓ **cup light mayonnaise**
- ¼ **cup grated Parmesan cheese**
- 2 **tablespoons seasoned breadcrumbs**

1   Preheat the oven to 400°F.

2   Coat a large baking dish with cooking spray. Arrange the chicken in one layer in the prepared dish.

3   Combine the soup mix, mayonnaise, and Parmesan in a small bowl.

4   Top the chicken with the soup mix mixture and sprinkle with breadcrumbs. Cover and bake for 35 minutes. Serve hot.

QUICK TIP: If the chicken is thicker than ¾ inch, you may need to bake it longer. Be sure to cook it until the juices run clear when pierced with a knife.

FOR KEEPS: Once assembled, this dish freezes well for up to 2 months. Bake the frozen dish by increasing the baking time by 40 to 50 minutes, or thaw the dish in the refrigerator overnight and bake as directed.

FAMILY MEALS AND ONE-POT DEALS

QUICK AND TENDER CHICKEN

This chicken is melt-in-your-mouth tender and creamy!

Prep time 10 minutes **Cook time** 40 minutes **Yield** 4 servings

4 **boneless, skinless chicken breast halves (1–1½ pounds)**

4 **slices Swiss cheese**

1 **(10.5-ounce) can low-sodium cream of chicken soup**

½ **cup water**

½ **cup (1 stick) butter**

2 **cups stuffing (any flavor)**

1. Preheat the oven to 350°F.
2. Coat a 9- by 13-inch baking pan with cooking spray. Arrange the chicken in the prepared pan; top each piece with one slice of Swiss cheese.
3. Mix the soup and water in a medium microwave-safe bowl; pour over the chicken.
4. In the same bowl, melt the butter in the microwave; add the stuffing and mix with a fork until combined. Place the stuffing mixture around and on top of the chicken.
5. Cover and bake for 20 minutes; remove covering and bake 20 minutes longer. Serve hot.

FAMILY PARTY CHICKEN

You may be surprised to see the cook time on this dish but you will be amazed by the finished product. An ultimately butter-tender chicken dish with little effort, and a good dish for any occasion.

Prep time 5 minutes **Cook time** 2 hours **Yield** 4 servings

8 **slices bacon**

4 **boneless, skinless chicken breasts halves (1–1½ pounds)**

1½ **cups reduced-fat sour cream**

1 **(10.5-ounce) can low-sodium cream of mushroom or cream of potato soup**

1 Preheat the oven to 300°F. Coat a 9- by 13-inch baking pan with cooking spray.

2 Wrap two slices of bacon around each piece of chicken; place in the prepared pan.

3 Mix the sour cream and soup in a small bowl; pour over the chicken.

4 Cover the pan and bake for 2 hours. Serve hot.

QUICK TIPS:

- **This recipe makes a lot of gravy, so serve the chicken over rice or egg noodles.**
- **Garnish with roasted red pepper slices.**

FOR KEEPS: **Prepare this recipe and freeze for up to 2 months. You can bake it frozen; just increase cooking time by 40 to 50 minutes.**

QUICK-CHICK PARMESAN

A quick and easy version of this classic Italian dish — always a kid-pleaser.

Prep time **10 minutes**   Cook time **30 minutes**   Yield **4 servings**

1 **egg, beaten**
¾ **cup seasoned breadcrumbs**
¼ **cup grated Parmesan cheese**
4 **boneless, skinless chicken breast halves (1–1½ pounds)**

1 **(28-ounce) jar prepared spaghetti sauce**
1 **cup shredded mozzarella cheese (about 4 ounces)**

1   Preheat the oven to 400°F. Coat a large baking dish with cooking spray.

2   Place the beaten egg in one bowl; combine the breadcrumbs and Parmesan in another bowl.

3   Pat the chicken dry with paper towels. Dip in the egg and then in the breadcrumb mixture.

4   Arrange the chicken in one layer in the prepared baking dish.

5   Bake uncovered for 20 minutes; pour the spaghetti sauce over the chicken and cover with the mozzarella. Bake covered 10 minutes longer or until juices run clear. Serve over pasta, couscous, or rice.

QUICK TIPS:

- If the chicken is thicker than ¾ inch, you may need to bake it longer. Be sure to cook it until the juices run clear when pierced with a knife.
- For more flavor, sprinkle the coated chicken with salt, pepper, cayenne, and garlic powder before baking.

FOR KEEPS: This fully-prepared dish freezes well for up to 2 months. Simply reheat in the oven or microwave.

EASTERN CROCKPOT CHICKEN

I try to schedule at least one slow-cooker meal each week during the cold Michigan winters. I cut up all the vegetables and meat, assemble the recipe the night before, and refrigerate everything. The next morning all I have to do is pull the crock out of the refrigerator and start the slow cooker before I leave for work. The addition of dried fruits to savory dishes is common in Eastern European countries.

Prep time 10 minutes   **Cooking time** 8 hours   **Yield** 4–6 servings

1	large onion, chopped
	Grated zest and juice of 1 large orange
2	tablespoons Worcestershire sauce
2	tablespoons low-sodium soy sauce
2	tablespoons Dijon mustard
1–2	teaspoons crushed garlic
½	teaspoon salt
4	chicken drumsticks
4	chicken thighs
1	cup diced dried fruit, your choice (prunes, dates, apricots, cherries, or raisins)

1   Put the onion into a slow cooker.

2   Combine the zest, juice, Worcestershire, soy sauce, mustard, garlic, and salt in a large bowl. Add the chicken and fruit; toss to coat.

3   Place the chicken mixture on top of the onion in the slow cooker and cook on low for 8 hours.

QUICK TIPS:

- **Serve with mashed potatoes and green peas.**
- **For a lower-fat, lower-cholesterol meal, remove the skin from the chicken.**

CHEESE-BAKED CHICKEN ENCHILADAS

These wraps have a creamy texture inside with great flavor throughout. They are simple to put together, too.

Prep time **12 minutes** **Cook time** **30 minutes** **Yield** **4–6 servings**

1 (8-ounce) package reduced-fat cream cheese, at room temperature

½ small onion, chopped

½ tablespoon garlic salt

1 (4-ounce) can chopped green chiles, drained

8 flour tortillas

2–3 cooked boneless, skinless chicken breast halves, shredded

2 cups shredded sharp cheddar cheese (about 8 ounces)

1 (10-ounce) can chopped tomatoes with jalapeño peppers, such as Rotel

½ cup milk

1. Preheat the oven to 350°F. Coat a 9- by 13-inch baking pan with cooking spray.

2. Combine the cream cheese, onion, garlic salt, and half of the chiles in a small bowl; mix well.

3. Lay the tortillas out on a work surface; spread each evenly with the cream cheese mixture. Divide the chicken and 1 cup of the cheese among the tortillas; roll them up and place them in the prepared pan.

4. Combine the tomatoes and their juices, milk, and the remaining chiles in the same small bowl. Pour over the tortillas and sprinkle with the remaining cheddar cheese.

5. Bake uncovered for 30 minutes and serve.

LICKIN' CHICKEN FINGERS

This is a great recipe for the youngsters in the family. Make a double batch, as these fingers freeze well before or after baking.

Prep time 15 minutes **Cook time** 25 minutes **Yield** About 15 fingers

1 **egg, beaten**
½ **cup milk**
1 **teaspoon Dijon mustard**
2–3 **shakes hot sauce, such as Tabasco**
½ **teaspoon garlic salt**

⅛ **teaspoon black pepper**
½ **cup all-purpose flour**
2 **cups cornflake crumbs**
12 **chicken breast tenders (about 1½ pounds)**
4 **tablespoons butter, melted**

1 Preheat the oven to 350°F.
2 Combine the egg, milk, mustard, hot sauce, garlic salt, and pepper in a shallow bowl; whisk in the flour.
3 Place the cornflake crumbs in another shallow bowl.
4 Dip the chicken tenders in the egg mixture and then roll in the cornflake crumbs, coating completely.
5 Place on a baking sheet and drizzle with the butter.
6 Bake for 25 minutes or until the chicken is cooked through and crispy on the outside.

QUICK TIPS:

- You can dip these chicken fingers in a prepared honey mustard sauce or combine ¼ cup each of honey, Dijon mustard, and mayonnaise for a quick dip; try Crazy Dipping Sauce (page 47) for another great dip idea.

- For a party, serve these fingers on toothpicks with some prepared mango chutney and blueberry mustard for dipping.

FOR KEEPS: Assemble and freeze up to 2 months in advance. To bake frozen fingers, place on a baking sheet and increase the baking time by 25 to 35 minutes. You can also freeze fully-baked fingers and reheat them in the microwave.

FAMILY MEALS AND ONE-POT DEALS

teen-friendly

HOT CHICKEN SALAD

I have used this recipe for so many years that it's become an old standby when I have leftover chicken and don't want the kids to know that I'm serving them last night's dinner.

Prep time 10 minutes **Cook time** 25 minutes **Yield** 6–8 servings

1 (10.5-ounce) can low-sodium cream of
   mushroom soup
½ cup light mayonnaise
2 tablespoons low-sodium soy sauce
2 tablespoons fresh lemon juice
2 cups cubed cooked chicken
1½ cups chopped celery
1 (8-ounce) can sliced water chestnuts, drained
1–2 bunches scallions (white and tender green
   parts), sliced
8 ounces elbow or similar pasta, cooked until
   just tender
1 cup chow mein noodles

1 Preheat the oven to 350°F. Coat a 9- by 13-inch casserole dish with cooking spray.

2 Combine the soup, mayonnaise, soy sauce, and lemon juice in a large bowl; blend well. Stir in the chicken, celery, water chestnuts, scallions, and cooked pasta.

3 Pour the chicken/pasta mixture into the prepared casserole dish and sprinkle with the chow mein noodles. Bake uncovered for 25 minutes or until heated through. Serve.

FOR KEEPS: Freeze the prepared dish up to 2 months in advance. Bake as directed, increasing the baking time by 40 to 50 minutes or until heated through.

FAMILY MEALS AND
ONE-POT DEALS

PIZZA STEAK

This recipe is a delicious, easy way to add great pizza flavor to a steak.

Prep time 10 minutes   Cook time 30 minutes   Yield 3 servings

4 tablespoons olive oil

3 teaspoons chopped garlic

1 (1 pound) thin-cut sirloin steak

3 tablespoons all-purpose flour

1 (15-ounce) can puréed tomatoes

1 tablespoon dried basil

1 tablespoon dried oregano

1 tablespoon dried parsley

Salt and pepper

1 Heat 3 tablespoons of the olive oil in a large skillet over medium heat; sauté the garlic for 1 minute.

2 In the meantime, notch the edges of the meat with a sharp knife to prevent curling.

3 Place the flour in a shallow bowl; dredge the steak lightly in flour.

4 Push the garlic to the sides of the skillet and add the steak. Increase the heat to medium-high and brown the steak quickly, about 4 minutes per side. Remove the meat from the skillet and keep warm.

5 Reduce the heat to medium and add the tomatoes, basil, oregano, and parsley to the skillet. Season with salt and pepper and simmer for 15 minutes, stirring occasionally.

6 Add the steak to the skillet; drizzle with the remaining 1 tablespoon of olive oil. Stir everything and cover; simmer on medium-low 10 minutes longer. Serve immediately.

FALL'S HARVEST:
A GIFT AT OUR DOORSTEP

I grew up deep in the city of Cleveland, which did not allow my family ready access to fresh produce. So in the fall we would take a drive into the country and pick tomatoes, apples, and Concord grapes. We'd drive home with over 20 bushels of fruit in the back of the family station wagon. The next two weeks were full of canning — over 100 quarts of tomato sauce and applesauce, and countless jars of grape jelly.

Today, I live in south-central Michigan, where within 2 miles of our home we can pick raspberries until the sun goes down. And just 4 miles up the road is a wonderful apple orchard with multiple varieties of apples throughout the fall. We are lucky to have this gift of harvest so close, and my kids know it. They never complain about the drive to the farm or the market and their friends are constantly over for a taste, a smell, or a meal every time I cook up one of my mom's favorite fall harvest dishes. Take advantage of what your local farms have to offer and support them.

FAMILY MEALS AND ONE-POT DEALS

HERE'S A GREAT FALL HARVEST DINNER MENU FOR 4:

Grilled Pork Loin Chops

Oven-Roasted Potatoes

Fresh Sautéed Apples

Corn on the Cob

GRILLED PORK LOIN CHOPS

½ cup soy sauce
½ cup orange juice
1 teaspoon ground ginger
2 teaspoons chopped garlic
4 pork loin chops, about ¾ inch thick

1 In a large ziplock freezer bag, combine the soy sauce, orange juice, ginger, and garlic. Add the pork and marinate for 4 to 8 hours.

2 Prepare a medium-hot fire in a gas or charcoal grill.

3 Discard the marinade and grill the pork for 4 to 5 minutes per side.

4 Serve with Fresh Sautéed Apples, Oven Roasted Potatoes, and Corn on the Cob (see recipes on the following page).

OVEN-ROASTED POTATOES

4–5 large russet potatoes, unpeeled, scrubbed, and cut into 2-inch chunks, or 2–3 pounds whole fingerling potatoes
2 tablespoons olive oil
Salt and pepper
Splash of balsamic vinegar

1 Preheat the oven to 425°F.

2 Place the potatoes in a large bowl and with your hands toss with olive oil, salt, and pepper.

3 Spread them out on a large baking sheet with 1-inch sides. Bake for 20 to 30 minutes, stirring occasionally. Pierce with a fork to test for doneness. The potatoes should be crisp on the outside and soft inside.

4 Immediately transfer the potatoes to a bowl and toss with a touch of sea salt and a splash of balsamic vinegar. Serve hot or at room temperature.

FRESH SAUTÉED APPLES

1–2 pounds tart local apples, cut into ½- to ¾-inch slices (peeling optional)
1–2 tablespoons butter
Pinch of salt
Pinch of cinnamon, optional

1 Melt the butter in a nonstick skillet over medium heat. Place the apples in the skillet; sauté over medium-high heat for 5 minutes or until barely tender.

2 Remove from the heat and sprinkle lightly with a pinch of salt and cinnamon, if desired.

3 Serve over pork chops.

CORN ON THE COB

It's so easy and the corn comes out perfect every time. When corn is cooked too long, it toughens up. *Always* buy the freshest produce available and you will have success when cooking.

4 ears local sweet corn, shucked

Place corn in a large pot of cold water. Bring the water to a boil and cook for 5 minutes (set your timer!). Remove the corn immediately and serve.

FAMILY MEETING POT ROAST

The key to this fantastic recipe is the cut of meat. A friend of mine substituted an expensive cut of meat; needless to say, the recipe turned out horribly. When I heard about this I quickly went out and purchased all of the ingredients, including the correct cut of meat, and brought everything to her house. That evening she prepared the meal and the entire family called me on the phone afterwards to rave about it. It's all about the meat!

Prep time **15 minutes**   **Cook time** **2 hours, 45 minutes**   **Yield** **6 servings**

 1 **(3–4 pound) bottom round beef roast**
 2 **tablespoons all-purpose flour**
 1 **tablespoon olive oil**
1½ **cups water**
 ¼ **cup balsamic vinegar**
 1 **(1.4-ounce) package instant vegetable soup mix, such as Knorr**
 1 **large red onion, quartered**
 4 **large baking potatoes, peeled and quartered**
 3 **large carrots, cut in half (peeling is optional)**
 ½ **teaspoon salt**
 ¼ **teaspoon black pepper**

1 Preheat the oven to 325°F.

2 Spray a large roasting pan with cooking spray; place the roast in the pan.

3 Combine the flour, olive oil, water, vinegar, and soup mix in a medium bowl; whisk until the flour and soup mix dissolve in the liquid. Pour over the roast and then place vegetables around the roast. Season with salt and pepper to taste.

4 Cover and bake for 2 hours and 45 minutes or until tender.

QUICK TIP: This dish is great served with steamed broccoli and crusty bread.

FOR KEEPS: Place any leftovers in a container, label it, and store it in the freezer. When the winter is dark and cold, take out the container and mix its contents with some beef soup starter, adjust the seasonings with some water and a tablespoon or two of bouquet garni (an item found in the spice section of the supermarket), add a bag of frozen mixed vegetables, simmer on the stove for a few hours, and serve the soup for dinner with a loaf of homemade country bread.

teen-friendly

AMERICAN ROAST BEEF

This is an easy meal to serve when you need a good source of protein and you have a lot of mouths to feed on a Sunday afternoon.

Prep time 5 minutes   **Cook time** 3–4 hours   **Yield** 6–8 servings

1   (3–4 pound) sirloin tip or rump roast
3–4 teaspoons crushed garlic
3–4 sprigs fresh Italian parsley
1   (4-ounce) can mushrooms, drained
1   (.87-ounce) package brown gravy mix
2–3 cups water
     Salt and pepper

1   Preheat the oven to 325°F. Spray a large roasting pan with cooking spray.

2   Place the meat in the pan; sprinkle the garlic and parsley on top of the meat (no need to chop the parsley).

3   Combine the mushrooms, gravy mix, and 1 cup of water in a small bowl; whisk until the liquid is smooth. Pour around the roast. Salt and pepper the roast to taste.

4   Cover and cook for 3 to 4 hours or until the meat is fork-tender. Add another ½ cup of water every hour to the juices in the pan (this will create a rich mushroom gravy when cooked). Add an extra cup of water 15 minutes before serving for a thinner gravy.

5   Let the roast rest for 10 minutes. Slice and serve.

QUICK TIP: During the last hour you can add peeled potatoes and carrots for a complete meal or serve with a Monster Potato Pancake (page 266).

FAMILY MEALS AND
ONE-POT DEALS

CLASSIC WILLIAMS POT ROAST

My husband grew up near the Williams family in Charlevoix, Michigan, and he had many Sunday afternoon meals at their house after a rough game of touch football or sledding in the middle of winter. Mrs. Williams, an outstanding cook, would serve this recipe (usually doubled) when her three sons and their friends tumbled into the house starving and looking for hot food. Mrs. Williams was kind enough to share this recipe and all of the stories that went along with it. I have chosen to leave the stories out so as not to embarrass my husband.

Prep time 5 minutes **Cook time** 3–4 hours **Yield** 6 servings

- 1 (4-pound) sirloin tip or rump roast
- 1 medium onion, chopped
- 1 (1-ounce) package au jus natural style gravy mix
- 1 cup water
- ¼ cup ketchup
- ½ cup dry red wine
- 2 teaspoons Dijon mustard
- 1 teaspoon Worcestershire sauce
- ¼ teaspoon garlic powder
- ¼ teaspoon salt
- ⅛ teaspoon black pepper

1. Preheat the oven to 310°F.
2. Coat a large Dutch oven or roasting pan with cooking spray and place the beef in the pan. Scatter the onion over the roast.
3. Combine the gravy mix, water, ketchup, wine, mustard, Worcestershire, garlic powder, salt, and pepper; whisk until combined.
4. Pour the gravy mixture over the roast, cover, and cook for 3 to 4 hours or until it is "butter knife" tender. Let the meat rest for 10 minutes and serve.

QUICK TIP: Add peeled carrots in the last hour of cooking for added sweetness.

CROCKPOT HUNGARIAN BEEF

The caraway seeds really make this dish unique. Serve with a salad and Better Buttered Noodles (page 240).

Prep time 10 minutes **Cook time** High 10 hours or Low 5 hours
Yield 4–6 servings

- 3 tablespoons all-purpose flour
- 1½ pounds stewing beef, cut into 1-inch cubes
- 1 beef bouillon cube
- ½ cup water
- 2 medium onions, chopped
- 1 medium green bell pepper, stemmed, seeded, and chopped
- 2 teaspoons chopped garlic
- 1 tablespoon paprika
- 1 teaspoon caraway seed
- ½ teaspoon salt
- ¼ teaspoon black pepper

1 Place the flour in a large ziplock freezer bag; add the beef and shake to coat. Transfer the meat to a crockpot.

2 Dissolve the bouillon cube in water; pour over the beef and onion. Add the bell pepper, garlic, paprika, caraway seeds, salt, and pepper.

3 Cover and cook for 5 to 6 hours on high or 10 to 12 hours on low.

LANSING CHILI

This is actually a version of Cincinnati Chili, but I thought that Lansing needed some press, too. The ingredient list is long but the preparation is very easy. This recipe yields a huge amount of chili, which freezes wonderfully and can be pulled from the freezer and heated in minutes for a last-minute meal.

Prep time 20 minutes   **Cook time** 1 hour 30 minutes   **Yield** 8–10 servings

2 pounds lean ground beef	2 tablespoons cocoa powder, (yes, cocoa powder!)
7 cups water	1 teaspoon chopped garlic
1 (32-ounce) can crushed tomatoes	2 tablespoons cider vinegar
1 (12-ounce) can tomato paste	2 teaspoons ground cinnamon
2 large onions, chopped	2 teaspoons ground cumin
2 bay leaves	2 teaspoons salt
4 tablespoons chili powder	½ teaspoon ground cloves

1   Place the beef and water in a large pot; stir to break up the meat.

2   Simmer over medium heat for 15 minutes or until the meat loses its red color; skim off any foam with a spoon. Stir in the remaining ingredients.

3   Simmer over low heat for 1 hour and 30 minutes, stirring occasionally; cover the pan partially so that the sauce does not get too thick. Serve immediately.

QUICK TIPS:
- **This recipe makes enough for 2 pounds of spaghetti.**
- **Serve this dish over spaghetti, topped with kidney beans, chopped onion, finely grated sharp cheddar cheese, and oyster crackers.**

FOR KEEPS: **Keeps well in the freezer for up to 2 months.**

CHILI STEW

When it's freezing outside and the family has been outdoors having crazy fun in the cold and snow, I like to warm everyone up with this dish. The recipe is a cross between chili and stew. It's fabulous served over noodles and soupy enough to sop up with a hunk of fresh bread. Add a green salad and your meal is complete.

Prep time 10 minutes **Cook time** 3 hours **Yield** 6–8 servings

2 tablespoons vegetable oil

3 medium onions, coarsely chopped

1 carrot, peeled and chopped

1 stalk celery, chopped

4 teaspoons minced garlic

3 tablespoons chili powder

1 (3–4 pound) beef tip roast, cut into 1-inch pieces

1 (32-ounce) can crushed tomatoes

1 cup water

1 can corn, drained or 1 cup frozen corn

1 (15-ounce) can dark red kidney beans

Salt and pepper

1 Heat the oil in a large saucepan over medium-high heat; add the onion, carrot, celery, and garlic; sauté for approximately 8 minutes or until the onions look soft and limp; stir occasionally.

2 Add the chili powder and sauté for 30 seconds, stirring continuously. Add the meat; stir to coat. Continue to cook the meat and vegetable mixture for 15 minutes, stirring occasionally. Juices will be released and create a sauce.

3 Add the crushed tomato and water to the saucepan; stir. Bring to a simmer; reduce the heat and cover to maintain a simmer. Simmer for 2 to 3 hours or until the meat is tender. Taste the dish 30 minutes before serving; season with salt and pepper.

4 For a thicker sauce, remove the lid for the last 30 minutes of cooking.

QUICK TIP: **You can add any of the following to this stew: mushrooms, potatoes, peas, sweet potatoes, or green beans.**

ZUCCHINI LASAGNA

Vegetarian

You will be surprised by how easy this recipe is. There will be a lot of juice with this dish so be sure to include a nice loaf of crusty bread to soak it all up.

Prep time 12 minutes   **Cook time** 40 minutes   **Yield** 4 servings

- ½ **pound lean ground beef or turkey**
- 1 **(8-ounce) can tomato sauce**
- 2 **teaspoons Italian seasoning**
- 1 **teaspoon salt**
- ½ **teaspoon garlic powder**
- 4 **small zucchini, sliced in ¼-inch discs (about 4 cups)**
- 1 **cup small curd cottage cheese**
- 1 **cup grated mozzarella cheese (about 4 ounces)**

1 Preheat the oven to 325°F. Coat an 8-inch square baking dish with cooking spray.

2 Brown the meat in a medium skillet over medium heat; stir in the tomato sauce, Italian seasoning, salt, and garlic powder.

3 Arrange half of the zucchini slices in the bottom of the baking dish. Spoon half of the meat sauce, half of the cottage cheese, and half of the mozzarella over the zucchini.

4 Repeat the layering, ending with mozzarella.

5 Bake uncovered for 40 minutes. Serve.

FOR KEEPS: **This dish can be assembled at the beginning of the day and refrigerated until ready to bake. Increase the baking time by 10 to 15 minutes.**

MEXICAN LASAGNA

Quick, easy, and great-tasting!

Prep time 15 minutes   **Cook time** 15 minutes   **Yield** 4–6 servings

- 2 **tablespoons vegetable oil**
- 1¼ **pounds lean ground turkey**
- 1 **medium onion, chopped**
- 1 **green bell pepper, stemmed, seeded, and chopped**
- 1 **(4-ounce) can green chiles, drained and diced**
- 1 **(1.25-ounce) package low-sodium taco seasoning mix**
- 1 **(10-ounce) bottle taco sauce**
- 10 **(6-inch) flour tortillas**
- 2 **cups grated cheddar, Monterey Jack, or Mexican cheese blend (about 8 ounces)**

1. Preheat the oven to 400°F. Coat a 9- by 13-inch baking pan with cooking spray.

2. Heat the oil in a large skillet over medium heat. Add the turkey and sauté until no longer pink, 6 to 8 minutes. Stir in the onion, pepper, chiles, and seasoning mix. Reduce the heat to low and cook for 3 to 4 minutes; stir occasionally.

3. Spread ¼ cup of the taco sauce over the bottom of the prepared baking pan; cover with 5 tortillas. Spread the tortillas with half of the turkey mixture, half of the remaining taco sauce, and 1 cup of the cheese. Repeat with the remaining ingredients (tortilla, turkey, sauce, and cheese).

4. Bake for 15 to 20 minutes or until heated through and the cheese is browned and bubbly.

FOR KEEPS: You can assemble this dish in the morning and chill until ready to bake. Increase baking time by 30 to 35 minutes.

TUNA SWISS PIE

This dish came from an old friend. She always cooked easy, carefree dishes that took minimal amounts of time so that she could visit with friends. I have since made this recipe for wedding and baby showers, as well as for Boy Scout potlucks.

Prep time 10 minutes **Cook time** 50 minutes **Yield** 6 servings

- 2 (6-ounce) cans chuck light tuna in water, drained and flaked
- 1 cup grated Swiss cheese, such as Gruyère (about 4 ounces)
- 1 bunch scallions (white and tender green parts), sliced
- 1 (9-inch) prebaked piecrust
- 3 eggs
- 1 cup light mayonnaise
- ½ cup milk

1 Preheat the oven to 375°F.

2 Combine the tuna, cheese, and scallions in a large bowl; toss together. Spread the mixture in the piecrust.

3 Beat the eggs, mayonnaise, and milk together in the same large bowl; pour slowly and evenly over the top of the tuna mixture.

4 Bake 50 minutes or until a knife inserted in the center of the pie comes out clean.

QUICK TIP: You can prepare this dish and freeze it. Reheat in the oven or microwave when ready to eat.

FAMILY MEALS AND ONE-POT DEALS

MARINADES

In this section you'll find some great marinades that you can use any time. For each of the recipes below, combine all of the ingredients with a whisk, add the meat, and refrigerate to use within 48 hours.

You can also marinate in the freezer. After combining the marinade and meat in a ziplock freezer bag, store in the freezer for up to 2 months. Then just thaw in the refrigerator on the day you're ready to cook.

GREAT COUNTRY MARINADE

Prep time 5 minutes
Yield Enough for 2–3 pounds of meat

For chicken or pork.

- ⅓ cup cider vinegar
- 2 tablespoons Dijon mustard
- 2 tablespoons vegetable oil
- 3 teaspoons dried basil
- ½ teaspoon salt
- 1 teaspoon freshly grated lemon peel
- 1 teaspoon chopped garlic

LEMON MARINADE

Prep time 2 minutes
Yield Enough for 2–3 pounds of meat

For chicken or pork.

- 1 (6-ounce) can frozen concentrated lemonade, thawed
- ¾ cup low-sodium soy sauce
- 1 bunch scallions (white and tender green parts), finely sliced, optional

ALL-PURPOSE MEAT MARINADE

Prep time 5 minutes
Yield Enough for 3–4 pounds meat

- ½ cup olive oil
- ¼ cup balsamic vinegar
- 3–4 teaspoons chopped garlic
- ¼ cup chopped fresh parsley, loosely packed
- ¼–½ teaspoon black pepper
- Salt

DRY RUBS

Dry rubs are mixtures of salt, herbs, and spices rubbed on the outside of raw meat for a few minutes or, even better, several hours before grilling or baking. The rub lends the meat deep flavor during cooking.

Here are some dry rub recipes that you can put together and use immediately, or store in an airtight container to use within 2 months, or freeze for up to 2 years. These rubs are great for chicken, pork, or fish. I like to massage a bit of olive oil over the meat or fish before applying the rub. This bit of oil helps the spices to adhere to the meat in an even layer.

ST. JOSEPH'S RUB

- 1 tablespoons garlic powder
- 1 tablespoon salt
- 1 tablespoon paprika
- 1 tablespoon oregano
- 1 tablespoon onion powder
- 2 teaspoons black pepper
- 2 teaspoons dried thyme
- 1 teaspoon cayenne pepper, or to taste

GARLIC-SPICE RUB

- 1 tablespoon brown sugar
- 1 tablespoon paprika
- 1½ teaspoons black pepper
- 2 teaspoons garlic powder
- 1 teaspoon salt

DESERT RUB

- 1 tablespoon brown sugar
- 2 teaspoons cumin
- 1½ teaspoons garlic powder
- 1½ teaspoons ground coriander
- 1 teaspoon ground ginger
- ½ teaspoon turmeric
- 1 teaspoon salt

MEDITERRANEAN RUB

- 1 tablespoon brown sugar
- 2 teaspoons fennel seeds, crushed
- 1½ teaspoons paprika
- 1½ teaspoons garlic powder
- 1½ teaspoons salt

JAMAICAN JERK RUB

- 1½ teaspoons salt
- 1½ teaspoons ground allspice
- 1 teaspoon sugar
- 1 teaspoon dried thyme
- 1 teaspoon black pepper
- ½ teaspoon garlic powder
- ½ teaspoon ground red pepper
- ¼ teaspoon ground cinnamon
- ¼ teaspoon ground nutmeg

ENGLISH RUB

- 1 tablespoon brown sugar
- 2 teaspoons garlic powder
- 2 teaspoons ground ginger
- 2 teaspoons paprika
- 1 teaspoon salt
- ½ teaspoon cinnamon
- ⅛ teaspoon ground cloves

PEPPERS, SPUDS, AND SAUSAGES

I have been eating this dish since I was a child; it's beautifully simple and I've made no changes to it. I sometimes put this in the oven at a slightly lower temperature (325°F) and take the kids to a quick soccer match or cross-country practice. When we arrive at home, dinner is done!

Prep time 15 minutes   **Cook time** 50 minutes   **Yield** 6 servings

2–3 **pounds russet potatoes, unpeeled, scrubbed, and cut into ½-inch slices**

2 **pounds uncooked Italian sausage, cut into 1-inch pieces**

3 **green bell peppers, stemmed, seeded, and thickly sliced**

2 **large onions, coarsely chopped**

2 **tablespoons olive oil**

Salt and pepper

1 Preheat the oven to 375°F.

2 Combine the potatoes, sausage, bell peppers, onions, and oil in a large nonstick baking dish. Season with salt and pepper to taste; toss to combine.

3 Bake uncovered, stirring occasionally if possible, for 50 minutes or until the potatoes are tender. Serve immediately.

QUICK TIP: If you like a lot of flavor, use a spicy Italian sausage in this recipe. You can also use Polish, chorizo, or kielbasa sausage as a substitute.

KITCHEN 411: Using a low-sodium, prepackaged sausage is a good bet, but if you have access to a butcher who makes handmade sausage, by all means give it a try. You are guaranteed a fresher product with fewer additives and preservatives.

ITALIAN-STYLE CHICKEN AND BROCCOLI

A quick and easy meal that makes great leftovers.

Prep time 5 minutes   Cook time 35 minutes   Yield 4 servings

2 tablespoons butter

1 (6.9-ounce) package chicken flavor Rice-a-Roni

2 cups water

1 teaspoon dried basil

1 teaspoon dried oregano

4 boneless, skinless chicken breast halves (about 1½ pounds)

2-3 cups broccoli florets

1 medium tomato, chopped

1 cup grated mozzarella or sharp cheddar cheese (about 4 ounces), optional

1 Heat the butter in a large skillet over medium heat. Add the Rice-a-Roni, reserving the seasoning packet; sauté until golden brown, about 8 minutes.

2 Add the water, seasoning packet, basil, and oregano; stir gently. Increase the heat to high and bring to a boil.

3 Add the chicken to the skillet, reduce the heat to medium-low, cover, and simmer for 12 minutes. Turn the chicken, adding ¼ cup of water if the rice is sticking to the pan; stir in the broccoli and tomato. Cover and simmer 10 to 12 minutes longer, or until the chicken is cooked through.

4 Remove from heat, sprinkle with cheese, if desired. Cover and let stand for 3 minutes; serve.

QUICK TIP: Cutting the chicken into smaller pieces will speed up the cooking process.

FAMILY MEALS AND ONE-POT DEALS

GRILLED PORK CHOP MEAL-IN-ONE

On our summer camping trips, I make this meal. It gives me more time to spend with the family, either hiking, fishing, or at the beach.

Prep time **10 minutes**   Cook time **30 minutes**   Yield **6 servings**

- **6 pork loin cutlets (about ½-inch thick)**
- **Garlic powder**
- **Salt and pepper**
- **¼ cup zesty Italian salad dressing**
- **1 large sweet onion, cut crosswise into 6 slices (I use Vidalia when in season)**
- **1 green bell pepper, stemmed, seeded, and cut into 6 slices**
- **2 large tomatoes, cut into 12 slices total**
- **Hard rolls**

1. Prepare a medium-hot fire in a charcoal or gas grill.
2. Cut six pieces of heavy-duty aluminum foil each about 16 inches long; spread the foil out on a work surface.
3. Rub both sides of the cutlets with garlic powder, season with salt and pepper, sprinkle with some of the Italian dressing, and place each on its own piece of foil.
4. Top each packet with 1 slice each of onion and bell pepper, then with 2 tomato slices. Season again with garlic powder, salt, and pepper. Drizzle any remaining Italian dressing over the tomato.
5. Tightly wrap each cutlet in the foil. Transfer the foil packages to the grill. Cook 15 minutes per side, turning occasionally.
6. Serve immediately with the rolls.

QUICK TIP: Make sure to fold the seams over 2 or 3 times to contain the juices in the packet.

FOR KEEPS: The foil packages can be assembled earlier in the day and refrigerated until ready to grill.

This dish freezes well after cooking.

KITCHEN 411: The French name for the cooking method used in this recipe is *en papillote* (meaning, "in paper"). You can also use this method with salmon or tilapia fillets in place of pork loin. In this case, reduce the grilling time to about 10 minutes if the thickest part of the fish is about 1 inch.

CREAMY HAM AND BROCCOLI CASSEROLE

This is a great dish to feed a group. It can be made ahead of time and popped into the oven when you get home. Double it when the whole team comes over!

Prep time 15 minutes   **Refrigeration time** 1–12 hours
Cook time 1 hour   **Yield** 8 servings

1 pound ham, cut into ½-inch cubes

1 (10-ounce) package frozen chopped broccoli, thawed and drained well

2 cups grated sharp cheddar cheese (about 8 ounces)

1 (6-ounce) package seasoned croutons

4 eggs

2 cups milk

1 cup whipped salad dressing, such as Miracle Whip

2 tablespoons all-purpose flour

2 teaspoons dry mustard

2 teaspoons dried basil

1 Preheat the oven to 375°F. Coat a 9- by 13-inch baking pan with cooking spray.

2 Layer the ham, broccoli, and cheese in the prepared pan; top with the croutons.

3 Combine the eggs, milk, salad dressing, flour, mustard, and basil in a medium bowl; whisk until blended. Pour the egg mixture over the croutons.

4 Cover and refrigerate 1 to 12 hours.

5 Bake uncovered for 1 hour. Serve immediately.

FOR KEEPS: This dish freezes well before or after baking. Bake the assembled frozen casserole by increasing the cooking time by 50 to 60 minutes. Warm a baked frozen casserole until heated through, about 25 minutes.

HEARTY CHOWDER

This great fall chowder is so filling that you can serve it as a main dish with a side salad and crusty bread.

Prep time **15 minutes**   Cook time **15 minutes**   Yield **4 servings**

- 1 **pound Italian sausage, spicy or sweet, casings removed**
- 2 **tablespoons olive oil**
- 1 **large onion, finely chopped**
- 1 **red bell pepper, stemmed, seeded, and finely chopped**
- 1 **pound russet potatoes, scrubbed and cut into ½-inch cubes**
- 1 **(14.5-ounce) can low-sodium chicken broth**
- 2 **cups whole milk**
- ¼ **cup all-purpose flour**
- 2 **(15-ounce) cans corn kernels, including natural juices**

1 Cook the sausage in a large soup pot over medium-high heat, breaking it apart with a wooden spoon, until browned, about 5 minutes. Remove the sausage from the pot and set aside.

2 Add the oil, onion, bell pepper, and potatoes to the pot; cover and cook for 5 minutes.

3 Whisk the broth, milk, and flour together in a medium bowl. Add to the pot and stir well.

4 Add the sausage and corn to the pot; bring to a boil. Reduce the heat to medium-low and simmer for 15 minutes or until the potatoes are tender. Serve immediately.

FOR KEEPS: This chowder freezes well for up to 2 months.

FALL CLEANUP SOUP

A lot of cleanup happens in and around our house during the late fall and everyone pitches in — raking leaves, cleaning gutters, storing patio furniture, and did I mention raking leaves? Inside, we clean windows, wash comforters, and dig out our winter clothes. Fall is also the time of year that I defrost the large freezer in the garage to make room for the coming holiday season.

It's quite interesting what I find in the bottom of this freezer. Any frostbitten items are thrown away. My kids claim the sweet stuff (leftover birthday cake, old holiday cookies, etc.) before I can warn them of the dangers of eating frozen mystery desserts, and the rest is made into soups like this one.

Prep time 10 minutes   **Cook time** 50 minutes   **Yield** 6 servings

2–3	tablespoons olive oil
1	large onion, coarsely chopped
1	large carrot, coarsely chopped
1	green bell pepper, stemmed, seeded, and coarsely chopped
1	stalk celery, coarsely chopped
1	medium zucchini or summer squash, optional
1	pound low-sodium Polish sausage, chopped
2	cups chopped cooked chicken or turkey meat
1	teaspoon minced garlic
6–7	cups low-sodium chicken broth
1–2	cups prepared spaghetti sauce
	Dried herbs, such as basil, oregano, marjoram
1	(16-ounce) bag frozen vegetables (any kind)
1	(15.5 ounce) can beans (pinto, kidney, or garbanzo)
½	pound cooked potatoes or cooked pasta
	Salt and pepper

1 Heat the oil over medium heat in a large soup pot. Add the onion, carrot, bell pepper, celery, and squash, if desired. Sauté for 8 minutes, or until softened. Add the sausage, chicken, and garlic; sauté 5 minutes longer.

2 Add the broth and spaghetti sauce; bring to a simmer. Sprinkle in the herbs, starting with 1 teaspoon of each. Let the broth simmer for 5 minutes, taste for flavor, and add more seasoning if needed. Simmer for at least 30 minutes.

3 About 20 minutes before serving the soup, add the frozen vegetables, beans, and potatoes or pasta. Season with salt and pepper to taste; serve immediately.

TALKING TURKEY

After Thanksgiving, it's turkey, turkey, everywhere! So I freeze the leftover meat in 2-cup quantities. Then I pull out as much as I need for a recipe such as this one. Leftover Thanksgiving turkey is a perfect substitute for practically any dish calling for cooked chicken.

vegetarian

VEGGIE CHILI

This recipe is for those who need a break from red meat chili. It is loaded with great, healthy ingredients and you won't miss the meat.

Prep time 15 minutes   **Cook time** 20–30 minutes   **Yield** 6 servings

¼ cup vegetable oil

2 large onions, chopped

3 (14-ounce) cans diced tomatoes

2 (7-ounce) cans mushroom pieces

2 cups chopped broccoli

2 medium zucchini, cut in half lengthwise and sliced

1 whole green bell pepper, stemmed, seeded, and chopped

¼ cup chili powder

1 teaspoon garlic powder

¼ teaspoon black pepper

¼ cup water

2 teaspoons all-purpose flour

2 (15.5-ounce) cans kidney beans, drained

1 Heat the oil in a large saucepan over medium-high heat. Add the onions and sauté until softened, about 8 minutes; reduce the heat to medium. Add the tomatoes, mushrooms, broccoli, zucchini, bell pepper, chili powder, garlic powder, and black pepper. Cover and simmer for 15 to 30 minutes, stirring occasionally.

2 Whisk the water and flour together in a small bowl. Stir into the vegetable mixture in the saucepan and add the beans. Cook until thickened, about 5 minutes, or until the beans are heated through, stirring frequently. Serve.

QUICK TIPS:

• **This chili can be served alone or over rice, pasta, or couscous.**

• **Try serving with sliced scallions, sour cream, or shredded cheddar cheese.**

CHICKEN CURRY CASSEROLE

Good friends of ours prepared and served this delicious casserole when we were visiting their gorgeous home on Lake Michigan. I love the combination of sherry and curry powder. They add exciting flavor and richness not usually found in simple casseroles. This dish can be prepared early in the day and refrigerated until your guests arrive. Pop it into the oven and serve with a crisp salad.

Prep time 10 minutes   **Cook time** 30 minutes   **Yield** 6–8 servings

3 (10-ounce) packages frozen broccoli spears

4 cups cubed cooked chicken (4 to 6 chicken breasts halves or 1 medium rotisserie chicken)

1 (10.5-ounce) can low-sodium cream of chicken soup

1 cup light mayonnaise

1 teaspoon fresh lemon juice

1½ teaspoons curry powder

1½ teaspoons sherry

1½ cups grated sharp cheddar cheese (about 6 ounces)

1 tablespoon butter, melted

¾ cup herb seasoned stuffing

1   Preheat the oven to 350°F. Coat a 9- by 13-inch baking dish with cooking spray

2   Arrange the broccoli in the bottom of the prepared baking dish; arrange the chicken evenly over the broccoli.

3   Whisk together the soup, mayonnaise, lemon juice, curry powder, and sherry in a small bowl. Spoon the soup mixture over the meat as evenly as possible — it will be thick. Sprinkle the casserole with cheese.

4   Mix the butter and stuffing in a small bowl; sprinkle over the cheese. Bake uncovered for 30 minutes. Serve immediately.

FOR KEEPS: This dish freezes well for up to 2 months before or after baking. Bake the assembled frozen casserole by increasing the cooking time by 50 to 60 minutes. Warm a baked frozen casserole until heated through, about 50 minutes.

FAMILY MEALS AND ONE-POT DEALS

vegetarian

BAKED PASTA

Perfect for when you have a lot of mouths to feed. If the whole track team is coming over, I suggest that you make two or three pans full!

Prep time 20 minutes   Cook time 55 minutes   Yield 6 servings

- 8 ounces elbow macaroni, cooked
- 1 (16-ounce) can tomato purée
- 1 cup water
- 1 tablespoon Italian seasoning
- 1 teaspoon garlic powder, divided
- 1½ pounds cottage cheese (4 percent fat), preferably small curd
- ½ teaspoon onion powder
- ½ cup grated mozzarella cheese (about 2 ounces)

1. Preheat the oven to 350°F. Coat a 9- by 13-inch baking pan with cooking spray.

2. Combine the tomato purée, water, Italian seasoning, and ½ teaspoon of the garlic powder in a small bowl; stir to combine. Combine the cottage cheese, onion powder, and the remaining ½ teaspoon of garlic powder in a medium bowl; mix well.

3. Spoon one-third of the tomato mixture into the baking pan, then layer half of the macaroni, all of the cottage cheese mixture, and another one-third of the tomato mixture. Add the remaining macaroni and cover with the remaining tomato mixture.

4. Cover and bake for 50 minutes. Remove from the oven, uncover, and top with cheese.

5. Let stand for 5 minutes. Serve.

FOR KEEPS: This dish can be assembled earlier in the day and refrigerated. Increase the baking time by 15 minutes and add a few extra tablespoons water to keep the dish moist.

FAMILY MEALS AND ONE-POT DEALS

CHICKEN TARRAGON CASSEROLE

This recipe is easy and comforting, and has a nice French flair with the tarragon flavor. It's a perfect solution on those winter nights when you're tired of cooking and you need a creamy casserole to fill everyone up. Use a low-sodium cream soup to avoid a lot of the hidden salt in canned soup.

Prep time 5 minutes   **Cook time** 1 hour   **Yield** 4 servings

- 1 (10.5-ounce) can low-sodium cream of mushroom soup
- 1¾ cups white rice, uncooked
- 1¼ soup cans of water
- 4 boneless, skinless chicken breast halves (1–1½ pounds)
- 1 tablespoon fresh tarragon
  Garlic powder
  Salt and pepper
  Paprika

1. Preheat the oven to 325°F. Coat a 9- by 13-inch baking pan with cooking spray.

2. Combine the soup, rice, and water in a medium bowl; pour into the prepared pan.

3. Set the chicken on top of the rice mixture; sprinkle with tarragon, garlic powder, and salt and pepper to taste. Garnish with paprika.

4. Cover tightly with foil and bake for 1 hour. Serve.

FAMILY MEALS AND ONE-POT DEALS

vegetarian

TORTILLA CASSEROLE

I am always looking for good vegetarian recipes to try. I found this one a couple of years ago and made some changes to suit what was in my pantry at the time.

Prep time **15 minutes**   **Cook time** **35 minutes**   **Yield** **6 servings**

2 **tablespoons vegetable oil**

2 **large onions, chopped**

2 **large green bell peppers, stemmed, seeded, and chopped**

1 **(14.5-ounce) can diced tomatoes**

¾ **cup picante sauce (or salsa)**

2–3 **teaspoons crushed garlic**

2 **teaspoons cumin**

2 **(15-ounce) cans black beans, drained**

12 **(6-inch) soft corn tortillas**

2 **cups grated sharp cheddar cheese (about 8 ounces)**

TOPPINGS

Diced tomatoes

Chopped scallions

Black olives

Sour cream

Cheddar cheese

1 Preheat the oven to 350°F. Coat a 9- by 13-inch baking pan with cooking spray.

2 Heat the oil in a large skillet over medium heat. Add the onion, bell peppers, tomatoes, picante sauce, garlic, and cumin; bring to a boil.

3 Reduce the heat to medium-low and simmer for 10 minutes; remove from the heat and stir in the beans.

4 Spread one-third of the tomato mixture on the bottom of the baking pan; top with half of the corn tortillas and then another one-third of the tomato mixture. Cover with the remaining tortillas and then the remaining tomato mixture.

5 Cover and bake for 30 to 35 minutes. Remove from the oven, sprinkle with cheese, and let stand for 5 minutes.

6 Serve with desired toppings.

FAMILY MEALS AND ONE-POT DEALS

BLT PIE

I have seen many versions of this recipe over the years, but I think the sharpness of the cheddar cheese combined with the bacon and tomato makes this one the best! Your kids will love the novelty of a sandwich in a pie.

Prep time **10 minutes** **Cook time** **35 minutes** **Yield** **6 servings**

8 **slices bacon, cooked and crumbled**
¾ **cup grated sharp cheddar cheese
   (about 3 ounces)**
1 **large tomato, chopped**
1 **small onion, chopped**
1 **tablespoon dried parsley**
1 **(9-inch) prebaked piecrust**
1 **egg**
⅔ **cup evaporated milk**
1 **small tomato, thinly sliced**
  Shredded lettuce

1 Preheat the oven to 350°F.

2 Combine half of the bacon, all of the cheese, and the chopped tomato, onion, and parsley in a small bowl; spoon into the pie shell.

3 In the same small bowl beat the egg with the milk; pour slowly over the pie filling; arrange the sliced tomato on top.

4 Bake for 35 minutes; remove from the oven and let stand for 10 minutes.

5 Top with shredded lettuce and the remaining bacon. Serve.

FOR KEEPS: This pie freezes well before or after baking. Remove the prepared pie from the freezer and place directly in a preheated oven. Increase the baking time by 40 to 50 minutes, or until a knife inserted in the center comes out clean. Reheat a baked frozen pie for 40 to 50 minutes in a preheated oven.

SOUTHWEST BEAN CASSEROLE

My sister lived in Phoenix for a couple of years and came back with a totally different outlook on food. This recipe, with its southwestern flair, was inspired by her transformation.

Prep time 10 minutes **Cook time** 45 minutes **Yield** 6–8 servings

3 boneless, skinless chicken breast halves, cut into 1-inch pieces

1 (1.25-ounce) package low-sodium taco seasoning

2 large green bell peppers, stemmed, seeded, and chopped

1 large red bell pepper, stemmed, seeded, and chopped

1 (10-ounce) package frozen corn

1 (16-ounce) jar spicy salsa

1 (15-ounce) can black beans, drained

1 (15-ounce) can pinto beans, drained

1 large jalapeño pepper, chopped

Tortilla chips

1 Preheat the oven to 350°F. Coat a 9- by 13-inch baking pan with cooking spray.

2 Combine the chicken with the taco seasoning in a large bowl; toss gently. Add the bell peppers, corn, salsa, beans, and jalapeño pepper. Arrange the chicken and bean mixture in the prepared baking pan.

3 Bake for 45 minutes, stirring halfway through. Serve with chips.

QUICK TIP: For a healthier dish, this recipe can be served with corn or flour tortillas instead of chips.

FOR KEEPS: The casserole can be assembled and stored in the refrigerator for up to one day, or up to two months in the freezer, before baking. If frozen, increase the baking time by 40 to 50 minutes or until the chicken is fully cooked.

STOVE TOP ITALIAN CHICKEN

This chicken dish is quick and tasty. The Italian seasonings are appealing to even the pickiest eaters.

Prep time **3 minutes**   Cook time **40 minutes**   Yield **4 servings**

3 **tablespoons olive oil**

4 **boneless, skinless chicken breast halves (1–1½ pounds)**

Salt free Italian seasoning

Salt and pepper

1 **(14.5-ounce) can diced tomatoes**

1 **(14-ounce) can low-sodium chicken broth**

1 **(5-ounce) package dry tomato soup mix**

½ **cup uncooked white rice**

1 Heat the oil in a large skillet over medium-high heat. Generously sprinkle both sides of the chicken with Italian seasoning and transfer to the skillet; season with salt and pepper. Cook until nicely browned, about 4 minutes per side.

2 Combine the tomatoes, broth, soup mix, and rice in a medium bowl; pour over the chicken. Bring the mixture to a boil, cover the pan tightly, and reduce the heat to medium-low.

3 Simmer, stirring once halfway through cooking, for 30 minutes.

4 If all of the liquid has not been absorbed, remove the lid and cook over medium heat for 5 minutes, stirring often, until moist but not soupy. Serve.

QUICK TIP: Dry tomato soup mix can be found in the soup section of the grocery store. If you can't find it, substitute 1 (10.75-ounce) can of condensed low-sodium tomato soup and decrease the chicken broth to 1 cup.

FOR KEEPS: This dish works well reheated the next day, and when cooked it freezes well for up to 2 months.

FAMILY MEALS AND ONE-POT DEALS

L.Z.'S ENCHILADA CASSEROLE

Prep time 30 minutes   Cook time 30 minutes   Yield 6–8 servings

- 1 (28-ounce) can mild enchilada sauce
- 8 (6-inch) soft corn tortillas
- 2 cups shredded cooked chicken
- 1½ cups grated Monterey Jack cheese (about 6 ounces)
- 1 bunch scallions (white and tender green parts), sliced
- 1 cup plain low-fat yogurt

1   Preheat the oven to 325°F. Coat a 9- by 13-inch baking pan with cooking spray.

2   Pour 1 cup of the enchilada sauce into a shallow bowl. Dip 4 tortillas in sauce and place in the bottom of the baking pan; sprinkle with the chicken, cheese, and scallions.

3   Dip the remaining 4 tortillas in the same enchilada sauce and place on top of chicken mixture.

4   Add the yogurt to the remaining enchilada sauce and stir to combine. Pour the sauce over the casserole, making sure to moisten all of the tortillas with sauce.

5   Bake for 30 minutes. Remove from the oven and let rest for 5 minutes before serving.

QUICK TIP: Serve with a green salad.

FOR KEEPS: When baked, this dish keeps well in the refrigerator for up to 2 days. Warm in the oven for 30 to 40 minutes, until heated through.

AUTUMN CHICKEN

This is a great dish for the fall, when sweet potatoes are at their peak.

Prep time **3 minutes**   Cook time   **30 minutes**   Yield   **4 servings**

2 **tablespoons vegetable oil**

4 **boneless, skinless chicken breast halves (1–1½ pounds)**

1 **cup low-sodium chicken broth**

2 **teaspoons Italian seasoning**

1 **large sweet potato, peeled and cut into ¼-inch discs**

1 **cup frozen green beans**

Salt and pepper

1 Heat the oil in a large skillet over medium heat; add the chicken and cook for 5 minutes per side.

2 Add the broth, seasoning, potato, and green beans; bring to a boil and reduce the heat to low.

3 Cover and simmer for 20 minutes or until the vegetables are tender. Season with salt and pepper to taste, and serve.

QUICK TIP: **You can cook this dish all at once in a crockpot, as well. (My friend is an emergency room doctor. To test this recipe, she threw all of the ingredients into a crockpot and cooked it at work. It turned out great, and the whole ER staff loved it.)**

SAUCY BEEF AND BROCCOLI

A perfect protein-rich dish for your young athletes, this Asian-style stir-fry produces enough sauce to enjoy with a big chunk of bread.

Prep time 10 minutes   Cook time 20 minutes   Yield 4 servings

     2 tablespoons vegetable oil
     1 pound beef sirloin steak, cut into ½-inch
        strips
     1 teaspoon chopped garlic
     1 medium onion, chopped
     1 (10.75-ounce) can low-sodium cream of
        chicken or mushroom soup
     1 cup water
    1½ tablespoons low-sodium soy sauce
     1 head broccoli, chopped (about 4 cups)

1 Heat the oil in a large skillet over medium-high heat. Add the beef and garlic; sauté for 4 to 5 minutes, stirring occasionally.

2 Add the onion; cook and stir for 5 minutes longer.

3 Add the soup, water, and soy sauce. Bring to a boil and reduce the heat to low; add broccoli.

4 Cover and simmer 5 minutes or until the vegetables are tender.

QUICK TIPS:

- **Serve with a loaf of French bread for sopping up the juices.**
- **For more servings, increase the meat to 1¼ pounds, add a can of drained water chestnuts when adding the soup, and serve with rice.**

VEGETARIAN SHEPHERD'S PIE

vegetarian

For vegetarians, the vegetable protein mix in this recipe does an excellent job of adding great flavor and texture to the dish. Make both pies even if you need only one for dinner; serve one and freeze the other.

Prep time 10 minutes **Cook time** 25 minutes total **Yield** 2 pies; each serves 4

1 (12-ounce) package ground beef substitute, such as Lightlife Smart Ground Original or Morningstar Farms Meal Starters, Grillers Recipe Crumbles

½ cup seasoned breadcrumbs

1 medium onion, finely chopped

¼ teaspoon garlic powder

1 egg, lightly beaten

2 tablespoons water

1 tablespoon Worcestershire sauce

¼ teaspoon salt

¼ teaspoon black pepper

2½ cups prepared mashed potatoes (instant works great!)

2 cups shredded sharp cheddar cheese (about 8 ounces)

1 (16-ounce) bag frozen mixed vegetables

1 Preheat the oven to 350°F. Coat two 9-inch pie pans with cooking spray.

2 Combine the ground beef substitute, breadcrumbs, onion, garlic powder, egg, water, Worcestershire, salt, and pepper in a large bowl, mixing with your hands until well blended.

3 Press the mixture into the bottom and up the sides of the prepared pie pans, forming a "shell."

4 Bake for 10 minutes. Remove from the oven; set aside.

5 Reduce the oven to 325°F.

6 Using the same large bowl, combine the potatoes, cheese, and vegetables; spoon the mixture into the pie pans.

7 Bake until heated through and the cheese begins to melt, about 15 minutes. Serve immediately.

Perfect Pasta Dishes and Sauces
That Your Kids Will Love

Almost every culture has its own version of pasta, from Polish pierogi to Asian rice noodles to the Italian pasta dishes in this chapter. Most recipes in this chapter are designed so that the pasta cooks while you do the remainder of the preparation — an efficient use of your precious time. When the pasta is done, you'll be ready to serve the meal.

Here are some tips for making perfect pasta:

- Be sure to use a big pot with plenty of water. If the pot is too small the pasta will stick together and to the pot.
- Always salt the water after it has come to a boil. This prevents pitting on the pan's surface and ensures that the pasta will be properly seasoned.
- Make sure the water is at a real rolling boil before adding the pasta; otherwise, you may end up with mushy noodles.
- Once you've added the pasta to the pot, give it a good stir. Then stir it a couple more times during cooking to keep it from sticking.
- For hot pasta dishes, don't rinse the pasta with water after draining. You'll rinse off the starch, which is essential for sauces to stick properly.

- Reserve about 1 cup of the pasta cooking water before draining the pasta. With its starch content, you can use a little of this water to slightly thicken and bind a thin sauce, or thin out a thick sauce. It also helps the sauce to stick to the pasta.
- For a real treat, look for fresh pasta in the refrigerated foods section of the grocery store. It is much more tender than dry pasta and cooks in just a few minutes for a quick meal — but it does cost quite a bit more than dry pasta. Fresh pasta will last just a few days, tightly wrapped, in the refrigerator, but it can be frozen for up to 1 month.

vegetarian

teen-friendly

SALSA CORN PASTA

I never thought of putting salsa on pasta until my son mentioned the idea when I was testing dishes for this cookbook. I ran out of energy while testing one evening and just wanted to put chicken on the grill and call it quits. My son bugged me to make pasta and I refused. He decided to make it himself and dug around in the pantry for ingredients. He ended up with this dish, which, by the way, went beautifully with my grilled chicken. It is now a mainstay of our dinner menu.

Prep time 5 minutes   **Cook time** 20 minutes   **Yield** 4–6 servings

1 **pound pasta, any style**
1 **(15-ounce) can black beans, drained**
1 **(15.75-ounce) can sweet corn, drained (or**
   1 (16-ounce) bag frozen corn, thawed)
1 **(16-ounce) jar salsa (about 2 cups)**
1 **bunch scallions (white and tender green**
   parts), sliced
½ **teaspoon chili powder**
1 **large avocado, pitted, peeled, and cut into**
   1-inch chunks
   Sour cream

1 Cook pasta in a large pot of salted boiling water until al dente.

2 Combine the beans, corn, salsa, scallions, and chili powder in a serving bowl large enough to hold the pasta.

3 Drain the pasta and transfer to the serving bowl with the other ingredients; toss well.

4 Gently toss in avocado and serve with a dollop of sour cream.

QUICK TIPS:
• Add some cooked, shredded chicken and extra salsa for a menu-stretcher. Cooked shredded pork works well, too.
• Add roasted zucchini, scallions, and sweet peppers for a vegetarian stretch.

PASTA, PLEASE!

CAESAR PASTA SALAD

An excellent pasta dish that can be served hot or cold. The Caesar salad dressing really adds zest to this salad.

Prep time 5 minutes   **Cook time** 20 minutes   **Yield** 4–6 servings

1	pound pasta, any style
½	cup light mayonnaise
¼	cup plain low-fat yogurt
½–1	cup light Caesar salad dressing
2	cooked boneless, skinless chicken breast halves, thinly sliced
	Romaine lettuce
1	large tomato, sliced
¼	red onion, thinly sliced

1   Cook pasta in a large pot of salted boiling water until al dente.

2   Whisk the mayonnaise, yogurt, and dressing together in a serving bowl large enough to hold the pasta.

3   Drain the pasta and transfer to the serving bowl with the dressing. Add the chicken, tossing well to coat.

4   Serve on a bed of lettuce; dress with tomato and red onion.

KITCHEN 411: Using ingredients such as salsa, soy sauce, salad dressing, and barbecue sauce in a dish gives an instant depth of flavor that typically would take all day to develop if working with individual spices. Use them sparingly, though, as their sodium contents can be high.

vegetarian

SUMMER CHOPPED VEGGIE PASTA

A light summer meal that can be prepared with either the homemade vinaigrette given in the recipe or with a good-quality bottled vinaigrette. Very fast, very easy, and very tasty. Did I mention that it's very good for you, too?

Prep time 5 minutes **Cook time** 20 minutes **Yield** 4 servings

1 pound pasta, any style

2 carrots, peeled and chopped

1 green bell pepper, stemmed, seeded, and chopped

1 cup frozen corn, thawed

1 medium tomato, chopped

1 bunch scallions (white and tender green parts), sliced

2 radishes, chopped

VINAIGRETTE

½ cup extra-virgin olive oil

¼ cup fresh lemon juice

1 tablespoon Dijon mustard

1 teaspoon dried oregano

1 teaspoon salt

¾ teaspoon black pepper

1 teaspoon chopped garlic

1 Cook the pasta in a large pot of salted boiling water until al dente.

2 Combine the carrots, bell pepper, and corn in the bottom of a colander.

3 Combine the tomato, scallions, and radishes in a serving bowl large enough to hold the pasta.

4   For the vinaigrette, combine the olive oil, lemon juice, mustard, oregano, salt, pepper, and garlic in a medium bowl; whisk well. Set aside.

5   Pour the pasta and cooking water over the carrots, bell peppers, and corn in the colander; transfer to the serving bowl; drizzle with dressing, tossing well to coat.

6   Serve warm or chilled.

QUICK TIPS:

- If you're making a veggie pasta dish like this one, you can place the veggies in the colander and simply pour the pasta and the cooking water over the vegetables; this will soften them slightly. Or if you are using vegetables that have longer cooking times, like broccoli and carrots — or if you prefer your vegetables a bit softer — add them to the boiling pasta water 2 to 3 minutes before the end of the cooking time.

- Add crumbled feta cheese to the pasta just before serving for a burst of flavor.

- Add shredded chicken, smoked salmon, or canned tuna for a change.

- If you don't care for chopped garlic in the vinaigrette, replace it with ⅛ teaspoon of garlic powder.

FOR KEEPS: The vinaigrette will keep in the refrigerator for up to 2 weeks. Use leftover dressing on tossed green salads.

CHICKEN PASTA SAUTÉ

No need to wrap the leftovers on this one — there won't be any!

Prep time **5 minutes**   Cook time **20 minutes**   Yield **4 servings**

½ **pound pasta, any style**

½ **(1.25-ounce) package fajita seasoning mix**

½ **red bell pepper, stemmed, seeded, and chopped**

3 **tablespoons water**

2 **cooked boneless, skinless chicken breast halves, thinly sliced**

¼ **cup light mayonnaise**

2 **tablespoons low-fat ranch dressing**

2 **tablespoons Italian dressing, the zestier the better**

1   Cook pasta in a large pot of salted boiling water until al dente.

2   Combine the seasoning mix, bell pepper, and water in a medium bowl; add chicken and toss to coat.

3   Sear the chicken mixture in a large pan over high heat for 3 minutes; set aside.

4   Combine the mayonnaise and both dressings in a serving bowl large enough to hold the pasta.

5   Drain the pasta, reserving ½ cup of the cooking water.

6   Toss the pasta in the serving bowl with the dressing, seared chicken, and reserved pasta water. Serve immediately.

QUICK TIP: For color and taste variations, try tossing the pasta with ¼ cup of grated carrots and ½ cup of chopped green bell pepper, or add some frozen vegetables to the pasta during the last 3 minutes of cook time.

PASTA, PLEASE!

ROTINI MEXICALI

Any kind of fun-shaped pasta is perfect for this Mexican-style dish.

Prep time **10 minutes**   Cook time **20 minutes**   Yield **4 servings**

1 **pound pasta, any type of fun shape**
½ **pound lean turkey breakfast sausage,
  removed from casings**
1 **teaspoon chili powder**
½ **teaspoon ground cumin**
1 **(28-ounce) can crushed tomatoes**
1 **teaspoon sugar**
1 **cup grated Monterey Jack cheese
  (about 4 ounces)**
3 **tablespoons chopped jalapeño slices,
  optional**
1 **large avocado, sliced**

1   Cook pasta in a large pot of salted boiling water until al dente.

2   Sauté the sausage in a large skillet over medium-high heat.
    Cook until no longer pink, breaking up the meat with a
    wooden spoon.

3   Add the chili powder and cumin to the meat and cook for
    30 seconds (the mixture will be dry).

4   Add the tomatoes and sugar to the meat; bring to a boil and
    reduce the heat to low. Cover and simmer for 15 minutes,
    stirring occasionally.

5   Toss the cooked and drained pasta in a large serving bowl with
    the sauce, cheese, jalapeño slices, if desired, and avocado.
    Serve immediately.

QUICK TIP: **A ready jar of jalapeño slices in the refrigerator adds
flavor and heat to all sorts of recipes.**

PASTA, PLEASE!

SPRING GREEN PASTA

This dish is great for a spring day when you get home from work and would rather spend time outside than in the kitchen. The fresh parsley adds a lively flavor.

Prep time **5 minutes**   **Cook time** **20 minutes**   **Yield** **4 servings**

1 **pound pasta (linguine or rigatoni)**
¾ **cup light mayonnaise**
3 **tablespoons Dijon mustard**
2 **tablespoons chopped fresh parsley**
½ **teaspoon dried thyme**
¼ **teaspoon salt**
½ **pound ham, diced**
1 **cup frozen corn, thawed**
1 **bunch scallions (white and tender green parts), sliced**

1   Cook the pasta in a large pot of salted boiling water until al dente.

2   Whisk the mayonnaise, mustard, parsley, thyme, and salt together in a serving bowl large enough to hold the pasta.

3   Add the ham, corn, and scallions to the mustard mixture.

4   Drain the pasta, reserving ½ cup of the cooking water. Toss the pasta into the serving bowl with the ham mixture and reserved pasta water. Serve hot, warm, or chilled.

EASY-CHEESY PASTA SALAD

If you want to take a popular pasta salad to a backyard barbecue, give this recipe a try.

Vegetarian

Prep time	5 minutes	Cook time	20 minutes
Chill time	1–2 hours	Yield	4–6 servings

1 **pound pasta, any short, chunky shape**
¾ **cup light mayonnaise**
½ **cup Molly McButter cheese-flavored granules**
¼ **cup pickle relish, sweet or dill**
1 **(16-ounce) bag frozen peas**
1 **red bell pepper, stemmed, seeded, and chopped**
Salt and pepper

1. Cook the pasta in a large pot of salted boiling water until al dente.

2. Combine the mayonnaise, cheese granules, and relish in a serving bowl large enough to hold the pasta.

3. During the final 3 minutes of pasta cooking time, add the frozen peas to the boiling pasta water.

4. Drain the pasta; rinse in cold water and drain again. Place in the serving bowl with the mayonnaise dressing; add the bell pepper and mix thoroughly. Season with salt and pepper to taste.

5. Cover and refrigerate for 1 to 2 hours before serving.

QUICK TIP: Add cooked, shredded chicken to stretch this dish. Or add some sautéed Polish sausage with the green bell pepper.
FOR KEEPS: Keep this salad for up to 5 days in the refrigerator.

PASTA, PLEASE!

KIDS-LOVE-THIS-PASTA PASTA

Everyone knows children who hate vegetables. This recipe conceals the goodness of broccoli in a cheesy, creamy sauce. The smaller you chop the broccoli, the more readily it will be accepted by picky eaters.

Prep time 5 minutes   Cook time 20 minutes   Yield 4–6 servings

- 1 **pound pasta, any style**
- 1 **head broccoli, chopped (about 4 cups)**
- 1 **(16-ounce) jar low-fat processed cheese, such as Velveeta**
- ⅛ **teaspoon garlic salt**

1   Cook pasta in a large pot of salted boiling water until al dente.

2   During the final 3 minutes of the pasta cooking time, add the broccoli to the boiling pasta water.

3   Drain the pasta and broccoli; transfer immediately to a serving bowl.

4   Add the cheese and garlic salt; toss until the cheese coats the pasta. Serve immediately.

QUICK TIPS:

- **The fresh broccoli balances the processed cheese to make for a satisfying and nourishing dish — especially when time is at a minimum and picky eaters are at a maximum.**
- **Add some cooked, shredded chicken to stretch this dish.**

BETTER BUTTERED NOODLES

Kids of all ages and picky eaters love plain buttered noodles. Doctor yours up by adding ⅛ teaspoon nutmeg, ½ cup of grated Parmesan cheese, and 4 tablespoons of butter to a pound of cooked pasta. Freshly ground black pepper finishes off the noodles nicely.

BOW TIES WITH CAESAR

Easy is the name of the game here. I used to make my own Caesar salad dressing for this recipe, but the prepared kind works great. Serve with a green salad.

Vegetarian

Prep time 5 minutes   **Cook time** 20 minutes   **Yield** 4–6 servings

- 1 **pound bow tie pasta**
- ½ **cup light Caesar salad dressing**
- 1 **(15-ounce) can tomato purée**
- ¼ **cup chopped fresh parsley**
- ¼ **cup red onion, thinly sliced**
- ½ **cup cherry tomatoes, halved**

1. Cook pasta in a large pot of salted boiling water until al dente.

2. Combine the dressing and tomato puree in a serving bowl large enough to hold the pasta.

3. Drain the pasta and add to the serving bowl with the dressing. Toss in the parsley, onion, and cherry tomatoes. Serve warm, at room temperature, or chilled.

QUICK TIPS:

- **Pass a bowl of freshly grated Parmesan cheese to sprinkle on this dish at the table.**
- **Add some cooked, shredded chicken or slices of grilled sirloin steak to help stretch this dish.**

CHEESY LINGUINE

This dish is so light and creamy your family will think that you slaved over it all day.

Prep time **5 minutes**   Cook time **20 minutes**   Yield **4–6 servings**

1 **pound linguine**
½ **cup light mayonnaise**
¼ **cup grated Parmesan cheese**
¼ **cup whole milk**
½ **teaspoon garlic powder**
½ **teaspoon dried basil**
1 **head broccoli, chopped (about 4 cups)**
1 **cup chopped ham**

1   Cook pasta in a large pot of salted boiling water until al dente.

2   Combine the mayonnaise, Parmesan, milk, garlic powder, and basil in a serving bowl large enough to hold the pasta.

3   During the final 3 minutes of pasta cooking time, add the broccoli to the boiling pasta water.

4   Drain the pasta and broccoli; toss in the serving bowl with the sauce. Add the ham.

5   Serve immediately or chill and serve as a pasta salad.

QUICK TIPS:

- **Do not substitute low-fat milk when preparing this recipe.**
- **In place of broccoli, try frozen peas, corn, or mixed vegetables.**
- **For a vegetarian version, omit the ham; the recipe will still taste great.**

TURKEY-VEGGIE FETTUCCINE

The smoked turkey is the key to this light and flavorful dish.

Prep time **5 minutes**   Cook time **20 minutes**   Yield **4–6 servings**

- 1 **pound fettuccine**
- 1¾ **cups skim milk**
- 1 **(8-ounce) package reduced-fat cream cheese, cubed**
- 1 **bunch scallions (white and tender green parts), thinly sliced**
- 1 **teaspoon Italian seasoning**
- ¼ **teaspoon garlic powder**
- 1 **cup cooked smoked turkey breast meat, cubed (deli-style works fine)**
- ½ **cup grated Parmesan cheese**
- 1 **cup broccoli florets**
- 1 **cup carrot slices**
- 1 **cup zucchini slices**
  Salt and pepper

1. Cook pasta in a large pot of salted boiling water until al dente.
2. Combine the milk, cream cheese, scallions, Italian seasoning, and garlic powder in a large microwave-safe bowl.
3. Microwave on high for 2 to 3 minutes, stirring every minute, until the mixture has a smooth consistency and is heated through.
4. Add the turkey and Parmesan to the cream sauce; stir to combine. Set aside.
5. During the final 3 minutes of the pasta cooking time, add the broccoli, carrots, and zucchini to the pasta pot.
6. Drain the pasta and vegetables, add to the serving bowl, and toss with the sauce; season with salt and pepper. Wait 2 minutes, toss again, and serve.

PASTA, PLEASE!

SHELLS AND CHEESE

Using ingredients you probably already have in your refrigerator and pantry, you can have a rich satisfying dish on the table in just over 30 minutes.

Prep time 10 minutes   Cook time 25 minutes   Yield 4 servings

12 ounces medium-size pasta shells

1 tablespoon olive oil

½ green bell pepper, stemmed, seeded, and diced

1 small onion, diced

½ teaspoon chopped garlic

1½ cups prepared spaghetti sauce

1 cup water

½ teaspoon oregano

1 tablespoon dried parsley

4 ounces American cheese, cut into ½-inch cubes

1 Cook the pasta in a large pot of salted boiling water until al dente.

2 Heat the oil in a large skillet over medium heat. Sauté the bell pepper, onion, and garlic until beginning to brown; 8 to 10 minutes.

3 Add sauce, water, oregano, and parsley; simmer 5 minutes.

4 Remove from the heat and stir in the cheese cubes. Drain the pasta and toss with the vegetable mixture in a serving bowl. Serve immediately.

QUICK TIP: To stretch this dish, add some cooked, shredded chicken. Sautéed zucchini and additional onion and peppers go well with this pasta.

PASTA, PLEASE!

SPINACH-FETA MOSTACCIOLI

The green spinach and salty feta taste just right served on the deck on a hot summer evening. Small portions are a perfect accompaniment to barbecued ribs or chicken.

Vegetarian

Prep time **5 minutes**   Cook time **20 minutes**   Yield **4–6 servings**

> 1 **pound pasta, such as mostaccioli or penne**
> 3 **large tomatoes, chopped**
> 1 **(10-ounce) package frozen chopped spinach, thawed and well drained**
> 1 **bunch scallions (white and tender green parts), thinly sliced**
> ¾–1 **cup crumbled feta cheese (about 4 ounces)**
> 4 **tablespoons olive oil**
>   **Salt and pepper**

1 Cook the pasta in a large pot of salted boiling water until al dente.

2 Combine the tomatoes, spinach, scallions, and cheese in a serving bowl large enough to hold the pasta. Toss gently.

3 Drain the pasta, reserving ½ cup of the cooking water. Add the pasta to the serving bowl with the vegetables and cheese. Toss with the oil, reserved pasta water, and salt and pepper to taste. Serve hot or at room temperature.

> **QUICK TIP:** Thaw the spinach in the microwave for quick results. Always remember to drain it well and squeeze the water out of thawed frozen spinach before using. Spinach tends to hold a lot of moisture and the excess water will alter a recipe considerably, creating unfavorable results.

PASTA, PLEASE!

Vegetarian

FAST SKILLET PASTA

This is one of my favorite recipes in this chapter. This version is for a side dish, but you can double it and serve it as a main dish topped with some roasted vegetables and a tomato salad on the side. It's also great with barbecued pork, grilled chicken, salmon, or steak. You can even use the leftovers in a pot of soup.

Prep time 5 minutes   **Cook time** 15 minutes   **Yield** 4 servings

- 2 tablespoons olive oil
- 2 bunches scallions (white and tender green parts), sliced
- ¼ large green bell pepper, stemmed, seeded, and chopped
- 2½ cups water
- 2 chicken bouillon cubes
- ½ teaspoon garlic powder
- 1 cup orzo (or other very small pasta)

1 Heat the olive oil in a medium skillet over medium heat. Sauté the scallions and bell pepper until tender, about 5 minutes.

2 Add the water, bouillon, and garlic powder to the skillet; bring to a boil. Add the uncooked pasta and return to a boil. Reduce the heat and simmer.

3 Cover and cook for 10 minutes or until the pasta is tender.

4 Serve hot, warm, or chilled.

QUICK TIPS:
- Very small pasta shapes such as orzo or acini di pepe work best in this recipe.
- Add some cooked, shredded chicken to stretch this dish.

QUICK, HOT PASTA SALAD

A great, versatile recipe that features the added bonus of helping you to clean out the vegetable drawer.

Vegetarian

Prep time **5 minutes**   Cook time **20 minutes**   Yield **2–4 servings**

- **8 ounces pasta, any style**
- **2 tablespoons olive oil**
- **⅓ cup creamy Italian dressing**
- **3–4 tablespoons grated Parmesan cheese**
- **½ cup chopped zucchini**
- **½ cup chopped broccoli**
- **½ cup chopped cauliflower**
- **½ cup chopped onion**

1. Cook the pasta in a large pot of salted boiling water until al dente.

2. Whisk the olive oil, dressing, and Parmesan together in a serving bowl large enough to hold the pasta.

3. During the final 3 minutes of the pasta cooking time, add the vegetables to the boiling pasta water.

4. Drain the pasta and vegetables; place in the serving bowl and toss gently until well coated. Serve immediately.

QUICK TIP: **Top with a grilled chicken breast for a heartier meal.**

PASTA, PLEASE!

vegetarian

PEAS, CHEESE, AND PASTA BAKE

This dish is a great make-ahead meal.

Prep time **5 minutes**   Cook time **35 minutes**   Yield **6–8 servings**

1 **pound pasta, any style**

1 **pound low-fat cottage cheese**

2 **cups grated mozzarella cheese (about 8 ounces)**

1 **(16-ounce) bag frozen peas**

¼ **cup grated Parmesan cheese**

3 **eggs, lightly beaten**

½ **teaspoon garlic powder**

½ **teaspoon salt**

½ **teaspoon black pepper**

1 **(28-ounce) jar meatless spaghetti sauce**

1 Preheat the oven to 350°F. Spray a 2½-quart casserole dish with cooking spray.

2 Cook pasta in a large pot of salted boiling water until al dente.

3 Combine the cottage cheese, mozzarella, peas, Parmesan, eggs, garlic powder, salt, and pepper in a medium bowl; mix well.

4 Drain the pasta and return to cooking pot. Toss the pasta with the entire jar of spaghetti sauce.

5 In the prepared casserole dish, layer half of the pasta and then half of the cheese mixture.

6 Cover with the remaining pasta and the remaining cheese mixture. Bake for 35 minutes or until hot and bubbly.

7 Remove from the oven and let stand for 5 minutes before serving.

QUICK TIPS:

• **For those who like a saucy dish, add an extra cup of spaghetti sauce.**

• **Serve smaller portions as a side dish with a grilled skirt steak.**

FOR KEEPS: You can prepare this dish up to 2 days in advance. To bake straight from the refrigerator, increase the cooking time by 20 to 25 minutes.

SAUSAGE AND MOZZARELLA LASAGNA

This dish takes a little more time to put together, but it's worth the effort.

Prep time 30 minutes   **Cook time** 35 minutes   **Yield** 8 servings

1 (15-ounce) container whole
   milk ricotta cheese
1 egg
¼ cup grated Parmesan cheese
1 tablespoon parsley flakes
¼ teaspoon salt
½ teaspoon black pepper
2 (28-ounce) jars spaghetti
   sauce

1 pound Italian sausage,
   casings removed, browned
   and crumbled
1 (9-ounce) box no-boil
   lasagna, about 16 sheets
3 cups grated mozzarella
   cheese (about 12 ounces)

1 Preheat the oven to 375°F. Spray a 9- by 13-inch baking pan
with cooking spray.

2 Combine the ricotta, egg, Parmesan, parsley, salt, and pepper
in a medium bowl; mix well.

3 To assemble the lasagna, pour 1 cup of sauce in the bottom of
the baking pan; spread evenly. Lay 4 lasagna noodles over the
sauce in a single layer. Cover with another cup of the sauce
and half of the sausage. Distribute one-quarter of the ricotta
mixture evenly over the sauce by spoonfuls, smoothing out
the lumps. Sprinkle ½ cup of the mozzarella cheese over the
ricotta cheese.

4 Repeat these steps three more times. Make sure that the top
layer is covered with the sauce and mozzarella. Cover the dish
with foil, making sure that the foil does not touch the top layer
of lasagna.

5 Bake for 25 minutes, remove the foil, and bake 10 minutes
longer or until the top is bubbling and golden. Let stand for
5 minutes before serving.

CHICKEN AND PASTA

A meal in itself. All you need to complete the dinner is a green salad.

Prep time 5 minutes   Cook time 20 minutes   Yield 3–4 servings

8 ounces pasta	1 teaspoon red wine vinegar
2 tablespoons olive oil	2 tablespoons butter
4 boneless, skinless chicken breast halves (1–1½ pounds)	2 tablespoons water
1 (.7-ounce) package dry Italian salad dressing mix	

1   Cook pasta in a large pot of salted boiling water until al dente.

2   Heat the oil in a large nonstick skillet over medium heat.

3   Reserve 2 teaspoons of the Italian dressing mix; set aside. Coat both sides of the chicken with remaining seasoning mix.

4   Cook the chicken in the skillet, about 8 minutes per side or until the juices run clear when cut through the thickest part. Remove the chicken to a serving platter and keep warm.

5   Add the vinegar, butter, and water to the skillet. Stir until the butter melts, about 10 seconds; set aside.

6   Drain the pasta, reserving ½ cup of the cooking water. Place the pasta in a large serving bowl and toss to coat with the butter sauce, reserved seasoning mix, and reserved pasta water.

7   Place the chicken on top of the pasta and serve.

QUICK TIPS:

- If you are short on time, cut up the chicken into small pieces and follow the recipe as usual. The chicken will cook in 5 minutes.

- You can make this meal without chicken for a vegetarian option. Sauté some zucchini, onion, and green bell pepper in place of the chicken and add a can of drained garbanzo beans to the serving bowl with the dressing.

vegetarian

DUO OF PEANUT SAUCES

Try either of these easy peanut sauces on pasta or chicken; even if it sounds strange, trust me — it's delicious. Both of these sauces are likely to accommodate whatever happens to be in your pantry. Combine with 1 pound of cooked pasta, enough for 2 to 4 servings.

CURRY PEANUT SAUCE

Prep time 3 minutes
Cook time 2 minutes
Yield About 1¼ cups

- ¾ cup creamy peanut butter
- ¼ teaspoon crushed red pepper flakes
- 1½ tablespoons low-sodium soy sauce
- 1½ teaspoons crushed garlic
- 1¼ teaspoons curry powder
- 1 cup low-sodium chicken broth

1. Combine all of the ingredients in a medium microwave-safe bowl, whisking lightly to blend.

2. Cover lightly with plastic wrap and microwave on high for 1 to 2 minutes, or until smooth and slightly thickened. If you prefer a thinner sauce, add a little more chicken broth.

GARLIC PEANUT SAUCE

teen-friendly

Prep time 5 minutes
Yield About 1½ cups

- ¾ cup creamy peanut butter
- 1¼ cups very hot water
- 1½ teaspoons crushed garlic
- 1½ tablespoons low-sodium soy sauce
- 2 teaspoons sesame oil

Combine all of the ingredients, mixing well to blend.

QUICK TIPS:

- Add steamed vegetables such as peas, broccoli, carrots, or water chestnuts to the tossed pasta for great texture and flavor.
- Crushed red pepper flakes can be added for the hot tongue in the family.
- Use as a dipping sauce for grilled chicken strips.

FOR KEEPS: These sauces freeze well for up to 2 months.

ROCKIN' SOCKIN' SOCCER SAUCE

I was planning to make beef and bean chili one evening for my son and his friend before their soccer game when I discovered that the friend would not eat beans. I came up with this sauce and served it over elbow macaroni. It was a big hit and I let the boys name it.

Prep time **5 minutes** **Cook time** **15–30 minutes**
Yield **About 5 cups, enough for 1½ pounds of pasta**

3 **pounds lean ground meat**
1 **large onion, chopped**
1 **tablespoon chopped garlic**
2 **(32-ounce) cans tomato sauce**
¼ **cup chili powder**
1 **tablespoon ground cumin**

1 Brown the meat in a large pot and drain off any fat.

2 Add the onion and garlic to the meat and cook until the onion is softened, about 5 minutes.

3 Add the tomato sauce, chili powder, and cumin to the beef mixture.

4 Simmer for at least 15 minutes or up to 2 hours. The flavor will vary depending on the cooking time.

FOR KEEPS: **Freeze this sauce in multiple containers so that you can pull out what you need for a fast dinner.**

WHITE CLAM SAUCE

How can something so good be this easy?

Prep time **5 minutes** Cook time **5 minutes** Yield **2–4 servings**

12 **ounces linguine**
3 **tablespoons butter**
3–4 **teaspoons crushed garlic**
1 **tablespoon all-purpose flour**
2 **(6.5-ounce) cans minced clams**
¼ **cup chopped fresh parsley**
¾ **teaspoon dried basil**
1⅓ **cups half-and-half**

1 Cook the pasta in a large pot of salted boiling water until al dente.

2 Melt the butter in a medium skillet over medium heat; add the garlic and sauté for 1 minute. Whisk in the flour.

3 Reduce the heat to low; add clams with their liquid, parsley, basil, and half-and-half. Cover and simmer on low, stirring frequently, for 3 to 4 minutes. Serve over the drained linguine.

QUICK TIPS:
- **Reserve about ½ cup of the pasta cooking water before draining pasta. Use the reserved water to moisten the pasta if it seems a little dry.**
- **Serve with freshly grated Parmesan cheese.**

FOR KEEPS: This sauce freezes well for up to 2 months.

PASTA, PLEASE!

SIMPLE
Side Dishes

Quick and Easy Side Dishes
to Eat at Home or Take to a Friend's

The recipes in this chapter are simple and uncomplicated, and use fresh or frozen vegetables to create the most convenient and nutritious side dishes possible. Side dishes can be the most creative part of dinner. I like to play with color, textures, and flavor when choosing a side dish to complement the main part of a meal. Sometimes the side dish even becomes the main dish. When I realize that I don't have enough time to prepare the main dish I was planning, I might double the vegetable side, toss it with a bowl of couscous, pasta, or rice, drizzle on some olive oil, balsamic vinegar, and a sprinkle of herbs, and voilà — dinner is served.

Take advantage of seasonal vegetables readily available at your grocery store year round. When you stick with what's in season you are rewarded with the best value, flavor, and nutrition. Even in the mid-west during the dead of winter, root vegetables such as onions, shallots, beets, and carrots make a wonderful roasted vegetable medley. Parsnips, turnips, carrots, and potatoes can all be boiled, drained, and mashed with a touch of butter and cream. Experiment with combining some of these other vegetables with your mashed potatoes. Look to your sides to turn simple meals into creative masterpieces.

GREENS AND CHEESE

Have the kids grate the cheese while you chop the broccoli. They will be more likely to eat their vegetables when they contribute to the preparation.

Prep time 5 minutes **Cook time** 10 minutes **Yield** 4 servings

1 **bunch broccoli, cut into bite-size pieces**

⅓ **cup low-fat evaporated milk**

1½ **cups grated sharp cheddar cheese (about 6 ounces)**

1 Pour about ½ cup water into a large skillet and bring to a boil over medium-high heat. Add the broccoli and cover tightly. Cook for 5 to 7 minutes, or until the broccoli is tender crisp.

2 While the broccoli is cooking, combine the milk and cheese in a small microwave-safe bowl. Microwave for 1 to 2 minutes, stirring occasionally, until the sauce is smooth.

3 Drain the broccoli, transfer to a serving dish, top with the sauce, and serve.

ITALIAN-STYLE GREEN BEAN SAUTÉ

Serve with grilled chicken in the summertime when green beans are in season.

Prep time 5 minutes **Cook time** 8 minutes **Yield** 4 servings

1 **pound fresh green beans**

3 **tablespoons olive oil**

1 **small onion, chopped**

1 **teaspoon crushed garlic**

¼ **cup grated Parmesan cheese**

3 **tablespoons red wine vinegar**

1 Steam the beans until tender crisp, 8 to 10 minutes. Keep them warm in a shallow serving dish.

2 Meanwhile, heat the oil in a medium skillet over medium heat. Add the onions and garlic; sauté for 8 minutes. Spoon over the beans in the serving dish and sprinkle with the Parmesan and vinegar. Toss well and serve immediately.

ZESTY BAKED CARROTS

Carrots are so easy to prepare and are loaded with vitamins and nutrients. The horseradish adds a zesty, spicy burst of flavor to this recipe.

Prep time 5 minutes   **Cook time** 15 minutes   **Yield** 4 servings

- 6 large carrots, scrubbed and sliced into ¼-inch rounds (about 4 cups)
- 2 tablespoons fresh grated horseradish
- 2 tablespoons grated onion
- ½ cup light mayonnaise
- 1 teaspoon salt
- ¼ teaspoon black pepper
- ¼ cup water
- ¼ cup breadcrumbs
- 1 tablespoon butter, melted

1 Preheat the oven to 375°F. Coat a 6- by 10-inch baking dish with cooking spray.

2 Place the carrots in a large, microwave-safe dish (the carrots should not be stacked more than two high in the bowl). Add 1 tablespoon water, cover tightly with plastic wrap, and microwave on high for 4 to 6 minutes, until tender crisp. Drain carrots and transfer them to the prepared baking dish.

3 Combine the horseradish, onion, mayonnaise, salt, pepper, and water in a small bowl, whisking to blend. Pour the horseradish mixture over the carrots; sprinkle with the breadcrumbs and butter. Bake 15 minutes. Serve immediately.

TARRAGON CARROTS

This carrot dish brings a touch of Mediterranean sophistication to the dinner table. Green beans work well with tarragon too.

Prep time **5 minutes** **Cook time** **About 8 minutes** **Yield** **4 servings**

6 **large carrots, scrubbed and cut into ½-inch rounds**

1 **tablespoon dried tarragon**

2 **tablespoons butter, at room temperature**

¼ **teaspoon salt**

1 Place the carrots in a shallow, microwave-safe casserole dish. Add 1 tablespoon water, cover tightly with plastic wrap, and microwave on high for 4 to 6 minutes, until tender crisp.

2 Add the butter, salt, and tarragon to the hot carrots; stir well to combine. Cover tightly with plastic wrap again and microwave for an additional minute. Serve immediately.

SAUTÉED CARROTS

A great way to dress up carrots.

Prep time **5 minutes** **Cook time** **10 minutes** **Yield** **6 servings**

½ **cup (1 stick) butter**

1 **large onion, sliced thinly**

6 **large carrots, peeled and thinly sliced**

1 **tablespoon sugar**

2 **teaspoons dried tarragon**

Salt and pepper

1 Heat the butter in large skillet over medium heat. Add the onion and cook for 3 minutes, stirring occasionally. Increase the heat to medium-high and add carrots; cook and stir until the carrots are tender crisp, 4 to 5 minutes.

2 Sprinkle with the sugar and tarragon and cook for 2 minutes longer. Season with salt and pepper and serve.

CHEDDAR ONION PUDDING PIE

My neighbor made this dish for me a long time ago when I lived in Detroit. I must have eaten half of the pie, which convinced her to give me the recipe on the spot! I have used different cheeses and added diced jalapeño or a can of green chiles. I've served this pie as a main dish with a salad on the side. My kids love it — even my daughter, who cringes at the sight of onions.

Prep time 10 minutes   **Cook time** 38 minutes   **Yield** 6-8 servings

4 tablespoons butter
1 large onion, chopped
1½ cups milk
1 egg, beaten
1½ cups Whole Grain Master Mix (page 33) or prepared biscuit mix, such as Bisquick

1 cup grated sharp cheddar cheese (about 4 ounces)
Salt and pepper

1. Preheat the oven to 400°F. Coat a 9 inch pie pan with cooking spray.

2. Heat 2 tablespoons of the butter in a medium skillet over medium-high heat; add the onion and sauté 8 minutes or until golden brown; set aside.

3. Combine the milk and egg in a large bowl; blend in the master mix, ½ cup of the cheese, and the sautéed onion mixture. Pour into the prepared pie pan and sprinkle with the remaining ½ cup of cheese.

4. Melt the remaining 2 tablespoons of butter and drizzle over the pie; sprinkle with salt and pepper. Bake for 30 minutes.

5. Cool slightly, cut into wedges, and serve.

QUICK TIPS:
- **This dish freezes well after baking.**
- **You can use Monterey Jack or Swiss cheese in place of the cheddar.**

CHEESY ZUCCHINI BAKE

A great recipe for when your garden is overflowing with zucchini.

| Prep time | 10 minutes | Cook time | 40 minutes | Yield | 4-6 servings |

- 2 **tablespoons vegetable oil**
- 1 **large onion, chopped**
- 4 **small zucchini, thinly sliced (about 4 cups)**
- 1 **tablespoon dried oregano**
- ½ **teaspoon garlic powder**
- ¾ **teaspoon salt**
- ¼ **teaspoon black pepper**
- 1 **cup grated mozzarella or provolone cheese (about 4 ounces)**
- ½ **cup whole milk ricotta cheese**
- 2 **eggs, beaten**

1 Preheat the oven to 350°F. Coat an 8- by 12-inch or 9-inch square baking dish with cooking spray.

2 Heat the oil in a large skillet over medium-high heat. Add the onion, zucchini, oregano, garlic powder, salt, and pepper; sauté for 5 minutes.

3 Remove from the heat and drain any liquid that may have collected in the pan. Add the mozzarella, ricotta, and eggs; toss gently, coating the zucchini well.

4 Fill the prepared baking dish with the vegetable mixture. Bake uncovered for 35 minutes or until the top is browned. Serve.

STOVE TOP ZUCCHINI

During the height of zucchini season I make this recipe at least twice a week and serve it alone or over pasta with a drizzle of olive oil and a sprinkle of sea salt. The dish has a slightly tart taste from the fresh zucchini. If you want a sweeter taste, use dried sweet basil in place of the oregano and add a pinch or two of sugar with the salt and pepper.

Prep time 5 minutes **Cook time** 15 minutes **Yield** 6 servings

2 **tablespoons olive oil**
4 **small zucchini, thinly sliced (about 4 cups)**
1 **large onion, thinly sliced**
2 **teaspoons dried oregano**
3 **tablespoons grated Parmesan cheese**
  Salt and pepper

1 Heat the oil in a large skillet over medium-high heat. Add the zucchini, onion, and oregano to the skillet; stir to coat.

2 Reduce the heat to medium; cover and cook for 2 minutes. Remove the lid and sauté for 10 minutes to cook off the moisture and lightly brown the zucchini.

3 Sprinkle with the Parmesan, and salt and pepper to taste. Serve.

CAMP VEGGIES

My husband's family loves camping. This recipe was inspired by one of their campfire cooking techniques. My family is carrying on the camping tradition, and I have taken the liberty of adding a few different seasonings for a new taste. You don't need to use the exact ingredients listed — experiment! If you're not actually camping, feel free to use your backyard grill.

Prep time 5 minutes **Cook time** About 15-20 minutes **Yield** 4–6 servings

- 2 large sheets of heavy-duty aluminum foil
- 1 large onion, chopped
- 2 small zucchini, chopped
- 2 green bell peppers, stemmed, seeded, and chopped
- 2 small yellow squash, chopped
  Handful of mushrooms, halved
- 1 small stalk broccoli, trimmed and chopped
- 2 teaspoons crushed garlic
- 1 teaspoon dried basil
- ½ teaspoon salt
- ¼ teaspoon black pepper
- 2–4 tablespoons margarine (the easy-squeeze kind is great for camping)

1 Lay out the sheets of foil on a work surface. Evenly distribute the vegetables between the 2 sheets; sprinkle with the garlic, basil, salt, and pepper.

2 Put 1 to 2 tablespoons of margarine on top of each mound of vegetables. Seal up tightly by double folding all the edges of the foil. The packets can be made up to 5 hours in advance.

3 Place the packets over the campfire or grill, turning every 3 to 4 minutes. Grilling time is between 15 and 20 minutes, depending on the level of heat.

4 Remove from the fire, open the packets, and serve.

QUICK TIP: Olive oil or butter can be used in place of the margarine.

APPLE NORTHERN BEAN BAKE

When looking for a sweet, savory dish to go with grilled sausages or roast pork, give this one a try.

Prep time **10 minutes** **Cook time** **1 hour** **Yield** **8–10 servings**

- 4 **tablespoons butter**
- 3 **cups Granny Smith apples, peeled, cored and chopped (about 3 large or 5 small)**
- 1 **red onion, roughly chopped**
- ¾ **cup firmly packed brown sugar**
- ½ **cup ketchup**
- 1 **teaspoon cinnamon**
- ¼ **teaspoon ground cloves**
- 1½ **teaspoons salt**
- 1 **(48-ounce) jar great northern beans, drained**

1   Preheat the oven to 375°F. Coat a casserole dish with cooking spray.

2   Melt the butter in a large skillet over medium heat; add the apples and onions. Cook for 10 minutes, stirring occasionally. Add the sugar, ketchup, cinnamon, cloves, and salt; stir well.

3   Place the beans in the prepared casserole dish. Pour the apple mixture over the beans and mix well. Bake for 1 hour. (Cover the beans during baking process if they dry out too much.) Serve immediately or let cool slightly.

FOR KEEPS: This recipe can be assembled and refrigerated up to 2 days in advance. Increase the baking time by 10 minutes. When prepared, the dish stores well in refrigerator for up to 2 days.

TEXAS BOY BEANS

A great recipe I picked up in Texas, where beans are an important accompaniment to barbecue.

Prep time 20 minutes   **Cook time** 30 minutes   **Yield** 8 servings

- **6 slices bacon**
- **1 large onion, chopped (about 1½ cups)**
- **½ cup ketchup**
- **¼ cup firmly packed brown sugar**
- **1 tablespoon vinegar (cider or white)**
- **½ teaspoon salt**
- **1 tablespoon prepared mustard**
- **1 (16-ounce) can baked beans**
- **1 (15.5-ounce) can kidney beans, drained**
- **1 (15.5-ounce) can lima beans, drained**

1   Preheat the oven to 350°F. Coat a 9- by 13-inch glass baking dish with cooking spray.

2   Cook the bacon in a large skillet until crisp. Remove the bacon, leaving the bacon fat in the skillet. Cool the bacon slightly, and crumble in a large mixing bowl. Add the onions to the same skillet and cook for 8 minutes, until softened.

3   Spoon out the cooked onions, discarding the grease, and place in the bowl with the crumbled bacon; add the remaining ingredients and mix well.

4   Pour the beans into the prepared baking dish. Bake for 30 minutes. Serve.

FOR KEEPS: This recipe can be assembled and refrigerated up to 2 days in advance; simply increase the baking time by 10 minutes. When prepared, the dish stores well in the refrigerator for 2 days.

KICKIN' SOUTHWEST BEAN BAKE

The lime juice and salsa add a great Southwestern flair to this dish.

Prep time 2 minutes   **Cook time** 15 minutes   **Yield** 8 servings

1 (16-ounce) can baked beans
1½ cups chunky salsa, any flavor
1 tablespoon fresh lime juice
1 cup crushed tortilla chips
1 cup grated Monterey Jack cheese
(about 4 ounces)

1   Preheat the oven to 375°F. Coat a 9- by 13-inch baking pan with cooking spray.

2   Stir the beans, salsa, and lime juice together in a large bowl. Pour the bean mixture into the prepared baking pan.

3   Sprinkle with the chips and bake for 12 minutes. Sprinkle with the cheese, and bake for 2 minutes longer. Serve.

FOR KEEPS: This recipe can be assembled through Step 2 and refrigerated up to 3 days in advance. Continue with Step 3 when you are ready to bake, and increase the baking time by 10 minutes. When prepared, the dish stores well in the refrigerator for up to 2 days.

MONSTER POTATO PANCAKE

The rosemary makes this a perfect side dish for roasted chicken. Quick, easy, and delicious — and the kids love the presentation. This recipe also makes a great accompaniment to any style of eggs at breakfast or Sunday brunch.

Prep time 10 minutes   **Cook time** 15 minutes   **Yield** 6–8 servings

4	tablespoons butter
4–5	medium russet potatoes, peeled and shredded
½	teaspoon dried rosemary, crumbled
½	teaspoon salt
¼	teaspoon black pepper

1. Pat the pile of shredded potatoes with paper towels to dry; place potatoes in a large bowl, and toss with the rosemary, salt, and pepper.

2. Melt the butter in a large skillet over medium heat. Spread the potato mixture evenly over the bottom of the skillet and pat down firmly with a spatula. Cook until the pancake is crisp on the bottom, 7 to 8 minutes.

3. Invert the pancake onto a serving plate and slide back into the pan to cook the other side. Cook 7 to 8 minutes longer, or until crisp.

4. Transfer the pancake to a plate and serve.

QUICK TIPS:
- You can use different spices instead of rosemary, such as oregano, tarragon, basil, or none at all. Most adults like the rosemary and most kids like it plain.
- Use a food processor to speed up the shredding process.

QUICK POTATO BAKE

Sometimes I want my potatoes plain and simple — soft and creamy on the inside and a bit crispy on the outside. This recipe is perfect for those times. Most of the cooking is done in the microwave to speed things up. The oven is used only at the end to add the right texture to the skins.

Prep time **5 minutes**   **Cook time** **15 minutes**   **Yield** **4 servings**

4   **medium russet potatoes, peeled and sliced ¼-inch thick**

2   **tablespoons olive oil**

¼   **teaspoon garlic powder**

¼   **teaspoon salt**

⅛   **teaspoon black pepper**

1   Preheat the oven to 350°F.

2   Toss the potatoes, oil, garlic powder, salt, and pepper in a microwave-safe and ovenproof casserole dish. Cover tightly with plastic wrap. Microwave on high for 5 minutes.

3   Remove the plastic wrap and transfer the casserole dish to the oven; bake for 10 minutes, or until potatoes reach desired crispness.

QUICK TIP: If you don't have time to bake these potatoes, you can serve them right from the microwave.

FOR KEEPS: Potatoes can be peeled and wrapped in damp paper towel and stored in a ziplock bag in the refrigerator for up to 3 days.

JOEY'S STUFFED PILLOW POTATOES

Our son Joe loves to make this recipe. It tastes great and when he offers to cook it, it's one less thing that I have to worry about for the dinner hour.

Prep time 15 minutes   **Cook time** 12 minutes   **Yield** 6 servings

3 **large russet potatoes**
3 **tablespoons butter**
½ **cup milk**
½ **teaspoon salt**
¼ **teaspoon black pepper**

2 **cups grated sharp cheddar cheese (about 8 ounces)**
3 **tablespoons grated Parmesan cheese, optional**

1   Scrub the potatoes and pierce with a fork several times. Place in the microwave and cook for 10 minutes, or until fork-tender.

2   Slice the potatoes in half lengthwise. While still hot, scoop out flesh with a spoon and place it in a medium mixing bowl (not necessary to get all the potato out of the shell). Place the shells on a baking sheet.

3   Mash the potato with butter, milk, salt, pepper, and 1 cup of the cheddar; spoon the potato mixture back into the shells.

4   Top with the remaining cup of cheddar and sprinkle with the Parmesan, if desired. Place under the broiler for 2 minutes or until the cheese melts.

5   Serve immediately or at room temperature.

QUICK TIPS:

- Top with crumbled bacon, spicy sausage, sliced scallions, roasted red peppers, kidney beans, sliced jalapeños, or barbecued pulled pork or chicken.
- For a fall tailgate party, make this recipe in advance and warm it over a grill with your choice of toppings.

CREAMY POTATO BAKE

This dish is a hit with kids and adults alike. I have made it in advance and frozen it for many Thanksgiving dinners. You can also make it *after* Thanksgiving, when you have leftover mashed potatoes. This recipe is rich, yummy, and everything you could want from a potato casserole.

Prep time 10 minutes   **Cook time** 30 minutes   **Yield** 4–6 servings

- 3 **cups hot mashed potatoes (instant potatoes work well in this dish too)**
- 1 **cup reduced-fat sour cream**
- ¼ **cup milk**
- ¼ **teaspoon garlic powder**
- 1 **cup grated sharp cheddar cheese (about 4 ounces)**
- ⅔ **cup canned French fried onions**

1 Preheat the oven to 350°F. Coat a 2-quart casserole dish with cooking spray.

2 Combine the potatoes, sour cream, milk, garlic powder, and ½ cup of the cheese in a medium bowl; fold together gently.

3 Place half of the potato mixture in the prepared casserole dish and sprinkle with fried onions. Place remaining potatoes on top.

4 Bake for 30 minutes; remove from the oven, sprinkle with the remaining ½ cup of cheese and let rest for 5 minutes. Serve.

KITCHEN 411: When mashing your potatoes, don't overbeat them. When they are mixed or beaten too much, they become rubbery, stiff, and heavy.

FOR KEEPS: This recipe can be assembled and refrigerated for up to 2 days or frozen for up to 2 months. Increase the baking time by 10 minutes if refrigerated and by 30 to 40 minutes if frozen. Check to be sure that the potatoes are heated through before serving.

POTATO TACO POPPERS

These potatoes have a great taco flavor. They can also be served as a snack.

Prep time 10 minutes   **Cook time** 14 minutes   **Yield** 4 servings

4–5 **large russet potatoes, scrubbed**

¼ **cup vegetable oil**

1 **(1.25-ounce) package low-sodium taco seasoning mix**

3 **tablespoons cornmeal (white or yellow)**

1 Preheat the oven to 450°F.

2 Pierce the potatoes with a fork and place in the microwave. Microwave for 6 minutes or until barely tender. Cut the potatoes into 1-inch cubes and set aside.

3 Combine the oil, taco seasoning, and cornmeal in a large bowl. Add the potato cubes to the bowl; turn to coat well.

4 Transfer the potatoes to an ungreased baking sheet. Bake 8 minutes or until golden brown.

QUICK TIP: You can use other seasoning mixes in this recipe. I found a great Southwestern savory pizza seasoning mix made by Little Caesars and used 2 tablespoons of it in place of the taco seasoning mix. I then tossed the potatoes with ½ cup of light mayonnaise and 2 stalks of finely chopped celery. In any form, this dish is a big hit in our family. It's the most requested addition to any outdoor picnic, barbecue, or family gathering.

POTATOES MONACO

This potato dish is a good complement to grilled chicken in the summer. It has a nice, light taste.

Prep time **15 minutes** **Cook time** **10 minutes** **Yield** **4 servings**

1¾ **cups milk**

4 **potatoes, peeled and cut into 1½-inch chunks**

½ **teaspoon salt**

¼ **teaspoon black pepper**

1 **tablespoon butter-flavored granules (found in the seasoning section of the grocery store)**

Salt and pepper

¼ **cup crumbled feta cheese**

1 **tablespoon seasoned breadcrumbs**

1   Preheat the oven to 350°F. Coat a 2-quart baking dish with cooking spray.

2   Combine the milk and potatoes in a large saucepan. Simmer over medium heat for about 10 minutes, until the potatoes are tender. Stir occasionally to avoid scorching the pan, adding more milk if necessary. Remove the saucepan from the heat.

3   Using a slotted spoon, transfer the potatoes to the prepared baking dish; reserve the milk.

4   Whisk the butter granules, salt, and pepper into reserved milk; pour the mixture over the potatoes. Sprinkle with the feta and breadcrumbs and bake for 10 minutes. Serve immediately.

MICROWAVE POTATOES

The green peppers add a distinct bite to this dish.

Prep time 5 minutes   **Cook time** 15 minutes   **Yield** 6 servings

- 4 **tablespoons butter**
- 1½ **teaspoons salt**
- ¼ **teaspoon black pepper**
- 4 **medium potatoes, peeled and sliced ⅛-inch thick**
- ½ **large green bell pepper, stemmed, seeded, and chopped**
- 1 **medium onion, chopped**

1. Melt the butter in the microwave in a medium microwave-safe casserole dish; season with salt and pepper. Add the potatoes, bell pepper, and onion; toss well to coat.

2. Cover and microwave on high 10 to 12 minutes, stirring every 3 minutes, until the potatoes are fork tender.

3. Let stand covered for 10 minutes before serving.

LOW-FAT CHEESY POTATOES

For those of you who are looking for a great potato dish with all the richness of an old-time potato casserole, but with a lot less fat, look no further. This is the best low-fat potato dish that I've yet come across in my many trials. It's creamy, rich, and loaded with flavor.

Prep time 15 minutes   **Cook time** 50 minutes   **Yield** 6–8 servings

1 cup low-fat cottage cheese	2 tablespoons all-purpose flour
4 ounces reduced-fat cream cheese, at room temperature	4 large potatoes, peeled and cut into ¼-inch thick slices
1 tablespoon dried basil	Salt and pepper
½ cup nonfat milk	⅓ cup grated Parmesan cheese

1   Preheat the oven to 400°F. Coat 9- by 13-inch baking pan with cooking spray.

2   Combine the cottage and cream cheese in a blender or food processor. Blend on high speed until smooth, scraping down the sides of the blender several times and adding 1 to 2 tablespoons milk if the mixture seems too thick. Add the basil and blend to combine.

3   Whisk the milk and flour in a small bowl until smooth; set aside.

4   Arrange one-third of the potatoes in the bottom of the pan. Spread the potatoes with half of the cream cheese mixture and season with salt and pepper.

5   Make a second layer with another one-third of the potatoes and the remainder of the cream cheese mixture. Add the final layer of potato and sprinkle with Parmesan; pour the prepared milk and flour over the top.

6   Bake uncovered for 50 minutes or until the potatoes are tender and golden brown. Serve.

273

SWEET POTATO CLASSIC

This dish is a classic on our Thanksgiving table. Instead of using fresh sweet potatoes, I opted for canned to make the preparation a bit easier.

Prep time 10 minutes   **Cook time** 20 minutes   **Yield** 4–6 servings

- 2 (29-ounce) cans yams or sweet potatoes, drained and cut into large chunks
- 4 tablespoons butter, melted
- ¼ cup orange juice
- ½ teaspoon cinnamon
- ¼ teaspoon salt
- ⅛ teaspoon ground cloves
- 15 large marshmallows

1 Preheat the oven to 350°F. Coat a 2-quart casserole dish with cooking spray.

2 Combine the potatoes, butter, orange juice, cinnamon, salt, and cloves in a large bowl; mix well. Spoon the potato mixture into the prepared dish. Bake for 20 minutes.

3 Sprinkle with the marshmallows and let stand for 5 minutes before serving.

QUICK TIPS:

- To make this dish in the microwave, cook the potato mixture on high for 4 minutes, stir, and cook for 4 minutes longer. Remove from the microwave and top with the marshmallows; let stand for 5 minutes before serving.
- Add 2 tablespoons of rum to the orange-juice mixture to add a caramel-like richness to the recipe.

HOP AND POP FRIED RICE

This recipe is great as a side dish with a deli-bought rotisserie chicken. It is also very mild and perfect for young kids. My son's Cub Scout pack was having an end-of-year picnic and I brought a huge bowl of this rice; it disappeared before any of the adults got through the food line!

Prep time 5 minutes **Cook time** 25 minutes **Yield** 6–8 servings

- 3 tablespoons vegetable oil
- 1 medium onion, diced
- 1 stalk celery, diced
- 2 eggs, beaten
- 1 cup frozen peas and carrots
- 6 cups cooked Instant rice, warm or room temperature
- 1 (14-ounce) can bean sprouts, drained
- 1 bunch scallions (white and tender green parts), thinly sliced
- 2–3 tablespoons low-sodium soy sauce

1 Heat the oil in a large skillet over medium-high heat; add the onion and cook for 5 minutes. Stir in the celery and cook for 5 minutes longer. Add the eggs and stir-fry until set, 3 to 4 minutes; break up the cooked egg.

2 Add the frozen peas and carrots, cover, and reduce the heat to medium-low; cook for 5 minutes.

3 Add the rice and stir until heated through, about 5 minutes.

4 Transfer to a serving bowl; add the sprouts and scallions and sprinkle with the soy sauce. Stir gently and serve.

QUICK TIP: A couple of tablespoons more of soy sauce can be added just before serving if the dish needs some refreshing.

VEGGIE RICE

This rice dish delivers a nice, creamy texture along with the crunch of vegetables!

Prep time 12 minutes **Cook time** 15 minutes **Yield** 6 servings

- 2 **cups chopped broccoli**
- 2 **carrots, peeled and sliced**
- 1 **red bell pepper, stemmed, seeded, and chopped**
- 1 **medium onion, chopped**
- 2 **tablespoons bacon bits**
- 3 **cups instant rice, cooked and kept warm**
- 4 **tablespoons butter**
- 1 **teaspoon dried oregano**
- ⅓ **cup grated Parmesan cheese**
  Salt and pepper

1 Steam the broccoli, carrots, bell pepper, and onion together until the broccoli is tender, 4 to 5 minutes.

2 Add the bacon bits to the steamer and steam 1 minute longer.

3 Transfer the vegetables to a large serving bowl; toss with the warm rice, butter, oregano and Parmesan. Season with salt and pepper to taste. Serve immediately.

QUICK TIPS:
- **This recipe can be doubled and served as a main dish.**
- **Omit the bacon bits for a vegetarian option.**

RIGHT-ON RICE

Here is my simple, foolproof, method for perfect rice:

For every cup of long grain white rice, bring 2 cups of water to a boil in a saucepan. Add the rice to the boiling water. Return the water to a boil, cover, and reduce the heat to medium-low. Set the timer for 7 minutes; stir. Set the timer for another 7 minutes; stir again. Remove from the heat, leaving the lid on the pot. The rice will keep warm, tender, and fluffy for up to 1 hour. For more flavor, add a chicken bouillon cube to the water before cooking.

For brown rice, increase the liquid to 2½ cups for every cup of rice and increase the total cooking time to 45 minutes, stirring once at the 20-minute mark.

REAL GARLIC BREAD

This is the real deal!

Prep time 5 minutes   **Cook time** 5 minutes   **Yield** 8 servings

- ½ **cup (1 stick) butter, at room temperature**
- ½ **cup Parmesan or Romano cheese, freshly grated**
- ¼ **cup chopped fresh Italian parsley**
- ¼ **teaspoon black pepper**
- 2–3 **teaspoons crushed garlic**
- 1 **large loaf Italian bread, halved lengthwise**

1 Preheat the oven to 450°F.

2 Blend the butter, Parmesan, parsley, pepper, and garlic well in a medium bowl.

3 Spread the butter mixture over the sliced sides of the bread; place on a baking sheet. Bake until bubbly and golden brown, about 5 minutes. Serve immediately.

QUICK TIP: Be sure to use fresh garlic and freshly grated Parmesan or Romano cheese.

FOR KEEPS: The butter mixture can be made and frozen for up to 2 months. The whole loaf can be assembled 1 day in advance and refrigerated or frozen for up to 1 month; simply bring to room temperature before baking.

teen-friendly

SEASONED GREEN BEANS

This green bean dish is beyond easy and transforms a simple bag of frozen green beans into a flavorful side dish that complements any meat or fish entrée.

Prep time **2 minutes** **Cook time** **About 8 minutes** **Yield** **6 servings**

1 **(16-ounce) bag frozen French cut green beans**
½–1 **teaspoon onion flakes**
½–1 **teaspoon dried minced garlic**
¼ **teaspoon salt**
⅛ **teaspoon black pepper**

1 Place the frozen beans in a microwave-safe bowl; sprinkle with remaining ingredients and toss to coat.

2 Cover the bowl with plastic wrap and microwave on high for 4 minutes; toss beans and microwave 4 minutes longer. Serve.

SEASONED BISCUITS

These biscuits feature a wonderful combination of herbs that work very well with chicken and lots of gravy.

Prep time 3 minutes   **Cook time** 14 minutes   **Yield** 8 biscuits

1 (10-ounce) container low-fat biscuits, such as Pillsbury Grand

2 tablespoons butter, melted

Select any combination of the following seasonings:

  ½ teaspoon dried rosemary, crushed

½–1 teaspoon garlic powder

  1 tablespoon grated Parmesan cheese

  ¼ teaspoon Italian seasonings

  ¼ teaspoon dried parsley

  ¼ teaspoon dried onion flakes

1 Preheat the oven to 375°F.

2 Place the biscuits in a single layer in a baking pan.

3 Combine the melted butter with the seasonings in a small bowl. Brush the seasoned butter over the biscuits.

4 Bake for 14 to 16 minutes or until golden brown (watching carefully not to burn the bottoms of the biscuits). Serve immediately.

QUICK TIP: A few of my favorite seasoning combinations:

Rosemary and garlic powder

Garlic powder, Parmesan, and minced onion

Italian seasoning and Parmesan

Garlic powder, parsley, and salt

Dessert on a Dime

Simple and Satisfying
Sweet Treats for the Whole Family

Who doesn't like dessert? In this chapter you'll find a lot of easy and delicious treats, from cakes and pies to cookies, fruit dips, and ice cream. Baking for coffee houses in several cities for more than 14 years has helped me to develop some very quick and handy methods that I have included in this chapter.

My philosophy is that if you're going to indulge in a sweet treat, the experience should be worth the calories. Fast and simple my recipes may be, but they are also fresh, satisfying, and homemade. You'll enjoy every last bite — I know I did!

CHEWY CHIP COOKIES

Here is my version of the classic Toll House recipe.

Prep time **10 minutes**   Cook time **10 minutes**   Yield **2 dozen cookies**

DESSERT ON A DIME

2¼ **cups all-purpose flour**

¾ **cup whole-wheat flour**

1 **teaspoon baking soda**

1 **teaspoon salt**

1 **cup (2 sticks) butter, at room temperature**

¾ **cup granulated sugar**

¾ **cup firmly packed brown sugar**

1 **teaspoon pure vanilla extract**

2 **eggs**

2–3 **cups semisweet chocolate chips**

1 **cup chopped pecans**

1 Preheat the oven to 350°F. Lightly grease a baking sheet.

2 Sift together the flours, baking soda, and salt in a medium mixing bowl. Set aside.

3 Combine the butter, granulated sugar, and brown sugar in a large mixing bowl; beat with an electric mixer for 2 minutes. Add the eggs; beat until fluffy. Gradually add the flour mixture; beat with the mixer for 1 to 2 minutes. Stir in the chips and nuts.

4 Drop by heaping teaspoonfuls onto the prepared baking sheet. Bake for 10 to 12 minutes, until the cookies are golden. Cool on a wire rack.

FOR KEEPS: Tightly wrapped, these cookies freeze well for up to 2 months.

PUMPKIN-PECAN BUNDT CAKE

This Bundt cake is moist, delicious, and so darned easy! I typically prepare the recipe, cut the cake into quarters, and freeze the pieces individually so that I can have smaller quantities on hand, depending on how many children or adults I am serving.

Prep time 12 minutes **Cook time** 60 minutes **Yield** 12 servings

DESSERT ON A DIME

- 3 cups all-purpose flour
- 2 tablespoons pumpkin pie spice
- 2 teaspoons baking soda
- 1 teaspoon salt
- 1 cup (2 sticks) butter, at room temperature
- 2 cups firmly packed brown sugar
- 4 eggs
- 1 (15-ounce) can pumpkin puree
- ¾ cup chopped pecans or walnuts

1. Preheat oven to 325°F. Coat a Bundt pan with cooking spray.

2. Sift together the flour, pie spice, baking soda, and salt in a medium bowl. Set aside.

3. Beat the butter and brown sugar together with an electric mixer until light and fluffy; about 2 minutes. Add the eggs and pumpkin; combine well. Gradually add the flour mixture and mix just until combined.

4. Sprinkle the nuts in the bottom of the prepared pan; spoon the batter gently into pan. Bake for 60 minutes or until a tester comes out clean.

5. Cool for 5 minutes, then invert onto a wire cake rack to cool completely.

QUICK TIPS:

- **To ice the cake, heat ½ cup canned vanilla or coconut-pecan frosting in the microwave. Drizzle over cake and let cool to set.**

- **If you don't have pumpkin pie spice mix, use the following combination of seasonings: 2 teaspoons ground cinnamon, 1 teaspoon ground ginger, and ½ teaspoon cloves.**

FOR KEEPS: **This cake can be wrapped tightly in foil, stored in a ziplock freezer bag, and frozen for several months.**

APPLE SUGAR CAKE

Sweet and simple to prepare, this cake is perfect for the family who wants to have their cake and eat it, too — especially when no one can be around all day to make a cake from scratch. It makes a great breakfast cake, too.

Prep time 10 minutes   **Cook time** 30 minutes   **Yield** 12 servings

1 egg, beaten

¼ cup milk

4 tablespoons butter, melted and cooled slightly

1 teaspoon pure vanilla extract

1 (18.25-ounce) box spice cake mix

1 large Granny Smith apple, peeled, cored, and sliced

CRUMB TOPPING

1 tablespoon brown sugar

1 tablespoon granulated sugar

1 tablespoon butter, at room temperature

½ teaspoon cinnamon

1   Preheat the oven to 375°F. Coat a 9-inch square pan with cooking spray.

2   Combine the egg, milk, butter, and vanilla in a large bowl; mix well. With an electric mixer set on medium speed beat in the cake mix for 1 minute, or until smooth.

3   Spread the batter in the prepared pan and arrange the apples evenly over the top.

4   Combine the brown sugar, granulated sugar, butter, and cinnamon in a small bowl, blending with your fingers until crumbs form. Sprinkle the mixture evenly over the apples.

5   Bake for 30 to 35 minutes, or until a tester comes out clean. Cool on a wire rack before cutting into squares and serving.

QUICK TIP: You can use a butter cake mix if you prefer.

FOR KEEPS: This cake can be made 2 days in advance. When cooled, store in an airtight container at room temperature. It can also be wrapped tightly and stored in the freezer up to 2 months.

APRICOT-STRUDEL CREAM CHEESECAKE

Anybody with a sweet tooth will love this wonderfully creamy and smooth cheesecake.

Prep time 20 minutes   **Cook time** 25 minutes   **Yield** 12 servings

2 (8-ounce) containers reduced-fat crescent rolls

2 (8-ounce) packages reduced-fat cream cheese, at room temperature

1 cup sugar

1 teaspoon pure vanilla extract

4 tablespoons butter, at room temperature

½ cup apricot preserves

TOPPING

½ cup all-purpose flour

¼ cup sugar

4 tablespoons butter, at room temperature

½ cup sliced almonds

1   Preheat the oven to 350°F.

2   Remove the crescent roll dough from 1 container and press it into the bottom of an ungreased 9- by 13-inch cake pan. Use your fingers to seal all the seams and press the dough to the edges of the pan.

3   Beat the cream cheese, sugar, vanilla, and butter with an electric mixer in a large bowl; blend until no lumps appear. Spread the mixture over the crescent roll base. Drop the apricot preserves by teaspoonfuls over the cream cheese mixture; spread evenly.

4   Open the remaining crescent roll container; place the dough on the work surface and press gently with your fingertips into a 9- by 13-inch rectangle. Place the dough gently over the top of the cream cheese mixture.

5   For the topping, combine the flour, sugar, and butter with a fork until crumbly. Toss gently with the almonds. Sprinkle the topping evenly over the dough.

6   Bake for 25 minutes. Cool in the pan for 5 minutes; serve.

CLASSIC MINI-CHEESECAKES

This recipe is a tried-and-true favorite and extremely easy to prepare. It's perfect for the mom who wants to make those special comfort foods, but who has limited time to do so.

Prep time 10 minutes **Cook time** 20 minutes **Yield** 30 cheesecakes

4 (8-ounce) packages reduced-fat cream cheese, at room temperature

1¼ cups sugar

2 tablespoons pure vanilla extract

4 eggs

30 vanilla wafer cookies

¾ cup mini chocolate chips, optional

1 (21-ounce) can pie filling, cherry or blueberry, optional

1 Preheat the oven to 350°F.

2 Beat the cream cheese, sugar, vanilla, and eggs in a large bowl until no lumps appear.

3 Line standard-size muffin tins with paper liners and place one wafer cookie in each cup.

4 Fill each cup three-quarters full with the cream cheese mixture. Bake for 20 minutes.

5 Top each cheesecake with a sprinkling of mini–chocolate chips, if desired. Cool.

6 Serve plain or topped with pie filling, if desired, or fresh fruit.

QUICK TIP: For a patriotic look that doesn't take much time, top each cheesecake with a teaspoon each of cherry and blueberry pie filling and whipped topping.

FOR KEEPS: These cheesecakes can be made 3 days in advance; simply cover and chill. They can also be stored in a sealed container and frozen for several months.

FOOL'S STRAWBERRY CHEESECAKE

Don't let this recipe's name fool you. Stack this dessert in a glass; you don't have to bake it! A long time ago a neighbor taught me the secret of combining strawberries with brown sugar and sour cream to create a luscious cheesecake flavor. I took the idea a bit further and came up with this dessert.

Prep time **15 minutes**   **Yield** **About 4 servings**

- **1 cup reduced-fat sour cream**
- **¼ cup firmly packed brown sugar, plus more for sprinkling**
- **3 cups sliced strawberries, rinsed and hulled**
- **1 cup low-fat vanilla yogurt**

1. Combine the sour cream and brown sugar in a medium bowl; mix well until the brown sugar is incorporated and no lumps appear.

2. In four parfait glasses or dessert cups, layer ⅓ cup of the strawberries, 2 tablespoons of the sour cream mixture and then 2 tablespoons of the yogurt.

3. Repeat the layers one more time.

4. Store up to 1 day in the refrigerator. Sprinkle with brown sugar right before serving.

QUICK TIP: Using clear glass dessert cups allows the simple beauty of this dish to show.

LET'S TALK: A deconstructed version of this recipe works well when you have a large crowd. Place large, whole, fresh strawberries in a clear glass or crystal bowl, leaving the stems intact. Spoon sour cream and crumbled brown sugar into two separate bowls and set them in front of the bowl of strawberries. Create a small card instructing guests to dip the strawberries in the sour cream and then into the brown sugar.

SUMMER CAKES

A very refreshing, healthy, and quick recipe. It's a perfect dessert after a meal of chicken salad and greens.

3 **kiwifruit, peeled and sliced**

1 **large banana, peeled and sliced**

1 **pint sliced strawberries (hulled), blueberries, or raspberries**

1 **(8-ounce) can pineapple chunks, drained**

6–8 **large shortcakes, homebaked or prepared**

Frozen low-fat whipped topping

1 Combine the kiwifruit, bananas, strawberries, and pineapple in a bowl the day of serving; keep refrigerated.

2 After dinner is served, split the shortcakes and dress with the fruit and any juices that have collected in the bowl.

3 Top with whipped topping and serve.

QUICK RICE PUDDING

Rice pudding was a special dish in our house when I was growing up. To prepare it, my mother would slave at the oven for more than an hour, stirring and stirring. It seemed to take all day. I have modified that recipe to make it easier and quicker for today's busy cooks. The secret is leftover cooked rice. Instant rice works too. I like to make this dish when my kids are studying for finals and they need a break. It's comforting and satisfying and it lasts for up to 3 days in the refrigerator.

Prep time 5 minutes   **Cook time** 15 minutes   **Yield** 6 servings

DESSERT ON A DIME

½ **cup sugar**
⅓ **cup all-purpose flour**
¼ **teaspoon salt**
2½ **cups milk**
2 **cups cooked rice**
2 **eggs**

½ **cup golden raisins, optional**
½ **teaspoon cinnamon**
¼ **teaspoon ground nutmeg**
1 **tablespoon pure vanilla extract**

1 Stir together the sugar, flour, and salt in a medium saucepan; whisk in the milk until smooth. Add the rice.

2 Cook over medium heat, stirring constantly, until the mixture comes to a boil, about 10 minutes. Boil for 2 minutes longer and remove from the heat.

3 Beat the eggs in a small bowl. Slowly add 1 ladle of the hot pudding into the eggs, briskly stirring the egg/pudding mixture. Slowly pour the beaten egg mixture back into the pudding mixture (still off the heat); mix quickly and thoroughly. Add the raisins, if desired, cinnamon, nutmeg, and vanilla.

4 Return the pan to the heat and cook for 3 minutes more, stirring constantly. Pour into a large shallow serving bowl.

5 Serve hot, warm, or chilled.

QUICK TIP: This pudding is a real treat when served cold with warm milk on top and a generous sprinkling of cinnamon.

FOR KEEPS: The prepared pudding will keep well in the refrigerator for 3 days.

INCREDIBLE DOUBLE-CHOCOLATE COOKIES

This recipe is made from scratch and prepared by hand — which, in this case, is actually quicker than using an electric mixer. Make sure that the butter is at room temperature and you will not have any difficulty stirring by hand.

Prep time 10 minutes   **Cook time** 10 minutes   **Yield** 3 dozen cookies

1½ cups semisweet chocolate chips

½ cup firmly packed brown sugar

¼ cup granulated sugar

4 tablespoons butter, at room temperature

2 eggs, lightly beaten

1 teaspoon pure vanilla extract

1¼ cups all-purpose flour

1 teaspoon baking powder

1 (8-ounce) package semisweet chocolate baking squares, coarsely chopped

2 cups chopped walnuts, optional

1 Preheat the oven to 350°F.

2 In a large microwave-safe bowl, melt the chocolate chips in the microwave: heat on high for 1 to 2 minutes, stirring every 30 seconds to prevent scorching.

3 Immediately stir the sugars, butter, eggs, and vanilla into the melted chocolate; mix until the butter is melted.

4 Sift the flour and baking powder together in a small bowl and add it to the melted chocolate mixture, stirring until thoroughly combined. Blend in the chopped baking squares and nuts, if desired.

5 Drop the batter by heaping tablespoons onto ungreased baking sheets. Bake for 10 minutes for soft cookies or 12 minutes for crisp cookies.

6 Remove from the oven; cool for 1 minute. Remove from the baking sheet and cool completely on a wire rack.

GINGER COOKIES

These cookies can be prepared in a snap and are a hit with the neighborhood kids. They keep forever and are great to take along on long rides to those out-of-town games.

Prep time 10 minutes   Cook time 10 minutes   Yield 3½ dozen cookies

⅔ cup vegetable oil

1¼ cups sugar

1 egg, lightly beaten

¼ cup molasses

2 cups all-purpose flour

2 teaspoons baking soda

½ teaspoon salt

1 teaspoon cinnamon

2 teaspoons ground ginger

1 Preheat the oven to 350°F.

2 Beat the oil, 1 cup of the sugar, the egg, molasses, flour, baking soda, salt, cinnamon, and ginger with an electric mixer until thoroughly combined.

3 Roll the dough into balls about the size of walnuts. Place on ungreased baking sheets; sprinkle the remaining ¼ cup sugar over the tops of the cookies.

4 Bake for 10 minutes; cool on wire racks.

QUICK TIPS:

- **These cookies will flatten while baking and cooling, so there is no need to flatten the dough balls.**

- **Serve with vanilla ice cream and a drizzle of chocolate sauce.**

FOR KEEPS: **Store cooled cookies in an airtight container on the counter for up to 1 week. These cookies also freeze beautifully for up to 2 months, stored in a sealed container.**

DESSERT ON A DIME

APPLESAUCE COOKIES

Soft and comforting, these cookies make a great after-school snack. I have been making them since my children were babies. I sometimes make a double batch and freeze a portion to pop into lunch bags or to offer to unexpected guests.

Prep time 5 minutes · **Cook time** 10 minutes · **Yield** 2 dozen cookies

- 1 **cup firmly packed brown sugar**
- ¾ **cup (1½ sticks) butter, at room temperature**
- 1 **egg**
- ½ **cup applesauce**
- 2¼ **cups all-purpose flour**
- ½ **teaspoon baking soda**
- ½ **teaspoon salt**
- 1 **teaspoon cinnamon**
- ¼ **teaspoon ground cloves**

1. Preheat the oven to 375°F. Lightly grease 2 baking sheets.
2. Cream the brown sugar, butter, and egg in a large bowl with an electric mixer on medium speed. Stir in the applesauce.
3. Sift the flour, baking soda, salt, cinnamon, and cloves together in a medium bowl. Add to the creamed mixture; mix well.
4. Drop the batter by heaping teaspoons 1½ to 2 inches apart on the prepared baking sheets.
5. Bake for 10 to 12 minutes, until cookies are golden. Remove from the baking sheets and cool on wire racks.

QUICK TIP: You can add ½ cup of walnuts and/or raisins to the batter when adding the flour. You can also drizzle icing over the cooled cookies for a fancy look.

FOR KEEPS: These cookies can be made 3 days in advance and stored in an airtight container at room temperature. They can also be stored in a sealed container and frozen for several months. Place waxed paper between layers of cookies so they won't stick together.

CARAMEL APPLE SQUARES

I have made these for years and the kids love them. The hardest part of the recipe is coring and slicing the apples. The rest is easy. The squares can be served with French vanilla ice cream or sweetened whipped cream.

Prep time 10 minutes **Cook time** 40 minutes **Yield** 18 slices

1 (18.25-ounce) box spice cake mix
1 cup old-fashioned rolled oats
1 cup chopped walnuts or pecans
1 egg
½ cup (1 stick) butter, melted

2 Granny Smith apples, cored and thinly sliced into ¼-inch pieces
3 tablespoons all-purpose flour
1 cup caramel sauce (or caramel ice cream topping)

1   Preheat the oven to 350°F. Coat a 9- by 13-inch pan with cooking spray.

2   Combine the cake mix, oats, and nuts in a large bowl with a fork. Blend in the egg and butter and mix with a fork or pastry blender until crumbly.

3   Press 3 cups of the cake mixture into the bottom of the prepared pan. Bake for 8 minutes. Remove from the oven and place apples evenly over top of crust.

4   Whisk the flour into the caramel topping and pour over the apples; sprinkle with the remaining cake mixture. Return to the oven and bake 30 to 35 minutes longer. Cool before slicing.

QUICK TIPS:

• If you choose to use quick oats in place of regular oats, use 2 tablespoons less.

• If you are short on time, you don't need to peel the apples. Just be sure that they are washed, dried, and thinly sliced.

FOR KEEPS: This recipe can be made 2 days in advance; simply store the squares in an airtight container, separating layers with waxed paper. They can also be frozen for several months.

SWEET TREAT COOKIE SANDWICHES

Surprise your kids with this easy, sweet treat. I sometimes make cookie sandwiches with ice cream, but this filling won't melt when you want to take the cookies to a game or a picnic. They are ideal for school birthday parties, too!

Prep time 10 minutes **Yield** 6 sandwiches

DESSERT ON A DIME

- 2 tablespoons butter, at room temperature
- 1 cup confectioners' sugar, sifted
- 2 teaspoons milk
- ½–1 teaspoon pure vanilla, peppermint, almond, lemon, or orange extract or flavoring

- 1 tablespoon multicolored candy sprinkles, optional
- 12 prepared chocolate chip cookies, about 2½-inch diameter

1 Beat the butter and ½ cup of the confectioners' sugar in a large bowl with an electric mixer until smooth. Add the milk, the remaining ½ cup confectioners' sugar, the extract, and the sprinkles, if desired. Beat until well combined.

2 Spread frosting on the bottom side of half of the cookies; top with the remaining cookies, making sandwiches.

3 Store the cookie sandwiches in the refrigerator; wrap in plastic when they are firm.

QUICK TIP: For a very pretty presentation, stand the assembled sandwiches on their sides and roll them through sprinkles, letting the colorful candies stick to the edges of the frosting.

FOR KEEPS: These cookie sandwiches can be made in advance, wrapped individually, and frozen. A great grab-and-go sweet treat!

WHITE JERSEY PIZZA

My kids have played for many soccer teams and have several different jerseys to show for it. My son and daughter were helping me to make this dessert pizza when they chose the recipe name because the white chocolate and marshmallow base reminded them of white jerseys they once wore on the soccer field. This is a popular treat at sleepovers.

Prep time **10 minutes** **Cook time** **About 2 minutes** **Yield** **16 servings**

10 ounces white chocolate
2 cups crisp rice cereal, such as Rice Krispies
1 cup miniature marshmallows
½ cup dry roasted peanuts
16 chocolate kisses
8 maraschino cherries, cut in half

1 Butter a 10- to 12-inch round pizza pan.

2 Melt the white chocolate in a large microwave-safe bowl in the microwave for 1 to 2 minutes, stirring the chocolate every 30 seconds to prevent scorching.

3 Blend the cereal, ½ cup of the marshmallows, and the peanuts into the melted chocolate. Spread the mixture across the pizza pan, making a circle about 10 inches across.

4 Put the chocolate kisses into a microwave-safe bowl and melt in the microwave; drizzle over the pizza.

5 Decorate the pizza with the maraschino cherries and the remaining ½ cup marshmallows.

6 Cool in the refrigerator for 15 minutes and serve.

QUICK TIP: **In place of peanuts, you could use almond brickle, roasted almonds, or ½ cup dried cherries. Also, try adding peanut butter chips for a different flavor.**

teen-friendly

BUTTERSCOTCH CRUNCH

This is one of the easiest recipes in this book. I have made it for many bake sales and potluck dinners. Those who try it always ask me for the recipe.

Prep time 5 minutes   **Cook time** 1–2 minutes   **Yield** 25 squares

1 **cup butterscotch chips**
½ **cup peanut butter (creamy or crunchy)**
1 **cup crispy rice cereal, such as Rice Krispies**
1 **cup dry roasted peanuts**

1 Line an 8-inch square baking pan with parchment or waxed paper, leaving enough to overhang the edges of the pan.

2 Combine the chips and peanut butter in a large microwave-safe bowl. Microwave on high for 30 seconds; stir well. Continue heating on high for 30 seconds at a time until the mixture is melted and combined.

3 Add the cereal and nuts; mix well. Pour the mixture into the prepared pan and refrigerate until firm.

4 Using the waxed paper as a handle, lift out the set square and cut it into 25 pieces; serve.

QUICK TIP: You can use blanched peanuts instead of dry-roasted peanuts. You can also use cocoa rice cereal in place of regular rice cereal. Experimenting is what makes this recipe so much fun.

FOR KEEPS: This recipe can be made 3 days in advance; simply store in an airtight container in the refrigerator, separating the layers with waxed paper. It can also be stored in an airtight container and frozen for several months.

CHEWY CHOCOLATE FRUIT CLUSTERS

These clusters make lovely holiday gifts. The recipe doesn't take much time to prepare and no baking is required. The best part is that not a lot of pans get dirty — a definite plus!

Prep time 10 minutes   **Cook time** 2 minutes   **Yield** 24 clusters

1 **cup semisweet chocolate chips**
½ **cup coarsely chopped walnuts**
⅓ **cup raisins**
½ **cup old-fashioned rolled oats**

1   Place the chocolate in a large microwave-safe bowl. Microwave on high for 45 seconds to 1 minute; stir halfway through the cooking time. Remove the chocolate from the microwave and stir it until it's smooth.

2   Add the nuts, raisins, and oats to the chocolate; stir until well combined.

3   Drop the chocolate mixture by heaping teaspoons onto baking sheets lined with waxed paper. Cool completely in the refrigerator.

QUICK TIP: Lightly salted cashews or pecans can be substituted for the walnuts, and dried chopped apricots or dried cherries make great substitutes for the raisins.

FOR KEEPS: These fruit clusters can be made up to 2 weeks in advance. Separate the layers with waxed paper, cover lightly, and store in a cool, dry place.

SIMPLE S'MORE DESSERT

When my son turned eight, we celebrated his birthday by hosting a camp cookout. He chose to have a s'more cake. All of the boys loved it! We actually made it over the campfire. This recipe is a bit more refined than the original, but still sticky, yummy, and messy, all in the same bite — just the way it should be!

Prep time 10 minutes   **Cook time** 25 minutes   **Yield** 12–16 servings

½ **cup (1 stick) butter, cut into 8 pieces**
1½ **cups graham cracker crumbs**
1 **(14-ounce) can low-fat sweetened condensed milk**
1 **cup semisweet chocolate chips**
1 **cup miniature marshmallows**

1   Preheat the oven to 350°F.

2   Place the butter in a 9- by 13-inch baking pan, and put the pan in the oven for 2 to 3 minutes to melt the butter. Remove the pan from the oven and sprinkle the crumbs evenly over the butter.

3   Pour the milk evenly over the crumbs; sprinkle with the chocolate chips. Press gently on the top to firm up the crust. Bake for 25 minutes.

4   Remove the pan from the oven and sprinkle with the marshmallows; bake for 2 minutes longer.

5   Cool completely before serving (if you can wait that long)!

QUICK COOKIE SQUARES

This is a great recipe to make with your kids. Have them choose the toppings and crumble the cookie dough. The finished pan of cookies will disappear before you can turn around. You may want to make two pans just in case!

Prep time 10 minutes **Cook time** 30 minutes **Yield** 25 squares

1¼ cups confectioners' sugar, sifted
1½ cups peanut butter
1½ teaspoons pure vanilla extract
1 (18-ounce) package refrigerated chocolate chip cookie dough

FILLINGS (CHOOSE 1 OR 2)
½ cup mini-M&Ms
½ cup butterscotch morsels
½ cup peanut butter chips
½ cup chocolate chunks
½ cup salted peanuts

1 Preheat the oven to 350°F. Coat a 9-inch square pan with cooking spray.

2 Blend the sugar, peanut butter, and vanilla together with an electric mixer in a medium bowl.

3 Using floured fingers, remove the cookie dough from the wrapper and press half of the dough into the bottom of the prepared pan. Press optional filling(s) into the dough. Spread the peanut butter mixture over the filling.

4 Crumble the remaining cookie dough over the peanut butter as evenly as possible. Bake for 30 to 35 minutes or until golden brown.

5 Cool completely in the pan on a wire rack; slice and serve.

QUICK TIP: **Try different kinds of refrigerated dough flavors for variety.**

FOR KEEPS: **These cookie squares can be made 3 days in advance; simply store in an airtight container. They can also be stored in an airtight container and frozen for several months.**

teen-friendly

COOKIE PIZZA

Another terrific recipe for your teens to make with their friends. Plan a total pizza night, with takeout pizza followed by scoops of ice cream served with wedges of cookie pizza.

1 (20-ounce) package refrigerated sugar
   cookie dough
½ cup chopped dry roasted peanuts
1 cup miniature marshmallows
1 cup semisweet chocolate chips
⅓ cup caramel ice cream topping

1 Preheat the oven to 350°F.

2 Slice the cookie dough as directed on the package. Use the cookie dough slices to form a 12-inch circle on a large baking sheet, overlapping the slices slightly. Fill in the circle with remaining sliced cookie dough; seal firmly with your fingertips. Bake for 16 to 18 minutes; remove from oven.

3 Sprinkle the cookie with peanuts, marshmallows, and chocolate chips; drizzle with the caramel topping.

4 Bake 2 to 4 minutes longer or until the marshmallows are golden brown.

5 Cool for at least 10 minutes and slice.

FOR KEEPS: This recipe can be made 2 days in advance; just wrap lightly with plastic wrap or aluminum foil and store at room temperature.

DESSERT ON A DIME

FRUIT PIZZA

Great and refreshing for after the game — when the kids are at your house drinking juice and eating, and eating, and eating some more!

Prep time 10 minutes   Cook time 14 minutes   Yield 8 servings

1 (20-ounce) package refrigerated sugar
   cookie dough
1 (8-ounce) package reduced-fat cream cheese,
   at room temperature
⅓ cup sugar
1 teaspoon pure vanilla extract
1 (20-ounce) can pineapple rings, drained
1 large banana, peeled and sliced
1 kiwifruit, peeled and sliced
¼ cup strawberries, raspberries or blueberries
¼ cup apricot jam

1 Preheat the oven to 350°F.

2 Press the cookie dough into a 14-inch pizza pan and bake for 14 to 16 minutes; cool.

3 While the cookie is cooling, beat the cream cheese, sugar, and vanilla with an electric mixer in a medium bowl; spread over the cooled cookie. Arrange the fruit on top of the cream cheese.

4 Microwave the jam in a small microwave-safe bowl for 15 to 20 seconds, until the jam melts. Brush it over the fruit.

5 Serve immediately or refrigerate up to 1 day covered loosely with plastic wrap.

QUICK TIP: **If not serving immediately, banana slices need to be dipped in or lightly brushed with fresh lemon juice to keep them from browning.**

DESSERT ON A DIME

DEBBY'S CARAMEL APPLE CHEESECAKE PIE

My sister-in-law loves to bake but doesn't always have the time because of her busy schedule. She made this recipe for Thanksgiving a couple of years ago and it was the first thing to disappear from the dessert table — even before the pumpkin pie!

Prep time 15 minutes **Cook time** 35 minutes **Yield** 8 servings

DESSERT ON A DIME

- 1 (21-ounce) can apple pie filling
- 1 (9-inch) reduced-fat graham cracker crust
- 2 (8-ounce) packages reduced-fat cream cheese, at room temperature
- ½ cup sugar
- ½ teaspoon pure vanilla extract
- 2 eggs, lightly beaten
- ⅓ cup caramel ice cream topping
- 12 pecan or walnut halves, optional
- 2 tablespoons chopped nuts, optional

1. Preheat the oven to 350°F.
2. Reserve ¾ cup of the apple pie filling. Spoon the rest of the filling into the piecrust; set aside.
3. Beat the cream cheese, sugar, and vanilla with an electric mixer in a medium bowl. Add the eggs and beat until smooth. Pour over the apples in the piecrust.
4. Bake for 35 minutes; cool completely.
5. Mix the remaining apple filling and caramel topping together in a small saucepan; bring to a boil. Cook for 1 minute while stirring gently and constantly. Gently and evenly spread the apple topping over the top of the cooled pie; decorate with pecan halves and sprinkle with chopped nuts, if desired.
6. Refrigerate until ready to serve.

FOR KEEPS: This pie can be made 2 days in advance; keep chilled. Wrap tightly in plastic wrap or aluminum foil and freeze for several months; thaw in the refrigerator before serving.

GO USA PIE

This is *the* pie to serve on the Fourth of July.

Prep time **10 minutes** Freeze time **1 hour minimum** Yield **8 servings**

1 (9-inch) prepared reduced-fat graham
    cracker crust
1 quart ice cream, (your favorite flavor),
    softened
1 cup frozen low-fat whipped topping, thawed
1 cup halved strawberries
1 cup blueberries
1 cup miniature marshmallows

1 Fill the crust with the ice cream and then gently cover with the
   whipped topping. Arrange the strawberries, blueberries, and
   marshmallows on top.

2 Place the pie on a baking sheet and put it in the freezer, on a
   level surface.

3 Freeze for at least 1 hour.

4 Remove from the freezer 10 to 20 minutes before serving.

QUICK TIPS:

- **You can use peaches and raspberries in place of strawberries and
  blueberries.**

- **You can use other ice cream flavors, too. Try pistachio, blueberry,
  and coconut; these flavors will complement the fruit in this pie.**

DESSERT ON A DIME

PICKET FENCE APPLE PIE

An easy-to-make pie with a real homemade taste.

DESSERT ON A DIME

6 cups Granny Smith apples, peeled, cored, and sliced (about 6 large)

1 tablespoon fresh lemon juice

¾ cup sugar, firmly packed brown or granulated

3 tablespoons all-purpose flour

½ teaspoon cinnamon

⅓ cup raisins, dried cherries, or chopped dates

1 (9-inch) piecrust, unbaked

TOPPING

1 cup old-fashioned rolled oats, or ¾ cup plus 2 tablespoons quick oats

½ teaspoon cinnamon

⅓ cup firmly packed brown sugar

⅓ cup butter, melted

1 Preheat the oven to 375°F.

2 Toss the apples with the lemon juice in a large bowl.

3 Combine the sugar, flour, and cinnamon in a small bowl. Add to the apples with your choice of dried fruit; toss. Pour into the pie shell.

4 Using the same small bowl, make the topping. Combine the oats, cinnamon, brown sugar, and butter with your fingers; sprinkle on top of the apples. Press down slightly to adhere.

5 Place the pie on a baking sheet and bake for 50 to 60 minutes or until the topping is browned.

6 Serve warm or chilled.

KITCHEN 411: Here's what to do to prevent burning your piecrust:

1. Arrange two 15-inch lengths of aluminum foil across each other in a T shape.

2. Place the assembled pie in the center of the foil.

3. Roll up the foil around the pie pan and crust edge, leaving the top of the pie exposed.

4. Five to ten minutes before the end of the baking time, unroll the foil to expose the edge of the crust.

If you follow these steps, the piecrust should brown nicely. Another benefit: the foil protects the pan from spillovers!

FOR KEEPS: Covered tightly, this pie will keep for 2 days in the refrigerator. Wrap tightly and freeze for up to 2 months.

DESSERT ON A DIME

PEANUT BUTTER PIE

This is one of my most popular desserts. Adults seem to love it as much as kids. I have had the recipe forever and every time I serve it, someone invariably asks for the recipe — so for those of you who asked, here it is!

Prep time 8 minutes   **Freeze time** 4 hours   **Yield** 6–8 servings

4 ounces reduced-fat cream cheese, at room temperature

⅓ cup creamy peanut butter

½ cup whole milk

½ cup confectioners' sugar, sifted

1 (8-ounce) container frozen low-fat whipped topping, thawed

1 (9-inch) prepared reduced-fat graham cracker crust

1   Beat the cream cheese with an electric mixer in a large bowl until smooth, about 1 minute. Add the peanut butter and beat 30 seconds longer. Add the milk and confectioners' sugar, alternately, beating after each addition and scraping the bowl occasionally.

2   Gently fold in the whipped topping.

3   Pour the entire mixture into the piecrust and freeze for 4 hours.

4   Serve chilled or frozen.

KITCHEN 411: In cooking terms, folding means incorporating a light, fluffy substance into a stiffer or thicker substance. The added air makes the whole mixture lighter. Folding can be performed with a flat whisk, a large flat spoon, a rubber spatula, or even a large serving fork. Use large, slow, rolling strokes to combine the two substances — kind of like folding a blanket over and over in your arms. Add about half of the fluffy substance, folding gently until the majority of it is incorporated. Then add the rest. The most important thing is to not stir or beat the mixture, as doing either will deflate the air that you just added.

FOR KEEPS: This pie can be made 1 day in advance. It will also keep in the freezer for up to 2 months.

FRESH PEACH PIE

One hot summer evening spent grilling and swimming, some friends came over and everyone brought one simple, easy dish. One family, originally from Georgia, brought this pie. It was gone before the main course was served!

Prep time **8 minutes**   **Chill time** **1 hour, 20 minutes**   **Yield** **6–8 servings**

4 **tablespoons butter, at room temperature**

1 **cup plus 3 tablespoons confectioners' sugar, sifted**

1 **tablespoon brandy**

1 **(9-inch) pie shell, baked and cooled as directed**

6 **large ripe peaches, peeled and sliced**

3 **tablespoons fresh lemon juice**

¼ **cup granulated sugar**

1   In a medium bowl, beat the butter with an electric mixer until creamy, about 1 minute.

2   Add 1 cup of the confectioners' sugar and the brandy; blend well. Spread the mixture in the piecrust; chill for 20 minutes.

3   Combine the peaches, lemon juice, and granulated sugar in a medium bowl; toss gently. Arrange on top of the mixture in the pie shell; chill for 1 hour.

4   Sift the remaining 3 tablespoons of confectioners' sugar on top for garnish; serve.

QUICK TIPS:

- **Peaches will come loose when slicing this pie; just rearrange on the plates when serving.**
- **Serve each slice with a scoop of vanilla ice cream.**

CHOCOLATE-CHIP COOKIE PIE

This pie is rich and a small slice is quite satisfying. To me, it is the perfect comfort dessert. Serve each slice with a dollop of whipped cream. This recipe is so easy to put together that you might as well make two pies and freeze one.

Prep time 10 minutes   **Cook time** 50–60 minutes   **Yield** 8 servings

2 **eggs**
½ **cup all-purpose flour**
1 **cup firmly packed brown sugar**
1 **cup (2 sticks) butter, melted and cooled**
1 **cup semisweet chocolate chips**
1 **cup chopped walnuts, optional**
1 **(9-inch) deep-dish pastry shell, unbaked**

1 Preheat the oven to 350°F.

2 Beat the eggs until frothy, about 3 minutes. Add the flour and sugar and beat well, about 1 minute. Add the butter slowly; blend well.

3 Stir in the chocolate chips and the walnuts, if desired; pour into the pie shell.

4 Bake for 1 hour. Serve warm or at room temperature.

QUICK TIP: **Whipped cream, ice cream, and chocolate sauce all make wonderful additions to this dessert.**

FOR KEEPS: **This pie can be made 2 days in advance and stored airtight at room temperature. Or wrap tightly and freeze for several months.**

FALL APPLE CRISP

Anywhere in the United States, apples are at their best in the fall. Take advantage of fresh, crispy apples to make this dish — in the microwave, to save time. Serve with vanilla ice cream.

Prep time 12 minutes **Cook time** 15 minutes **Yield** 8 servings

6 **Granny Smith apples, peeled, cored, and sliced**
1½ **cups graham cracker crumbs**
¾ **cup firmly packed brown sugar**
½ **cup old-fashioned rolled oats**
½ **cup all-purpose flour**
1 **teaspoon cinnamon**
½ **teaspoon ground nutmeg**
½ **cup (1 stick) butter, melted**

1 Place the apples in a 2-quart microwave-safe baking dish.

2 Combine the graham cracker crumbs, brown sugar, oats, flour, cinnamon, nutmeg, and butter in a medium bowl; mix well. Sprinkle over the apples and microwave on high for 6 minutes. Rotate the dish and microwave for 7 minutes longer or until apples are tender.

3 Serve warm.

FOR KEEPS: This crisp can be made one day in advance; just cover and chill.

APPLE POPPER

This recipe is an excellent and delicious way to use canned biscuit dough without revealing the shortcut. Kids love the simple flavors and it makes a terrific dessert after a family meal.

Prep time 12 minutes   **Cook time** 25–30 minutes   **Yield** 8 servings

- ¾ **cup firmly packed brown sugar**
- 2 **teaspoons cinnamon**
- 6 **tablespoons butter, melted in the microwave**
- 1 **(16-ounce) container reduced-fat biscuit dough**
- 2 **large Granny Smith apples, peeled, cored and sliced ¼-inch thick wedges**
- ½ **cup chopped walnuts, optional**

1. Preheat the oven to 350°F. Coat an 8- by 12-inch or 9- by 13-inch baking pan with cooking spray.
2. Combine the brown sugar and cinnamon in a shallow bowl.
3. Remove the biscuit dough from the container and brush both sides of each biscuit with the melted butter. Roll the biscuits in the brown sugar mixture to coat. Reserve the leftover butter and sugar.
4. Arrange the biscuits in the prepared baking pan in a single layer; it's okay if they are tightly packed.
5. Arrange the apple slices between, around, and on top of the biscuit dough. Sprinkle with nuts, if desired, and then with any remaining brown sugar and butter.
6. Bake for 25 to 30 minutes, or until golden brown. Serve warm.

FOR KEEPS: You can prepare this recipe earlier in the day and refrigerate until ready to bake. Allow 3 to 5 minutes additional baking time.

DESSERT ON A DIME

BAKED APPLES

A simple and perfect preparation for fresh fall apples, kids and adults alike love this dessert.

Prep time **10 minutes** Cook time **40 minutes** Yield **4 servings**

4 large tart apples, such as Granny Smith
¼ cup firmly packed brown sugar
1 teaspoon cinnamon
4 teaspoons butter

1 Preheat the oven to 375°F.

2 Remove the cores to within ½-inch of the bottom of each apple and transfer the cored apples to a baking sheet.

3 Combine the sugar and cinnamon in a small bowl; spoon into the core of each apple. Place 1 teaspoon of butter on the top of each apple.

4 Bake, uncovered, for 40 to 45 minutes, or until tender.

5 Remove from the oven and baste several times with any pan juices before serving.

QUICK TIP: Serve with vanilla ice cream and caramel sauce.

DESSERT ON A DIME

EASY FRESH FRUIT TARTS

An easy, healthy dessert, you can make the tart "crust" in advance — simply fill when you're ready to serve.

Prep time 20 minutes   **Cook time** 6 minutes   **Yield** 12 mini tarts

12 **wonton skins**
 2 **tablespoons apricot jam**
 1 **cup low-fat yogurt (your choice of flavor)**
1½ **cups cut-up fresh fruit**

1   Preheat the oven to 375°F. Coat 12 mini-muffin cups lightly with cooking spray.

2   Press 1 wonton skin into each muffin cup, letting the edges hang over the side of the muffin tin.

3   Spray the wonton skins lightly with cooking spray. Bake for 6 to 8 minutes or until lightly browned. Carefully remove the baked wonton cups from the muffin tin and transfer to a rack to cool.

4   Heat the jam in the microwave until melted, about 20 seconds. Spread the jam in the bottoms of the cooled wonton cups; fill them with yogurt and fresh fruit.

5   Serve immediately.

FOR KEEPS: The wonton cups can be baked and stored in an airtight container up to 1 week in advance.

KITCHEN 411: Wonton skins can usually found in the produce section of the grocery store, near the tofu or Asian vegetables.

EASY LEMON ICE CREAM

I make this dessert for Christmas Day and serve it after the big meal. Everyone finds it very refreshing and it serves as a nice complement to the Christmas cookie tray. No one will ever know how quick and easy this recipe is — unless you tell them.

Prep time 10 minutes **Freeze time** 4 hours **Yield** 8–10 servings

2 **cups (1 pint) whipping cream**
1 **cup sugar**
Freshly grated zest of 1 lemon
⅓ **cup fresh lemon juice (juice from 2 to 3 lemons)**

1   Combine the cream and sugar in a medium bowl. Whisk until the sugar is dissolved (this may take up to 5 minutes).

2   Add the lemon zest and juice; stir for 10 seconds. The mixture will begin to thicken.

3   Pour into a container with a tight-fitting lid; freeze for at least 4 hours. Serve.

QUICK TIP: This recipe works only with *fresh* lemon juice — no substitutes.

FOR KEEPS: This ice cream will keep in the freezer for up to 3 months when sealed in an airtight container.

KITCHEN 411: To zest a lemon, use the finest holes of a box grater to remove the outer yellow peel, leaving the white pith on the fruit. After zesting, the lemon is softened from the friction and easier to juice. It's very hard to zest a cut lemon, so be sure to zest first and juice after.

If you need lemons for juicing only, shop for ones that have a slightly orange tint and smooth skin. These lemons tend to be riper and juicier, with a thinner skin. If you need lemons strictly for their peel or zest, shop for ones that have a bright yellow color. Such lemons tend to have thick, firm skin that is good for zesting.

SANDWICH COOKIE ICE CREAM

I have had this recipe forever and do not remember where it came from. This is one of my favorite ice cream desserts because it covers all the bases for me — cookies, whipped cream, and simplicity!

Prep time 10 minutes **Freeze time** 6 hours **Yield** 8 servings

2 cups (1 pint) whipping cream

3 large egg yolks

1 (14-ounce) can low-fat sweetened condensed milk

2 tablespoons water

4 teaspoons pure vanilla extract

1 cup coarsely crushed chocolate sandwich cookies, such as Oreos

1 Whip the cream in a large stainless steel bowl (preferably chilled) until soft peaks form; set aside.

2 Line a 9- by 5-inch loaf pan with aluminum foil.

3 Beat the egg yolks in a large bowl for 1 minute. Stir in the sweetened condensed milk, water, and vanilla; fold in the cookies and whipping cream. Pour into the lined loaf pan. Freeze for 6 hours, or until firm.

4 When you are ready to serve, remove the block of ice cream from the pan. Peel away the foil, slice the ice cream, and serve.

QUICK TIP: To crush the cookies, put them in a ziplock freezer bag and smash with a mallet or rolling pin.

FOR KEEPS: This recipe will keep up to 2 months in the freezer.

SHREVES'S BEST-EVER FUDGE SAUCE

This is a recipe from Karen Shreves, a good friend of mine from way back. Karen always had ice cream in her freezer and this fudge sauce came in handy when she wanted a good treat to serve. I have modified the recipe for the microwave to make it easier.

Prep time 3 minutes **Cook time** 2 minutes **Yield** About 1 cup

- 4 **tablespoons all-purpose flour**
- ¾ **cup sugar**
- ¼ **cup cocoa**
- 1 **cup water**
- 4 **tablespoons butter, at room temperature**
- ⅛ **teaspoon salt**
- 1 **teaspoon pure vanilla extract**

1 Sift the flour, sugar, and cocoa together into a large microwave-safe bowl; add the water. Whisk until the mixture is smooth, about 30 seconds. Microwave on high for 2 minutes.

2 Remove from the microwave immediately and whisk constantly for 1 minute.

3 Add the butter, salt, and vanilla, whisking until smooth.

4 Serve hot or cold over ice cream.

FOR KEEPS: This sauce will keep in the refrigerator for 3 weeks. Store in the freezer for up to 2 months.

CARAMEL APPLE FLUFFY

My daughter, who can smell something sweet a mile away, thinks this dish is heaven on earth. Don't think of the calories — just the fun of serving it!

Prep time 10 minutes   **Yield** 10 servings

6 apples, peeled, cored, and chopped
1 (20-ounce) can crushed pineapple, drained
½ cup finely chopped pecans
1 cup caramel apple dip (found in produce section)
1 (8-ounce) container frozen low-fat whipped topping, thawed

1 Combine the apples, pineapple, and pecans in a large bowl.
2 Combine the caramel dip and whipped topping in a medium bowl; mix well. Pour the topping over the apple mixture, stirring to incorporate.
3 Refrigerate until ready to serve.

QUICK TIPS:
• You can serve this dish with additional nuts, cherries, and drizzled caramel.
• Granny Smith apples are my favorite for this recipe because of their tartness, but you can use any type of apple.

FOR KEEPS: This recipe can be stored in the refrigerator for up to 3 days.

DESSERT ON A DIME

DESSERT DIP

This is a super-quick dessert that you can whip up whenever you have guests and you don't want to serve the kids the tiramisu that you slaved over, which they probably wouldn't like anyway.

Prep time **5 minutes**   Yield **2½ cups**

1 **(3.4-ounce) box instant chocolate pudding mix**
2 **cups cold milk (whole or 2 percent)**
4 **tablespoons creamy peanut butter**
  Marshmallows, cookies, fruit slices, and graham crackers, for dipping

1 Prepare the pudding according to the package directions, using milk. Add the peanut butter, stirring until creamy; chill.

2 Transfer to a serving bowl and serve with dippers.

QUICK TIP: If you are really pressed for time, you can always use prepared "lunch box" puddings instead of the pudding mix called for in the ingredients.

FOR KEEPS: This recipe can be made up to 3 days in advance.

DESSERT ON A DIME

Special Thanks

This book represents a very long journey. It started in the driveway of my good friend Lauren Zaworksi. She had this great idea to write a cookbook for soccer moms who are constantly running around taking their kids to and from practices and games and such, and who consequently have very little time to provide their family with quick, healthy, nutritious meals.

I agreed to work with her on this incredible idea and pretty soon we were off. Trying to write a book about a hectic lifestyle while you are actually living it, however, is no easy task. Lauren and I both had children involved in many extracurricular activities including soccer, piano lessons, swimming, trumpet lessons, Boy Scouts, basketball, softball, baseball, Girl Scouts, ballet, tap dance, flute lessons, and football.

We quickly realized that soccer moms aren't the only ones having this time-crunch problem — it's an issue that affects *everyone* living today's busy lifestyle. We plugged away for a couple of years on the project, making headway between sports, family activities, jobs, and academic seasons.

Family and personal issues became increasingly more important than our book as time went on. Lauren regretfully bowed out of the project to focus all of her energies on surviving breast cancer. Lauren is the most courageous, positive, and strong-willed person I know. She was determined to lick this disease — and she did. Without her initial contributions and inspiration, this book would not be in your hands.

This special dedication is to Lauren and to all women who have faced breast cancer. My hope is for a cure in our lifetime.

Metric Conversion Charts

Unless you have finely calibrated measuring equipment, conversions between U.S. and metric measurements will be somewhat inexact. It's important to convert the measurements for all of the ingredients in a recipe to maintain the same proportions as the original.

General Formula for Metric Conversion

Ounces to grams	multiply ounces by 28.35
Grams to ounces	multiply grams by 0.035
Pounds to grams	multiply pounds by 453.5
Pounds to kilograms	multiply pounds by 0.45
Cups to liters	multiply cups by 0.24
Fahrenheit to Celsius	subtract 32 from Fahrenheit temperature, multiply by 5, divide by 9
Celsius to Fahrenheit	multiply Celsius temperature by 9, divide by 5, add 32

Approximate Equivalents by Volume

U.S.	Metric
1 teaspoon	5 milliliters
1 tablespoon	15 milliliters
¼ cup	60 milliliters
½ cup	120 milliliters
1 cup	230 milliliters
1¼ cups	300 milliliters
1½ cups	360 milliliters
2 cups	460 milliliters
2½ cups	600 milliliters
3 cups	700 milliliters
4 cups (1 quart)	0.95 liter
1.06 quarts	1 liter
4 quarts (1 gallon)	3.8 liters

Approximate Equivalents by Weight

U.S.	Metric	U.S.	Metric
¼ ounce	7 grams	1 gram	0.035 ounce
½ ounce	14 grams	50 grams	1.75 ounces
1 ounce	28 grams	100 grams	3.5 ounces
1¼ ounces	35 grams	250 grams	8.75 ounces
1½ ounces	40 grams	500 grams	1.1 pounds
2½ ounces	70 grams	1 kilogram	2.2 pounds
4 ounces	112 grams		
5 ounces	140 grams		
8 ounces	228 grams		
10 ounces	280 grams		
15 ounces	425 grams		
16 ounces (1 pound)	454 grams		

Index

OTHER STOREY TITLES YOU WILL ENJOY

Fix, Freeze, Feast, **by Kati Neville and Lindsay Tkacsik.**
Great recipes that start with a warehouse club tray pack of meat
and end with a freezer full of delicious meals, ready for thawing
anytime.
256 pages. Paper. ISBN 978-1-58017-682-8.

Let's Get Together, **by DeeDee Stovel & Pam Wakefield.**
Simple recipes for stress-free gatherings with friends, from picnics
to open houses to potlucks.
288 pages. Paper. ISBN 978-1-60342-029-7.

Mom's Best Crowd-Pleasers, **by Andrea Chesman.**
The latest in a best-selling series — a relaxed approach to feeding
casual gatherings of every size.
208 pages. Paper. ISBN 978-1-58017-629-3.

Mom's Best One-Dish Suppers, **by Andrea Chesman.**
More than a hundred recipes that satisfy comfort-food cravings,
with minimal fuss and clean-up.
208 pages. Paper. ISBN 978-1-58017-602-6.

Munchies, **by Kevin Telles Roberts.**
Great recipes for the student with a small grocery budget, a tiny
kitchen, and limited time.
192 pages. Paper. ISBN 978-1-58017-536-4.

Picnic, **by DeeDee Stovel.**
A cornucopia of seasonal picnic ideas, from the informal to the
elegant, plus more than 125 recipes for soups, salads, entrées,
and desserts.
192 pages. Paper. ISBN 978-1-58017-377-3.

**These and other books from Storey Publishing are available
wherever quality books are sold or by calling 1-800-441-5700.
Visit us at *www.storey.com.***